The Video Game Writer's Guide to Surviving an Industry That Hates You

There have been many books written about how to write for games, but just as important as creating the deliverables is knowing how to do the job itself. In an industry that can seem like it's stacked against a game writer's professional survival, knowing how to navigate the choppy waters of building schedules, interfacing with other team members, getting actionable feedback, and putting yourself in a position to do your best work without killing yourself is vital information.

This book is a guide to identifying, approaching, and triumphing over those tasks beyond just laying down words as well as finding the power and joy in writing for video games. By turning humorous, horrifying, and hopeful, this is a user's manual to a role that is frequently misunderstood and underappreciated. Drawing on over two decades' experience in the game writing trenches, Richard Dansky takes you on a journey through the things you must know in order to survive and thrive as a game writer.

A 25-year veteran of the video game industry, **Richard Dansky** has written for franchises, including *The Division*, *Assassin's Creed*, *Far Cry*, and *Splinter Cell*. He has published eight novels and two short story collections and was a key contributor to the classic TTRPG setting *The World of Darkness*. Widely regarded as a leading expert on game narrative and writing, he is currently the Narrative Director at Romero Games. Richard lives in North Carolina.

"Angry but thoughtful, blunt but considered, THIS is the guidebook every game writer needs."

– **Antony Johnston** (*Dead Space, Middle Earth: The Shadow of Mordor, Resident Evil Village*)

"Richard Dansky has seen it all in his decades as a writer, and he's here to tell you the unflinching truth about the good, bad, and downright ugly of writing for video games. This book is a must-read for video game professionals and hopefuls alike."

– **Anna Megill,** Lead Writer, Author, and Game Narrative Veteran

"This is 'On Writing' for videogames."

– **Olivier Henriot** (*Assassin' Creed, Far Cry, Watch Dogs*)

"This really is the book our industry has been waiting for."

– **Rhianna Pratchett**

"The book that could revolutionize our industry."

– **Leanne Taylor-Giles**

The Video Game Writer's Guide to Surviving an Industry That Hates You

Richard Dansky

CRC Press
Taylor & Francis Group
Boca Raton London New York

CRC Press is an imprint of the
Taylor & Francis Group, an **informa** business

Designed cover image: Getty Images

First edition published 2026
by CRC Press
2385 NW Executive Center Drive, Suite 320, Boca Raton FL 33431

and by CRC Press
4 Park Square, Milton Park, Abingdon, Oxon, OX14 4RN

CRC Press is an imprint of Taylor & Francis Group, LLC

ISBN: 978-1-032-97262-6 (hbk)
ISBN: 978-1-032-97261-9 (pbk)
ISBN: 978-1-003-59298-3 (ebk)

DOI: 10.1201/9781003592983

Typeset in Times New Roman
by Apex CoVantage, LLC

Dedicated to my peers in the noble craft of video game writing, for all that you have done, are doing, and will do in the future to do good work and make great games. These words are for you.

Contents

Acknowledgments

I would like to say thank you to all of the friends, peers, coworkers, and fellow travelers who made this book possible. Starting at the beginning, thank you to David Weinstein for getting me to apply to Red Storm in the first place, and to Brian Upton and Kevin Perry for letting me grow on the job there. Thank you to the Red Storm game design team, a stellar bunch of folks, and especially Michael Fitch and Jay Posey, whose intelligence and skill helped inform my craft. I'd also like to thank Steve Reid and Elizabeth Loverso at Red Storm for letting me pursue a unique career path that led me here.

Thanks go to Alexis Nolent, Olivier Henriot, and Julien Charpentier, my champions at Ubi HQ over the years, and to all the writers I worked with, including Anne Reid, Navid Khavari, Mike Lee, and so many other talented people that I can't list you all. I would also like to thank David Fifield for turning me loose in the swamps of horror at Crytek and to the members of the *Hunt: Showdown 1896* Narrative team for their creativity and excellence.

Much appreciation goes to those industry veterans and luminaries who were so kind and generous when I first joined the industry. Noah Falstein, Patricia Pizer, Lee Sheldon, Bob Bates, Steve Meretzky, Eric Goldberg, and more – thank you.

Thanks, too, to Susan O'Connor for asking me to join the advisory board of what was once the Game Writers Conference, and to my fellow board members over the years for their dedication to promoting our craft. A big shout-out also goes to Dustin Clingman for getting me onboard at the late lamented ECGC. And of course, to Wendy Despain, Chris Bateman, and the rest of the folks who founded and supported the IGDA Game Writers SIG.

More thanks go out to all of the friends I've made through the craft over the years, who have continually encouraged and inspired me, and to the students who submit to the Student Narrative Analysis Competition at GDC every year for keeping me optimistic about the future.

In addition, I absolutely must thank Toiya K. Finley for championing this book to her publisher and the rest of the board and attendees of a certain unofficial unconference that remains one of my guiding stars, year after year.

A tip of the cap to all the non-game writer friends who listened to me blather about this book for the better part of a year. Looking at you, Jeff Strand, Bridgett Nelson, and Rena Mason; at you, Victor Jimenez; and most of all at you, the endlessly patient Ellen Williams.

And last but not least, a huge round of thanks goes to those souls kind enough to look at parts or all of the whole manuscript and offer their thoughts, corrections, encouragement, and screams of horror. Jesse Scoble, Lucien Soulban, Antony Johnston, Olivia Wood, Andrew Walsh, Jonathon Myers, Peter Woodworth, J.D. Sovari, Alexander Bevier, and Chris Thacker, thank you.

I couldn't have done it without you.

1

The Dreaded Introduction

1.1 What Is This Book?

I know what you are thinking:

"Oh God, not another book on video game writing."

I can understand that sentiment. There are plenty of books on writing for video games. Some are good. Some are not. Many are comprehensive and detailed. There are those that are high-level and conceptual instead. Some are written from a place of experience, while others offer a slightly more theoretical view. It can be hard to separate the wheat from the chaff or to figure out which ones might be most useful to you from among the many options. The last thing you need, it would seem, would be yet another book on the subject, even one with a dazzling and provocative title.

The good news is, though, that this is not one of those books.

Because this is not a book about game writing. It will, by and large, not teach you how to do the specific tasks asked of a game writer from a craft perspective nor will it offer exercises that will help you hone your skills.

Instead, this is a book about *being* a game writer, and there is a real and important difference between the two topics. While there are classes that can teach you how to write effective and concise dialog, there is no class in the world that will teach you the proper way to wrangle a Creative Director whose wild idea for a change to the story would wreck months of established work. Simply put, there are very few resources out there for the actual techniques, best practices, and survival skills needed to do the job, day in and day out. Those skills are important ones, the ones that allow a working writer to establish the boundaries, feedback loops, and confidence necessary to be allowed to create successfully.

Or, to put it another way, it helps a lot to know how the system works and where the exploits are. Too many talented individuals have washed out of the games industry, not because they weren't good at writing, but because they were bad at writing in a way that matched the needs of the game they were working on and the process of turning that writing into part of a game. Being able to navigate expectations and work around long-held industry illusions goes a long way toward getting enough time and resources to do the actual writing tasks right. It's all well and good to be a great writer of games content, but if you can't present your ideas cogently and appealingly to the team and management, you're dead in the water.

DOI: 10.1201/9781003592983-1

This, then, is a guide to deciphering the professional code that game writers must understand in order to do their actual job. It's about being able to convince people to let you do your best work, about building the relationships and feedback loops that allow your work to be polished and iterated on such that it is the best it can be. It is about the common roadblocks and misconceptions that game writers face and how to get around them – or, if necessary, bulldoze straight through them. It's about scoring the time and resources that you need to do the job right when all around you is chaos and short deadlines. And it's about all the little tasks that somehow become big tasks when no one is looking, about being the lone defender of concepts like character voice and narrative logic and character arcs. It's about being a functional, productive, and quality writer in spite of all the obstacles the foibles of the industry will inevitably throw in your way.

Because make no mistake, there are obstacles. It's a truism that "everyone thinks they're a writer," but there's a lot of truth in that statement. In too many companies, there is little to no understanding of what game writing is, what it needs to be good, and how long it takes. The same people who turn to ChatGPT to write their emails will tell you to your face that writing is easy and never see the irony. So many of the game writers I know have the same horror stories: Of being given inadequate time or resources to do insanely complicated tasks, of being rewritten by people who are not writers, of being ordered to do things that actively make the writing worse, of being cut out of conversations that are vital to doing the job right. I can tell you stories from my experience about having team leads demanding script rewrites while I was sitting in the studio because they didn't like particular word choices, of games where features were redesigned after the dialog was recorded and where there was no budget, will, or interest in doing pickup shoots to correct the now-glaring errors that shipped with the game, of games where the mandate to the writer was "We have unused levels from these other games, put them together to make a story and use at least three of them twice."

The list goes on. You'll hear a few more of those stories as you get deeper into the book. But the fact remains that no other discipline in game development has to deal with the entrenched opposition and disdain that writing does. I have been told to my face that game writers expect to have their stuff go into a game untouched, which anyone who has ever listened to – not talked to, but listened to – a game writer knows is arrant nonsense. I have had senior team leadership tell me that they have no idea what character voice is or why it matters when trying to shoehorn an idea into a game that makes absolutely no character sense. I can tell you about a writer friend who had a character in a game he was writing swapped from a Black American to an urbane Englishman the day of the voice shoot without anyone informing him, because it's not like writing dialog takes character background into account. Supposedly they spent half an hour trying to get the poor actor to say "Boo-yah" before finally giving up and going with "Nice shot." You get the idea.

This is why game writers need a survival tool kit. They need to know how to talk to people in positions of power who don't understand writing. They need to be able to communicate their vision and effort to other members of the team in a way that demonstrates their value and doesn't come across as trying to dictate terms. They need to be able to work fast and flexibly, to take feedback from a million different directions and make it work, and to be able to gently shoot down bad ideas in a way that won't get them labeled stubborn or "not a team player." They need to know all the things that will let them do the work as much as they need to know how to do the work itself. The best writing in the world never comes to fruition if it gets shortchanged, messed with, or left unpolished.

And that's what this book aims to be. Along the way there will be examples. There will be fist-pounding manifestos about aspects of game writing, which don't necessarily seem obvious. There will be anecdotes that you may or may not believe but that I can assure you are all 100% true (though they may have had the serial numbers scraped off for obvious reasons). And there will be a constant thread reaffirming the value of the game writer, with support for those brave souls who voluntarily take on that role.

For you.

1.2 Why This Book? And Who Am I?

All of that being said, one question remains: Why am I writing this book? The simplest answer I can give is because I've been doing this for a quarter of a century, I've seen things behind the scenes that you can't imagine, and I want to give back to the craft of game writing so those who come after me have it easier than I did.

When I first came into video game design and writing, I was 28 years old, coming off a critically successful but sales-challenged run as a tabletop roleplaying game designer for White Wolf Game Studios. I was in charge of various games at various times, most notably the ghost-themed tabletop role-playing game (TTRPG) *Wraith: The Oblivion*. I applied to the Tom Clancy-founded Red Storm Entertainment for a designer role at the recommendation of my friend Dave Weinstein, who worked at Red Storm, and I was frankly terrified when I did so. I knew that as much as I knew about TTRPG design and writing, I didn't know much about what went into the sausage-making process of video games, and I knew I didn't know it. As a result, I was frankly stunned when, the day after my on-site interview, the head of Red Storm HR called and said, "Don't go anywhere. We're going to make you an offer on Monday."

Sure enough, Monday rolled around, and they made me an offer. I thanked them and then called my manager at White Wolf. He was soft-spoken and Canadian, a Napoleonic miniatures game fanatic, and a very laid-back kind of guy. When he picked up, I told him I had an offer from a video game company for significantly more than White Wolf was paying me, but that I loved working at the Wolf and wanted to give him a chance to respond.

There was silence on the line for a minute, and then he said, "Take it. Go. Now. Seriously."

So I did, and I have never looked back. I knew I was inexperienced, and I was eager for help to enable me to do my job better. Thankfully, I got that help. I got it at Red Storm from folks like Brian Upton and Kevin Perry. And in early 2000, I got it at my first-ever GDC from people who were already established in the industry and had no need to reach down from Olympus in order to give me encouragement and a hand. Some of these were the very men and women who had created the games I had played obsessively as a teenager. Their bones were made. And yet, they were kind and generous enough to offer me advice, encouragement, and direction at a time when I was convinced I was the Velveteen Game Designer who would never get to play with the real ones.

The first game I worked on, *Anne McCaffrey's Freedom: First Resistance*, was a disaster for reasons beyond counting. As lovely as Ms. McCaffrey was to work with, the license was literally a freebie, derived from her seventh- or eighth-most popular series, and almost worth every penny we paid for it. The team had all sorts of issues, ranging from inexperience on one end to burnout on the other, to a rotating cast of producers leading the project, to the very strange idea of bolting a dialog and puzzle engine on top of the *Rainbow Six* tactical shooter game engine in the first place. During the development cycle, Red Storm was purchased by Ubisoft, who decided that the game needed to be shoved out the door as soon as possible, regardless of level of polish, in order to free up resources to complete the nascent *Ghost Recon*. There was even a brief moment of Internet notoriety when a gaming humor/review/snark site got an advance copy of the game somehow and claimed it blew up their monitor (it didn't). They also said that the entire dev team needed to die in a fire, along with their families, which no doubt helped set the tone for the reasoned, rational, generous online discussion of games we have to this day.

Years later, when I was manager of Red Storm's game design group, I interviewed a designer who purposely brought up that review and made a point of telling me repeatedly how hilarious he thought it was.

He did not get the job.

But I digress. I only mention this to note that in certain ways, I started at the bottom, with a game that is still referred to as "The Game Which Shall Not Be Named" by those who were there at the time. I learned a lot of lessons from that and from the games I was assigned to after that, and then before long there was a need for a writer who could serve as the central lore-keeper, authority, and resource on all things Tom Clancy. Ubisoft was expanding development on Clancy-branded games to multiple studios, and they needed someone to keep their stories straight. And that was me.

Fast forward roughly two decades, and here I am. I have worked on roughly 70 games in my 25 years in the industry. Some saw daylight, some didn't. Some were hits, and some were flops. Some were critically praised, some were panned, and some were trashed at the time but got reassessed years later as actually having been ahead of their time. I have written millions of words for games ranging from high fantasy to hardcore military shooters to horror to however the heck you define *Assassin's Creed*, and I have edited a bunch more. I have worked solo on projects, and I have worked with teams spread out across multiple continents. I have been on projects from the beginning, and I have written the dialog for brand-new features in the studio the day we had to record it. I was there for the founding of the IGDA Game Writers' SIG, the first professional group dedicated to supporting game writers, and I have lectured on game narrative at conferences around the world. I sit on the advisory board of the

Game Narrative Summit at GDC, I curated the narrative content at the late lamented East Coast Game Conference, and I judge the annual Student Narrative Analysis Competition at GDC, which gives the winners the chance to attend the conference and present their work.

In short, I have a wide and varied experience that I would like to share. I have indeed seen the elephant in its many guises, and each encounter has taught me something new. I have seen moments of pure magic when a team meshed and the synergy between writing, level design, and gameplay created breathtaking magic. I have seen it all go horribly wrong, and I've seen things that even a decade or more later I still struggle to make sense of. I nearly died on a work trip to brainstorm about a game that never got past the concept stage, I had my work complimented by actor Dwight Schultz, whose portrayal of "Howlin' Mad" Murdock on *The A-Team* lit up my childhood television screens, and I once had to write multiple missions' worth of dialog featuring a character voiced by an actor whose contract was up and who had no interest in doing further voice sessions.

In short, when it comes to game writing, I think I know my stuff pretty well. I have been in the rooms. I have pulled the all-nighters. I have had the moments of "Aha!" inspiration, and I have screwed things up. All of that, though, gets filed under "useful experience," which I have been able to draw upon, transform, and use to make my work always better as I have gone forward.

I care deeply about the craft of video game writing. I firmly believe it is a unique craft, one with its own special demands, requirements, and skills. I believe that while writers from other media can learn how to become good game writers, their experience elsewhere absolutely does not translate perfectly or immediately, and that folks who are trained from the get-go to understand how to write in an interactive space do in fact have a professional advantage and value. I believe there are game writers who have created work that can reasonably be called "art," and I believe that there is much more to game writing than dialog for cut scenes that isn't funny. And I believe that, because of all that game writing has given me over the years, it is my responsibility to try to codify some of what I have learned and to pass it along in a way that those who come along behind me don't have to reinvent the wheel. After all, I've got dozens of perfectly good wheels just sitting around the place, and I am happy to share. I believe what I have to offer is of value, and I would like to share it with you.

1.3 The Secret Is I'm Always Angry

At the same time, I confess I am angry. Angry at the low esteem my craft, and the craft of so many talented people I know and respect, is held in. Angry at the waste of time, effort, and money. Angry at the way the contributions of hard-working game writers are shown disrespect and not supported. Angry at the waste that comes from having to teach the same lessons over and over again.

Angry at the sheer, utter nonsense that we have to go through in order to do this job that we, despite it all, love. I can think of an instance where a writer was literally shoved out of his chair by a producer, who sat down, typed a few words, and supposedly said, "See? It's only dialog. I just wrote some. What's taking so long?"

That anger, I think, needs expression. Part of my intention is to pull back the curtain and demonstrate the problems game writers face so they (the problems, not the game writers) can be confronted and overcome. Quiet acceptance has, for decades, gotten us nowhere. It's time to shout it from the rooftops and in the team meetings that this sort of thing is, indeed, bullshit, unprofessional, and counterproductive, and that it needs to stop so we can make better games. Frankly, I don't care about the stuff that has happened to me along the way. By now, it's pretty much all water under the bridge. Still, I hate to think of the same mistakes, the same wasteful actions, being repeated again and again and again because no one ever stood up publicly and said, "Knock it off already."

1.4 The Manifesto

There you have it. What I want to do, why I want to do it, and why I think I am the right person at this place and time to be the one to do it. And, because I am, above all, a writer, I invite you to journey with me through this book as I share the stories of my experience and how they reflect the points I am trying to make about how to do this crazy, often thankless job well. Because, so help me, I cannot think of a better feeling than seeing a fully realized game being played and hearing dialog that you've written come out of characters' mouths and watching players react to it in all the ways you imagined when you were writing. The famous cut scene from the opening of *The Division* wherein police Captain Benitez tells Division agent Faye Lau that he doesn't want to throw her people to the wolves, and she responds with the iconic "We are the wolves?" That was written in the studio, as the actors were putting on their mo-cap suits after a series of frantic rewrites in the taxi ride over to the studio, and it wound up being quoted again and again by players, makers of fan videos, and more. The response to that put a smile on my face for ages. And then there's the story of Sand Guy from the original *Far Cry* . . . but I digress.

I warn you now, strap in. I'm going to digress a lot.

So that is it, in a nutshell. What this book is, why it is needed, and why I think I'm the right one to write it. Do I know all the answers? No, because I have not had all the experiences. But I have seen an awful lot on my long and winding road that can maybe be the start of your own take on this.

You should know that this book is not going to be gentle. I will pull no punches in calling out faults or misconceptions or willful bad behavior. There are places where I am going to provide behind-the-scenes examples that you probably won't believe, and that's OK. I didn't believe them either, and I was there. My mission is not to coddle; it is to inform you, to arm you for your future in game writing, and maybe, just maybe, to give you a few laughs from the stories of my misadventures along the way.

All right. Take a deep breath. Get ready. And remember, there's much more to this job than you ever might have imagined.

2

Why People Think Game Writing Sucks and Why They Are Almost Always Wrong

2.1 Stating the Myth

The narrative experience delivered by video games is not always as clean, as polished, or as smooth as the other aspects of games. To be honest, many times it is not as good. However, many people take this observation and draw the immediate, obvious, and incorrect conclusion, stating that the writing is always the problem.

This, by and large, is not the case. I mean, sure, in many cases the writing can be improved, but a good percentage of the time, it is not the actual arrangement of words that is the real problem. The issue is instead the *presentation* of the writing to the player, which is something very different. Understanding that difference is the key to understanding a lot of where video games go wrong in their assessment of and support for writing and for game narrative in general.

Because an awful lot of the written words never reach the player or get waylaid or damaged along the way. There are plenty of steps between the act of composition, when the words get laid down, and what comes out the other end when the player boots up the game, and many of those steps have the potential to be very bad for the very words they are theoretically trying to gussy up for their big moment.

2.2 Summoning the Ghost of Shakespeare

When I first got started on the Internet, it was a message board truism that as soon as someone referenced Shakespeare in a writing-based thread, that thread was functionally over. It was the equivalent of swatting a fly with a tank. And yet, here I go, because I think it's important to establish right off the bat that it has never been the writing's fault every single time. Sometimes, yes, but that's not the proposition we're examining here.

With that in mind, let us consider Shakespeare. William Shakespeare, unless you are a literature conspiracy theorist, is widely considered to be possibly the finest writer the English language has ever seen. His body of work is staggering, and the brilliance of his writing remains cogent and impactful even to modern audiences hundreds of years after his death. In other words, Bad Bill was pretty damned good at writing, and his stuff remains the gold standard for putting pen to paper.

And all of this is well and good, until someone like Kenneth Branagh comes along and casts Billy Crystal or Keanu Reeves in one of his Shakespeare adaptations. If you have seen them, you know that the results of those scenes can best be described as "dire." And no, the problem isn't the words. The

DOI: 10.1201/9781003592983-2

words are fine. The words are exactly the same words they were when the script of *Hamlet* or *Much Ado About Nothing* was getting praised to the skies for being foundational to English literature. The problem is that the words were put into the mouths of actors who simply could not handle them and who, as a result, gave miserable, deadening performances.

Nobody blames Shakespeare for Reeves' affectless Don John in *Much Ado*. Nobody blames Shakespeare because Billy Crystal mangled the Gravedigger's language from pillar to post, producing an unintelligible mess that made audiences cringe.

No matter how bad those scenes turned out, nobody pointed fingers at the writing. This was because, surprise of surprises, the writing was not the actual problem. The problem was in the transmission of the script as written to the audience by means of actors and Directors, and they're the ones who fumbled the handoff. They're the ones who, rightfully, got pilloried for this awfulness – not dear old Bill Shakespeare.

I am not saying that any video game writing ever done has a patch on the man who gave us Caliban, Horatio, Titania, and the like. What I am saying is that if *his* words can be mistreated, mangled, and misrepresented badly enough that they come off like a container of month-old tuna salad, then it is possible that the writer isn't always the one who is at fault.

That's not to propose the argument that there is no such thing as bad game writing. It exists, and it is far too common. But there are reasons a lot of it exists, reasons that often come from outside the writing team.

And let us take a moment to note that just as there are writers who are below the salt, so too are there artists, engineers, animators, producers, and representatives of every discipline who cannot get the job done. Game development, like anything else, is subject to the notion of a normal distribution. Not everyone can be good. It's baked into the math.

2.3 Bad Game Writers

I will freely grant that there are bad game writers who do bad game writing. Some are just bad writers and simply do not have the chops to produce good dialog or story. Some never got the training they needed and were punished for failing at tasks they were never prepared for. Some may excel in other media, particularly linear ones like screenplays or novels, but can't come to grips with all the challenges and needs of writing for an interactive medium.

This, incidentally, is true of even some of the most decorated and critically acclaimed writers of other forms. Some went in respectfully and with a willing spirit. Some loudly announced – to the point where it became a bit of a running joke to established game writers with "Who's going to tell us how to do our jobs this week?" – that all game writing was crap and that they were going to show us how it was done . . . until they didn't. Very few of them appear to have returned for round two.

And sometimes it's a case of a normally competent or even good writer being put in a place where it is impossible for them to do good writing under the imposed circumstances.

The variations often escape the outside observer. They look at the end result, and that's their right. For those on the inside, though, a smarter, more considered approach is necessary.

2.4 How It Breaks

Like I said, there are a lot of ways for writing to get broken on its way from composition to play session. Let's run them down.

One reason for a lot of bad narrative content in games is that the production is not set up to allow for good writing. For whatever reason, there is this obstinate myth in game development that writing deliverables can be pumped out quickly, easily, and perfectly in one go.

None of these are true.

But, since the people making the schedules sometimes feel that way, the sad truth is that composition and polish time get squeezed or disregarded. Too often, you can trace the ancestry of bad game writing to a deliverable schedule that demanded that the writer hop to it and hammer the text out as quickly as humanly possible without having the time for table reads, editing passes, or iteration. These short schedules then backed directly up against immovable demands for the finished script. There's localization, for example, an exercise that requires both time and precision as the game script is translated into foreign languages, and their deadlines are largely immovable. Or maybe there are recording sessions already booked and paid for that cannot be moved except at great expense and that run the risk of losing one or more of the actors to another, already scheduled gig if they do move. Honestly, it's details. What matters is that, for whatever reason, the time set out for composing scripts is short and there are not a lot of options.

If time for narrative to work on a script is short, there are a bunch of things that fall out of that proposition. One is that there is no time for iteration or polish. A first draft of a script may be good. It may even be very good. Or it may be utterly terrible. The immutable truth remains, however, that it is never as good as it could be with multiple drafts and iterations. The point being, the purpose of a first draft is to exist. You hammer it out, you squeeze it out of the printer or typewriter or whatever, and you get to the end. First drafts are full of inspiration but often rife with errors, overstuffed with extraneous ideas, and loaded with awkward sentence construction that turns people off from actual listening. The idea is for all of that to be there so you can go to work on it. It can then be cleaned up in succeeding passes until the finished product is deemed shippable. The less revision time the writers get – the less time other eyes spend on it, the less time there is for actionable feedback, the less time there is to do multiple versions – the less polished the end product is going to be.

Production schedules, which are created by producers and team leads and generally not by the narrative team, often lay the groundwork for bad writing by not allowing the time for good writing to happen. Bear in mind that other disciplines within game development have far fewer concerns with this sort of thing. It is understood, and rightfully so, that building maps takes time, that getting lighting right requires multiple passes and feedback sessions, and that gameplay balance is an endless process of implementing, trying, and then implementing slightly differently. All of these, and indeed pretty much any other aspect of game development, are afforded the time needed to do the job right through feedback and iteration.

Writing, though, doesn't necessarily get the same benefit, and the end result is that the product isn't as polished as, say, a character model that's gone through four rounds of reviews with hawk-eyed criticism processes in place to ensure that even the tiniest flaws are addressed before the asset moves forward.

Which means the schedule version of the Death Star trash compactor chugs into action. Level building takes a little longer. That pushes back mission design. And that pushes back something else, and at the end of the train, the caboose, is writing. The problem is, even as other stuff gets pushed into writing time, writing can't take a chunk out of something else's time by sliding back itself. Those studio dates are locked in. Those actors are booked. The deadline, in many cases, cannot move except at great expense and upheaval. The front end moves and the back end stays the same, and the writing time gets compressed as a result.

2.5 Mandates and Missions

That is just the start. Yes, the squeeze on good writing can start at the very beginning, in what is supposed to be a safe space for the generation of verbiage. In some cases, the issues arise during the act of composition. Direct mandates from above, from studio or company management, from team management, or from creative direction, can prevent issues in the long run. They can clarify and establish vision, they can set up collaboration with other disciplines, and they can build the walls of the sandbox out of adamantium and spiky bits. Being told that the studio can't or won't work with a specific actor prevents you from writing that actor's character from a preceding game into the script. Being told that one of the features the game wants to show off is dynamic weather effects keeps you from setting part of the story in a desert where it never rains. And so it goes.

However, these mandates can also be made from a position of imperfect knowledge and understanding. These external demands can have a bad habit of showing up out of the blue at the last minute, or of contradicting previously done work, or of even formalizing a bad decision in a way that the repercussions of that particular decision will be felt far beyond what was originally intended.

For example, one game that I worked on had a clearly defined arc for the main character, who was supposed to go from lone wolf operative to leader of a pack working in harmony. After some moments of friction along the way, his arc would include moments of self-awareness, acts of reconciliation, and then renewal as the protagonist finally matured into a leadership role so his entire team could finally rise to the occasion of the globe-spanning threat. Every one of the supporting characters got an arc that played off this; the moments of tension along the way could inform mission design harmoniously, and the player would get a unified experience where each aspect reinforced the other.

But.

The feedback I got on pretty much every scene boiled down to a single sentence: "Where's the conflict?" Never mind that there was conflict in the prior conversation, and the one before that, and the one after that, too. Never mind that one particular conversation was intended to be a quiet, conflict-free interlude where the main character could let down his guard and have a heart-to-heart with someone who might be too dangerous to trust but whom he has to trust because there are no other options. Never mind, even, that the tonal shift was deliberate, to allow for a change in dynamic and to let the player relax a bit before the tension got amped back up.

No, the feedback was always "Where's the conflict?" and the scripts didn't get approved until the conflict was cranked to 11 in every single scene. The end result was that the main character's arc was reduced to a series of arguments, and the emotional payoff didn't have anywhere near the impact it should have. The players noticed, too, asking why the main character was always an angry, shouty guy. They didn't know what had been planned instead, but they recognized something was missing, and that what it had been replaced with was less interesting and less powerful. Unfortunately, water flows downhill, and when the mandate comes from on high, the writer has to follow it.

Sometimes, someone will get a wild hair and insist on something that the writing professionals would not have chosen to do. There's a moment in the director's commentary on the DVD of the old "comedy" *Hudson Hawk* where the Bruce Willis character spits out what is possibly the least funny joke in the history of film. And the director, who up till that point had been pretty restrained, said roughly, "We had a lot of funny jokes there, but Bruce wanted that one." It's one of the few moments in my life where I could actually hear someone's soul shrivel in real time.

The same thing happens in games. Someone in a position of authority, formal or not, has an idea for something a character should say, and then suddenly the pressure is on to include it. Often, these folks have no idea what character voice is or why it is important, or why it would be problematic for a certain character to say a certain thing. They just know they want the line in the game come hell or high water, and if the writer won't provide it, they'll often dust their hands and rewrite things themselves. At best, this leads to clunky, weird dialog, as a character suddenly says something wildly inappropriate for their personality and background. At worst, it can step on legal toes and get people in a whole bunch of very expensive trouble if, say, a song quote is involved.

We will leave aside, for the moment, instances where non-writers decide to rewrite writers and send their stuff on to be recorded instead. That's a whole other topic, even though it, too, can lead to the writing being blamed. The thing is, in that case the player is absolutely correct. The writing is the problem. The writer, in that case, isn't.

2.6 Beyond the Lighted Page

That, however, is the first step on the journey, creating the writing. Once that's done, there's the matter of casting, recording, and performance.

Not every actor is a good fit for the role they are cast for. The casting process for games is rickety, to say the least. Often the folks in charge of making casting decisions – a motley crew including everyone from Realization Directors to writers to audio engineers to creative Directors to whoever else winds up on the list – get a series of samples, either audio or video, from prospective actors. What is supposed to happen is everyone listens to or watches all of the samples, and then there's a spreadsheet or survey wherein everyone inputs their choices and feedback. What *actually* happens a too-large proportion of the time is that half the folks in the inevitably too-large loop are afraid to post their opinions until someone else has said something first for them to riff off of. Then and only then do they pile on. Smart early birds have figured this out and jump on the opportunity to get their preferences in first, thus setting the tone for the conversation. If the person at the tip of the spear has a good ear and eye, then this can streamline awkward decision-making. If they don't, bad things can happen.

Plus, there's the fact that many audition samples are made at home by the actors. This affords them the luxury of infinite takes to get it right, with no way for the folks on the team to know if they're listening to gold or heavily refined, carefully polished pyrite.

What this means is that it's easy to make bad casting decisions. Large groups often comprise folks who are not experts at this sort of thing, making decisions based on group voting that has functionally been logrolled, and decisions based on audition materials of unknown provenance can lead to some nasty surprises once you get on set.

I can think of one game I worked on where an actress for a key role absolutely wowed everyone in the casting loop. We got on set for the first day of shooting, set up the intricate blocking and architecture for the full-body mo-cap of her big scene, started rolling, and on the very first take she called out "line" because she couldn't remember the first line of her character's speech.

The rest of the shoot was not an improvement. It quickly became clear that her fabulous audition video was the result of innumerable takes, the sort of thing that, thanks to our tight shooting schedule, we could not afford to do. After the day's work, the Director was so depressed he went back to his hotel and locked himself in his room with a bottle of scotch. The next day, we were forced to start the casting process all over again, now several weeks behind where we needed to be.

And on the flip side, on one of the original Tom Clancy's games, the team was very insistent on getting an actress for a very particular role who could channel the character of Vasquez, the tough-as-nails female space marine from the movie *Aliens*. That was the direction given on the audition materials, that was the hope, and when the audition files came in, there were a lot of pretty decent Vasquez impressions on there. One audition, however, stood out – in a bad way. Everyone involved agreed that this person simply had no idea what we were talking about when the team had asked for Vasquez, that she was totally wrong for the role, and that she never should have been asked to audition in the first place.

This was, of course, the audition tape of Jeanette Goldstein, the actress who played Vasquez. Which just goes to show you that in the end, it can be a crapshoot.

In any case, bad casting yields bad acting. Sometimes, the team gets lucky and there is enough time and budget to do a recasting. Sometimes, however, that is off the table. You have to live with what you've got and hope for the best. And there are further complications. There are studios that try to get talent on the cheap, which by and large backfires when they wind up with precisely the sort of talent they are willing to pay for. There are studios that will only cast local talent, even if the local talent pool is shallower than the tail end of the Colorado River during a drought.

On the flip side, there are times when money will be spent to bring in a celebrity voice actor without consideration for whether or not they are a good fit. The point of the stunt casting is often to generate PR – when actor David Duchovny and rapper Eve were cast in Ubisoft's adaptation of the French graphic novel series *XIII*, I was told point blank that the whole point was to get coverage in magazines and media that a game like that wouldn't normally receive. The fact that the excellent Duchovny is a largely physical actor whose delivery is often deadpan didn't seem to enter into the equation. As a result, without his trademark physicality, his performance in the game came across as flat and uninteresting. The game suffered as a result.

What it boils down to is that bad actor choices can play into bad presentation of writing and of narrative content in general. Bad direction can be a problem, too. The finest script in the world, if the Director sends the actors down the wrong road, can seem strange, uninteresting, or overcooked. Sometimes it's subtle decisions, like not reading character sheets before a shoot and mistakenly describing the villain of a game as a friendly helpmate to the actor playing the protagonist. (Yes, this happened to a game I was on.) Sometimes, it's not thinking about the context of line readings and how they will fit together throughout the ebb and flow of a game's storyline.

This, for example, is how you will sometimes get games where the characters are shouting all the way through it. You can pretty much always trace that back to the actor constantly getting feedback on each line reading to make it bigger and badder and bolder and louder. But if each line is bigger and bolder and badder and louder, then all the lines are bigger and bolder and badder and louder, and inevitably they become this monolith of impenetrable white noise from which neither nuance nor subtlety can escape. And sometimes they're plain weird.

I've found that the best recording booth/soundstage scenarios happen when there is only one voice in the actors' ears – that of the Director. Everyone else funnels their feedback and observations to the Director, who then parses it for the actors and passes it on, if appropriate, in usable form. With a good and attentive Director, this model works spectacularly well. Sometimes this model breaks down, though, depending on who else is in the studio. There's sometimes a weird prestige attached to being at a recording session – especially if it's taking place someplace cool or there's star-level talent involved that people want to interact with. That can lead to an overloaded booth or people who should be there being crowded out. And once the recording gets started, folks who aren't familiar with recording best practices can degrade the process, even with the best of intentions.

All of which can be summed up as "bad direction, regardless of source, can lead to bad performances." Bad performances are frequently read as bad writing. And that's another place the train of attribution of responsibility can get derailed.

2.7 Weaving It In

It's not the last one, though. The dialog, once it has been recorded, processed, and otherwise made usable, still needs to be integrated into the game. Each line needs to be placed so that it plays at the right time. For bespoke dialog, like in cinematic cutscenes or lines that trigger when a player reaches a certain point on a map, the lines often need to be individually placed.

In theory, this is good, allowing for infinite care in the timing of lines and their effect. It can, however, go both ways. If the lines trigger too fast, they pile up on top of each other and sound weird and robotic. If the lines are placed in such a way that there's too much dead time between them – and we are talking just a second here and a second there – then the dialog comes across as stilted, slow, and clumsy. Either of these gets read as bad writing. Again, it's a question of delivery, not the content itself, but that's a hair too far to split for some.

Let us also not forget the question of barks. Barks, or systemic dialog, are something unique to video games. They are the automatic response lines that play when there is a state change in the game world that the player should know about. Functionally, this is why every guard in every stealth game says ten variants on "What was that?" when he goes from resting to alert state and why he then says "Must have been my imagination" or a variant thereof when he switches back into resting state. Barks are simple in concept but complex in execution.

With that in mind, however, bark writing is always carefully planned in terms of what state changes are called out, how many variants of that call-out there are, and how many versions of the guard or other character will be calling them out. All of that adds up to immense line counts in a hurry, which then translates to big recording sessions, big audio tasks, and lots of time and money. I know of games that have had literally over a hundred thousand barks along with all the effort and expense that went along with that. Hell, I even worked on one.

This means there is a pressure to keep numbers of barks low while still providing as much coverage of gameplay events as possible, and one of the ways the team agrees on how many variants there are is by having a rough idea of how often a given bark instance is going to get called. Are the guards going to be super jumpy but easily calmed down, bouncing back and forth between states constantly, and calling out every time they do? Or are they going to be relatively chill, not notice much, and thus require much shallower bark pools because they won't be used as often? Good planning here can lead to efficient use of resources and a streamlined, positive experience. Bad planning – anticipating the guards will be relaxed and writing in that direction and then having their detection sensitivity turned all the way up – can lead to bad reviews, player mockery, and the occasional widely distributed web comic calling out the situation with bad intent.

Again, it's a situation where the writing team produces exactly what is asked of them, decisions external to the writing process are made, and suddenly the writing is expected to cover a task it was never designed for. To the player or reviewer who hears constantly yammering guards draining their bark pools and recycling them multiple times in a single encounter, however, it comes across as bad writing. This then gets communicated and repeated and acquires its own momentum. The beat, or the beatdown, goes on.

2.8 The Outer Limits

Then there are the outlier cases, when decisions are made far outside of the writer's orbit that nonetheless impact how the writing is ultimately received by the player. I can think of at least one game where the story elements were placed in the game, complete with cut scenes, in the wrong order. This, unsurprisingly, scrambled player understanding a little bit. I know of games with dialog that was locked, recorded, and implemented before the design of the game was locked. Subsequent design changes rendered the recorded dialog inaccurate, to the point where it would tell players the wrong way to do key aspects of the game. However, there was no way to do a pickup voice recording session to correct these mistakes. There wasn't even a writer left on the team at that point to do the corrections. As a result, the game shipped with inaccurate dialog, which, of course, got absolutely hammered.

Unfortunately, "It was working when I left it" doesn't play as an excuse. The only thing that matters is the player experience, and it's too easy to be the one left holding the bag.

2.9 Summary

All of which is a very long way of saying that there are a great many steps in between a writer coming onto a project and the moment when the player experiences the writing. Each of those steps is a chance for something cool and wonderful to happen. Feedback and iteration can produce better and better work. Great casting, acting, and direction can make lines sing. Smooth integration with visuals and gameplay can cement writing as unforgettable if it plays at the right moment. The opportunity is there.

It is also, however, a chance for something horrible, destructive, and negative to the player experience to happen. Sometimes, all it takes is one slip along the way for the narrative to come across as suboptimal. All it takes is one meme-worthy slip-up, and the fertilizer can hit the fan. Then again, sometimes the writing hits every branch on the screw-up tree on the way down, and the results are epic in a very bad way.

Again, this is not to say there is no bad game writing. I have said this before, and I will say this again. There absolutely is, along with bad art, bad lighting, bad engineering, bad sound, bad animations, and bad production and creative direction. Sometimes, a writer is too inexperienced to do the job or was never trained properly on how to approach a particular task. Some writers are good writers but bad fits for the subject matter. After 23 years of tactical shooters, I shudder to think of what my writing would look like on a kids' game. And sometimes the writer isn't very good. There are times when it is absolutely appropriate to blame the writer for not writing well.

That's thankfully not the case all of the time. I don't think it's the case even the majority of the time, but most consumers of game content have no idea this is even an issue. It's the obvious read, and an awful lot of game devs and even writers can fall into this trap. They reflexively pivot to blame bad writers when there are other authors of failure whose actions remain unexamined and thus excused.

Now, though, you've got no excuse.

So if the writing comes across as bad, don't leap to the conclusion that the writing is the problem. Pay closer attention. Is it the performance? The presentation? Or something else?

Because blaming the writing without thinking, and thus the writer, masks all these other problems and issues. If everyone, including the executives at the company who made the game, leaps to that dismissive conclusion, then the actual problems that can crop up along the way never get recognized, let alone identified and fixed. If they don't get fixed, they happen all over again.

If you take one thing away from this chapter, it should be that issues with narrative presentation can pop up anywhere in the production pipeline and that there is a good chance the source of those problems is not the writer. The ones who are responsible, particularly those who sandbag the process at the beginning by refusing to allocate the proper time and resources to getting a good deliverable out of the writing team, need to be identified, called out, and either educated or replaced by folks who will do a better job of allowing for good writing deliverables as part of a fruitful game development process.

The cost of not changing, of not identifying all these concerns and doing something about them, is too damn high.

3

What Is a Game Writer? Brutal Realities of the Job

3.1 Asking the Question

Ask a dozen different game developers what a game writer's actual job is, and the best you will get is a sort of fuzzy "Well, they . . . write." Writing seems to occupy this hazy, mystical space in production, and nobody seems very clear on what it is writers do day to day. This mystery, and the reluctance to investigate it in order to get a clearer picture, leads to painful misunderstandings.

Admittedly, there are some writers who relish the whiff of strangeness that hovers about the role, using that mystique to abstract their work from input from others. In the end, this approach is counter-productive. Going full Wizard of Oz actively hinders efforts to integrate writing with other aspects of the game, like art and audio. Far better, then, to seek to promote understanding.

But if you want to help people understand what a game writer does, you have to know it yourself before you can tell them. Bear in mind that the details of the role can and do shift from studio to studio and project to project. Some studios want their writers inputting dialog in the engine after it's approved. Others are horrified at the notion of a writer-type touching the versioning software at all and insist that they stay as far from it as possible. It all depends on the culture and needs of the team.

That being said, certain basics have parallels throughout the industry, from AAA monsters to small indie games. And one is that the job is completely unique.

I cannot say this often enough: Being a video game writer is like nothing else, either in video games or in the larger field of writing. Certain other roles have similarities, but the job of pounding out words for a video game is something that is pretty much its own freaky thing. Writing for games has its own special language, its own unique types of deliverables, and its own needs. The fact that it is an interactive, not a linear, medium has a massive impact. So, too, does the fact that in games, writing is seldom the origination point or the focus of the project as a whole. Yet, people persist in comparing apples to horny melons and dragon fruits, and trying to make congruencies with other forms of writing where none exist.

There are lots of different types of writers. There are television and movie writers. There are fiction writers, some of whom specialize in long-form projects and some of whom prefer shorter ones. There are tabletop RPG and board and card game writers. There are poets. There are movie reviewers and people who compose novels on smartphones and more. The list goes on. Some writers are able to switch effortlessly between genres or even between forms. Some are not.

DOI: 10.1201/9781003592983-3

However, what is implicitly understood in the case of all of these other types of writers is that they are specialized, specific, necessary roles. The skills that enable you to succeed at one form do not mandate or even necessarily help provide success in another. No one in their right mind would hand a lyric poet a contract and a deadline to blast out the script for a US$200 million action movie script based solely on the fact that it's a job for a "writer." Hell, it's hard enough getting taken seriously if you're a horror writer and want to write straight-up high fantasy novels for a change. (Ask me how I know.) Still, the misconception persists that you can pluck any writer out of any other sub-discipline of writing and plop them down in video games to good effect.

I am here to tell you this is 100% false.

3.2 The Game Writer Stands Alone

There are indeed writers of movies and television and novels and TTRPGs who have transitioned seamlessly to writing for video games, but even the best of them needed time and training to be able to do the job right. Others simply never get what a video game needs that is unique to the form. There is nothing in their experience that prepares them for, say, the necessity to write systemic dialog or to take interactivity into account. As such, they flounder. I have been brought in to clean up after big-name writers from another field who simply couldn't hack it in games. Does this make any of them a bad writer? Absolutely not. I had nothing but respect for their work in other fields, much of which I have read or watched and enjoyed. The thing is, they weren't very good in *this* one, and they weren't willing or able to learn. Just like you wouldn't take a chef specializing in red sauce Italian cuisine, hand him a pile of raw fish, and tell him to create high-end sushi right now because the couple at table 12 is hungry, you can't plop a writer of some other form down into games and expect immediate perfection.

And to speak a hidden truth, sometimes when a "name" writer gets brought in, they don't do a lot of work in the actual trenches. They're more likely to be involved in high-concept work but producing few or no actual deliverables. The point of their involvement is a Marketing exercise. I can think of one game where the involvement of a notable Hollywood personality was trumpeted to the skies, but a friend on the project confided in me that the guy's contribution was limited to once in a while passing along cryptic two-line notes that would have made the Oracle at Delphi go "Huh?"

Another professional friend was working on a project that had a tight, professional game narrative team making good progress when a "name" from another medium was brought in to juice the games awareness. The "name" then proceeded to alienate the team, trash all of their work, destroy all of the work pipelines that were in place, and replace everything with stuff that was his and his alone. Unsurprisingly, this new direction glaringly reflected his lack of understanding of games, required tons of work to be discarded and replaced at great cost, and generally set things back by months if not years. In the end, the project went nowhere, with the narrative nonsense from this expensive millstone being a major contributor to the disaster.

Let's be clear: Game writer is a real, distinct, and serious job. It requires a particular set of skills that can be acquired and honed nowhere else but the games space. These go in addition to the base writer skills that require you to be able to write at a professional level. To think otherwise is to invite calamity. I can think of one project that I was initially the writer on but got removed from because I made the mistake of questioning the narrative mandate from on high. They canned me, brought in a Hollywood writer, and then proceeded to pay him a lot more than they had been paying me, only to receive months of zero results. Eventually, they had to fire him and bring me back, and lo and behold, we ultimately got a game out of it. Lesson learned, or so you'd think, but the cycle keeps repeating.

3.3 This Means Something. This Is Important

At this point, it is important to establish what being a working game writer means and what it does not. Let's start with the negative definitions, as they're easier to get out of the way. Besides, it's more fun to end on a high note.

First and foremost, unless you are very senior on a game that is specifically narrative-driven or you are an auteur (and thus likely doing more on a game than strictly writing), you are not the primary driver of the game's content or concept. A game writer, as valuable as that role is, is not the engine that powers everything else. It is, instead, a complementary element, intended to work in harmony with other elements to create a synergistically better whole. The rest of the team is not a collective pair of hands there to bring your vision to life. You are not there to give orders, demand things that you are not necessarily entitled to, or otherwise throw your weight around in a way that negatively impacts the production as a whole. Do that, and you will find yourself ignored at best, unemployed at worst.

Simultaneously, you must remember at all times that you are there to make a *game*. Yes, the game may be part or even the cornerstone of a new intellectual property, laying out the groundwork for novels, television shows or movies, comic books, and more, but at the end of the day, if you're a game writer, you're there to make the actual game. That means you write game stuff. Some of that will never be seen by players because it is directed at other team members. Some of it needs to be directed squarely at the player base. None, or at least very little of it, needs to exist up front to flesh out stuff that neither the player nor the rest of the team will ever see and that does not impact the moment-to-moment experience the player has interacting with the game content. Writing for your own delight, enjoyment, or obsessive-compulsive mania does not serve the purpose you were hired for.

There is nothing wrong with writing stuff you find delightful. In fact, I hope you feel that way about most of your writing. (If you take endless delight in writing endless variants on "Grenade!," though, I might start to worry.) If pleasing yourself is the only end goal of your work with no room for "do the job you were hired to do," then you're not doing the job right.

Let me be clear: There is nothing wrong with creating detailed backstory elements chock full of story hooks that can be attached to later as needed. It's that there *is* something wrong with taking the time and effort away from stuff that will ultimately be player-facing to instead painstakingly craft bits of the universe's lore that no one except you will ever see or care about. If your long-gone demon empire is indeed long gone and nothing remains of it but some ruins, then you don't need to spend time and money on detailing out how their irrigation systems worked. Just say there were ruins, put a pin in it so you can come back to it later if there is a need, and move on. It's a matter of focusing your time and effort on what you are actually supposed to be doing for the game as a whole.

3.4 Small Gear, Big Machine

Ultimately, you need to accept that you are a part of a much bigger machine, and you are far from the biggest part. You must embrace the idea that you will be working with internal customers as well as external ones, that your work is necessary to making the game but not what the game is about, and that you must inevitably bow to the greater collective needs. Your work needs to be a part of the game, not outside it or in conflict with it, and you must collaborate with everyone else who will be actualizing your writing. It's sad, but magic pixies are not going to convey your story to players psychically without you talking to the audio team or UI or whoever else is actually making in-game assets.

If you do not fundamentally understand that you are one part of a team – if you cannot accept and even take pride and joy in that – then you are in trouble. Yes, the stereotype of the writer has always been of the lone scribbler in a dark room, feverishly typing away under a swinging, burned-out light bulb. Or maybe it's the Emily Dickinson cliché, tying poems up with neat ribbons in solitude, to be discovered by the universe postmortem so everyone can recognize your genius once you're gone and feel sorry they didn't beforehand. As far as game writing is concerned, this is dangerous bunk.

While fiction and other writing forms may be solo to start, even they involve collaboration sooner or later. The comics writer needs the artist (assuming they aren't the artist to begin with), the letterer, and the inker. The scriptwriter may write the script, but it's going to get marked up and rewritten on set; there will be endless notes, and it takes the actors, Director, cinematographers, and everyone else to make it into a movie. Even the poet needs an editor and a publisher, and if they're doing a book, most likely a cover artist.

Collaboration with other team members from other departments is not anathema. The difference here is that it is wired into the job's DNA to happen before and during composition as well as after, and some people find that to be an intrusion on their creative integrity. If that's how they feel, that's how they feel, but the truth is that's how the sausage gets made, and if you want to be in the figurative room, you have to accept that it's not your room and you won't be alone in there.

3.5 The Negative and the Way Forward

All of this sounds very negative, to be sure, and there's a reason. While it's nice to pretend that we're all one unified community marching forward in harmony and refusing to criticize each other, the truth is that some folks are better and some folks are worse, and some folks can do the job and some folks can't. Sometimes, even, folks who can't do the job get hired and promoted and hired again, while folks who can and have knocked it out of the park are left out in the cold by corporate politics or nepotism or prejudice or numbers crunches or things that went wrong on a previous project that they were in no way responsible for. With that being the case, you need to understand *what* you are there to do if you intend to continue doing it.

It is worthwhile, then, to call out the bad in order to differentiate it from and elevate the good. Furthermore, I think a lot of bad game writers aren't bad by choice or inclination but instead got dumped in the deep end without help and have nonetheless found a way to survive. If this book can help them, I'll be happy.

Unfortunately, yes, there are game writers who do it wrong and whose bad behaviors need to be eradicated going forward for the good of the craft and its practitioners.

Do I think the majority of game writers are bad? Of course not. Furthermore, I abhor the practice of victim-blaming that the game writing community seems to have adopted. In my online series of posts about game writing, the comments sections can fill up with working writers chiming in to tear down other writers as unworthy or unprepared or needing to do this thing better or that, when a significant portion of the time, the things that lead to bad writing deliverables come from elsewhere. And those same writers eager to turn on juniors for the crime of being juniors seem almost pathologically afraid of calling out producers for creating bad schedules or Creative Directors for giving inconsistent feedback.

That needs to stop. Where writers can and should improve, they need to be called out and given the tools and opportunities they need to improve. If they won't improve, they need to start on a high, fast trajectory out of the industry to make room for someone who will do it right. As for the rest of us, we need to celebrate the good our fellow writers are doing and reinforce it, which leads us to the positive aspects of the role of game writer, and they are many.

Let's start with the big one. As a game writer, you get paid to tell stories to thousands, if not millions, of people. Your job is literally to help people you have never met have fun, feel emotions, create moments of excitement that they will remember and share, and generally be an instrument of joy in a world sadly in need of it. Sometimes achieving this means doing work that is, in and of itself, less than entirely fun, but the end result is so often worth it.

The big picture role for a game writer breaks down to this. Your job is to use words to communicate and enhance the vision of the game to your team members in order to help them collaborate with you and do their jobs, and to the audience in order to give them the best play experience possible. Yes, that is a very long sentence, but the core idea is simple and clear. Use your words to make good stuff. That's it. Everything else is details.

How you use those words, though – that's the sticky part. Depending on the needs, platform, size, budget, and other aspects of the game you might be working on, the writing needs can fluctuate. Not every game needs all the writing in the world. This is a canard frequently recited by people who do not understand game writing and how it works and who use the missing middle fallacy to suggest that there is nothing between the immense verbiage of *Baldur's Gate 3* and the mute elegance of *Tetris*.

Some games just need a frame story or occasional on-screen caption. Some need a strong central narrative that requires fleshing out through dialog and cut scenes. Some need a locust swarm of barks before you even start writing mission dialog. It varies, and it is your job as a game writer to be prepared to create everything that might be on the menu.

3.6 The Actual Deliverables

One of the enduring myths about game writing is that you're just writing the big, exciting stuff. Everyone looks at trailers and cinematics and thinks that's the main course, but it really isn't. Moments like that, where you're writing the splashy stuff that gets played once in the game and that's all, are a relatively small part of the job. They're a vital and hopefully a quotable part, yes, but a small one. A huge portion of your work as a game writer never gets in front of the player at all, at least not if you can help it.

(I once had a series of working world notes for a game that I had written largely for self-reference and the use of other writers get picked up by the Marketing department, poured into a book with lots of art, and released, thankfully, without my name on it. Those notes were unpolished, unedited, and never meant for public consumption, and I remain aghast to this day that the book ever happened. At least someone was kind enough to sneak me a free copy for my brag shelf.)

Those documents that the player never sees but which set up huge chunks of the game are often your purview. They may not be sexy, but they are absolutely necessary. You are responsible, as noted earlier, for transforming vision into actionable words, and that includes things like character designs and backstories that can then be picked up by concept artists, modelers, and animators in order for them to work their own magic. These are foundational documents for the game, and so much gets built on them that they require craft as elegant as the most expensive cut scene, even if they go to a mere half-dozen readers.

As such, when you write them, as with anything you write, you need to keep in mind who you are writing for. Something you write about a character for the fanbase will focus on certain things, but those are not the same things the person drawing the concept art needs to know.

As a result, make sure that if you're writing a document that will be used to create a character's appearance, you describe their looks, their clothes, their style, and their unique features. Don't be prescriptive and write out every last detail down to the color of their shoelaces and the exact text on the labels in their clothes – you don't want to reduce a concept artist to the equivalent of a short-order cook – but do call out key things as needed that the concept can't survive without.

Similarly, if the document is going to get handed to animation to show how a character (or monster) moves, then make sure you give good descriptions of those movements that make a character, who the player may only see from the back for 100-plus hours, unique and cool. Don't skimp on the stuff that will be useful down the line, the voice notes and personality traits, and even some basic personal history that someone writing or recording this character will need. Be aware that you don't need to front-load all that, and you will have the capability to add it in elsewhere when it is needed.

And now for a little heresy: The bulk of your work is words, yes, and absolutely should be. With that in mind, there is no reason not to do what you can as a writer to help people digest and connect with your words. That, when you're dealing with artists, means visual reference. Or, in the language of the rest of the world, pictures and even video clips. You should seek to back up what you are trying to describe for an artist with images that either display what you want or inspire it. Make sure you make clear what the images are there for – a headshot of a movie actress to reference her hairstyle for a character in one game turned into a snowball effect that ended up with her eventually being cast as our main villain, haircut and all – but it is never cheating to make your case to best effect. Do the same thing with videos for animators, by the way. Get your point across, and if words alone are not going to do it – I once worked with an artist who literally deleted Microsoft Word off his hard drive so he had an excuse to never, ever read a document – pictures will definitely help.

3.7 Narrative Fantasy

Another key task of the role is the presentation of the narrative fantasy. Remove the narrative from a video game, and all you've got is button mashing on a piece of plastic. Every game has some narrative framing, even something as open and plotless as *Minecraft*. What *Minecraft* (or *Tetris*, because they *always* reference *Tetris*) does not have is a *plot*, which is not the same thing at all. The fact that you are given a pickaxe and a sword in that game is, much to many people's surprise, an expression of narrative. The choice of those two implements over, say, a Black and Decker Multitool and an AR-15 firmly establishes you in a non-technologically advanced, non-modern space, and that allows everything else that happens in that space to flow naturally as a result. The same is true for pretty much every game, large or small.

With writing comes the narrative fantasy, the role the player takes on, and the things they want to do in game. A lot of times, this is simple. The player wants to step into the shoes of a space marine and shoot aliens, or an elf archer and shoot mind flayers because everybody hates mind flayers, or a post-apocalyptic survivor and shoot zombies, or . . .

I'm mostly kidding with the examples, but the point stands. The role and the key action should be inextricably intertwined. Your job as a writer is to make sure that they are and then that they are in alignment with what the game is designed and intended to do well. You have to make the player want to do for narrative reasons what the game is designed to have them do, do well, and often do repeatedly.

If your game mechanics are centered around stealth and detection and silent kills, and your main character is therefore a spy, it is your job as a writer to craft that spy's story so that it is natural and interesting and desirable to sneak and be stealthy and do silent kills. If you write a character in that situation who is best suited to spray-and-pray gunfire, you have detached the narrative fantasy from the game, and things will go very badly as a result. The player will want to do things the game is not set up for them to do, the content that does exist does not get accessed by players looking to run and gun, and the whole thing ends up being a mess. The fantasy is not fulfilled, the player is frustrated, and they either ignore the writing thereafter or quit the game because it's not providing what they were promised.

Instead of doing that, make the whole thing seamless. The player should want to do for story reasons what the game does well because the character they want to inhabit and whose story they want to experience is skilled at those things. I have long held that the supposed antagonism between gameplay and story is, in fact, pure organic fertilizer. Both are elements of the overall player experience, and both should work together to reinforce each other to create the best player experience possible. Competition between or separation of the two yields a more disjointed, disconnected experience with unusable exit hatches every which way.

3.8 Character Voice

One more thing that falls to you as a game writer is establishing and using character voices. Each character should have a unique and appropriate voice, and by voice I mean how they express themselves. This includes lots of different elements, starting with but not limited to accent, diction, syntax, grammar, length of sentences, length of paragraphs, how often and how long they speak, how much profanity and/or slang they might use, how technical their language might be, any emotional underpinnings that inform the words they use, how fast they speak, and what pop culture elements they are likely to understand and reference. All of that comes together to form a unique mode of expression that should allow a character to be instantly identifiable. It should provide direction on their age, background, social status, education, and more, and it should feel appropriate as a logical outgrowth of those character details.

Or, to put it another way, some stuff sounds right coming out of a particular character's mouth. On the other hand, some stuff doesn't, and it is up to you to make sure you produce the former and not the latter.

Functionally, this means deciding on a character voice's elements, locking them down, and then communicating them to everyone else who might touch that character. This goes for Marketing to ensure that the character's presentation in ads and trailers is consistent; it goes for Art (so they don't, say, put a modern teenager in stuff they remember as being cool from their school days in the 1990s); it goes for animation (meaning if they're creating dances for the character, they give the old guy the Electric Slide or maybe the Achy Breaky and don't have them doing the latest craze instead, except maybe for humor value); and on and on.

It also means building something that another writer can pick up and run with right out of the box because you cannot guarantee that you will always be the only one to write a given character for all eternity. That's just not how the business works – you can move on from a company, a company can move on from you, you can get moved off a project, or you can be assigned different deliverables and need other writers to step in to pick up what you laid down. It doesn't matter. The professionally responsible thing to do is to prepare each and every character you write in such a way that if you have to hand them off, you can do so knowing that there is a strong reference base for whoever comes after.

3.9 The Other Invisible

Beyond this, there are a ton of game writer tasks that are invisible to outside eyes. You need to champion the writing constantly and broadly to the rest of the team so that they see value in what you do and want more of it. You need to propose, establish, reinforce, and defend processes for writing that will get your words from your screen into the game. That covers everything from helping set reasonable deliverable schedules to creating a good process for feedback and lining up things like table reads. You need to build bridges with other writing-adjacent groups on the team you are on.

Do this, and they will take your work into consideration when doing theirs and vice versa in hopes of creating a gloriously unified whole. You need to write the documents that other team members need to do their jobs, like character descriptions for concept artists and map element histories for level builders. You will almost certainly be heavily involved in crafting character count-appropriate text strings for UI, and you will probably be fielding all the questions from localization about what a given line of dialog actually means, allowing the spirit of the line to be translated instead of the letter. You will be thankful for this, by the way, because the alternative is an idiomatic usage in your script that gets translated literally and produces an international flame war incident.

And that's just the start. You will need to do research, lots and lots of research, particularly if you are working on a game that either draws on real-world stuff or has a deep body of existing lore. I recall one game I worked on where there was a raging war among players over whether the gun models had been created with the right color of electrical tape wrapped around their bits. You may or may not be asked, depending on the team and the tools, to implement your writing in-engine and get your hands dirty on the technical side of things. There is a non-zero chance, depending on the scope of your project, that you will go into the recording studio to offer support, context, and on-the-spot rewrites – more on this later. You will even, and this pretty much never gets listed in the job description, get called in to help with Marketing deliverables to produce catchphrases and punch up interview answers and the like.

You may have noticed, if you've gotten that far, that I have largely forgotten to mention the basic task of a game writer thus far, which is to say "writing." There's a reason for that.

What it comes down to is that the actual act of writing as a game writer is obvious. It's right there in the title. Too often, people think that's all there is to it; as a result, they think that all a game writer has to do is sit down and scribble, and then the rest is dark sorcery that needs no human intervention. By putting this last, I am deliberately elevating all the other, non-intuitive tasks that you absolutely have to do to survive as a professional writer of games. These are things you have to be aware of. These are the things you absolutely have to know how to do. These are vitally intrinsic aspects of the job, and if you're not prepared to do them – or not able to learn them when asked – then you might be setting yourself up for failure down the line.

3.10 Oh, and the Writing

Remember, the head-down, words-out writing always does matter. When everything else boils away under the heat of deadlines, you are the champion of words, and you must use those words for the benefit of the game.

You will be asked to write all sorts of words. Be prepared to be versatile because they all matter in a way that doesn't exist in any other medium. The common misconception, again, is that all the writer does is the cool, expensive stuff, and that could not be further from the truth. Yes, there is often dialog that goes along the Golden Path of the player experience to direct and reward them. There are sometimes very pretty, very expensive cinematics or scripted sequences that call for what is essentially movie-style dialog since in those moments, interactivity is often lacking. Those are the sexy, high-profile parts of the gig. But they are not the most important, and they are not the largest, and if you are not prepared to write all the other totally necessary stuff, then this is not the job for you.

If you think you are too good or too creative to write barks, then you need to re-examine your understanding of your role. Yes, barks are short and repetitive, and the best ones are aggressively devoid of personality because the last thing you want is to hear the same witty one-liner called out ten times by five different mooks in a single firefight, but they are also the dialog the player hears most in the game. They are what provides the information the player uses to react moment to moment. They are incredibly important and quite possibly the most important writing in the game. Yes, coming up with new and kind of exciting ways to say "I've been shot!" isn't creating deathless prose, but it is creating something valuable for the game through your words. That's the sort of challenge a good game writer embraces.

That's just looking at some of the material the player encounters. There's a ton I haven't even gone into depth on, because it's mostly variations on a theme. Writing audio logs, for example, offers a unique episodic writing challenge. Writing spray-painted graffiti on a bombed-out, post-apocalyptic city wall is a fun collaboration with art and level design to come up with the right words presented in the right place and font and color and style. It doesn't matter if it offers a key plot hint or not; it's still got to be good. And of course (and this was briefly mentioned earlier), there is the task of creating text strings for the UI, which is a game of coming up with interesting, game-metaphor-appropriate ways of saying the same stuff over and over again, with the added limitation of brutal character count limits. You have not lived as a game writer until you have gotten the frantic "This item name is six characters too long! We have to think of the German version!" message (because German words for game stuff are generally much longer than English ones) in the middle of the night.

3.11 Writing for the Team – Specifics

Let's take a step back and look at the writing you do that the public never sees. A lot of writers who don't know better think of this as drudge work, as something unimportant because it's not flashy and uninteresting. They think this because it often is descriptive and supportive instead of being "creative," whatever that means.

Nothing could be further from the truth. If the game is the gourmet meal presented to a player, this is the equivalent of writing the menu, buying the ingredients, and making sure no one has gotten wacky with the spice rack. All sorts of tasks for a game writer live in this space, from the tiny to the immense.

There is a good chance, for example, that you will be asked to contribute to, if not take charge of, a document called a bible. This is a touchstone document for the game's narrative content, laying out who, what, how it works, and on and on, all in one well-organized and easily readable place (or at least such is the theory). This document serves as a central reference for teams, Marketing, licensing partners, and more, and as such has to be on the money and accessible. Writing (and updating) it is a major task, requiring encyclopedic knowledge of the setting (which helps anyway), the ability to write concise content (because this is not the place for lengthy in-depth descriptions; it's a taste, not the whole meal) and the ability to organize what is literally a world's worth of content.

And if that wasn't enough, there are character descriptions to write and world history to create. There's stuff the art team needs to know about, say, the history of a particular building on a map, and there's stuff the animators need to know about how a character moves. There's material for the level-building team that can be anything from a broad overview of a space to "[T]hese are the five species of trees we should see on the map if we don't want to get pilloried online, and I'm telling you this now so you don't accidentally build the wrong trees instead." If your game has magic – and your game probably has magic or the science fiction/horror equivalent – there are metaphysics to codify with the help of Design, a basic primer on "how all this stuff works in the world" that might inform character dialog but should never be just blasted at the player. The list goes on.

Your writing for the team is very different than the stuff you need to create for the game and ultimately the players. While you do have to take care to present your content in a way that is respectful, accessible, and open, you don't need to indulge in the level of polish that player-facing deliverables require. In fact, this can be an active hindrance to getting the job done: An infinite polish job on a doc that just needs to be functional, not a crystalline manifestation of immortal prose that will be looked to as inspiration down the ages, bottlenecks production, forces the people who will be using your writing to create other assets to wait, and reinforces the negative stereotype of writers as snooty perfectionists who don't understand how a game gets made. And if you think that I made that sentence deliberately overcomplicated to prove a point, you're starting to get it.

All of this and more is as much a part of the game writer's job as the shiny, prominent bits. All of it matters, and devaluing a task because it's not going to get your name in front of the fans as much as writing a cut scene might is not going to do your professional reputation any good. The industry is small, and people talk, and word gets around as to who is willing to put in the work and who isn't. And not just some of the work – all of it.

Because in the end, you have to do it all, you have to do it fast, and you have to do it right no matter how thoroughly the production deck is stacked against you. These are the brutal realities of the big picture. On a very real level as a game writer, you are creating assets that happen to be made of words instead of 3D models or lines of code. As a game writer, you are a contributor, a gear in a much larger machine.

If that sounds like I'm diminishing the job, well, I'm not. Game writers are cogs, but take that cog out of the larger machine and you'll start to hear grinding noises as the system breaks down. It is an important role. It's just one that needs to be understood for what it is and why it can be hard. Fail to see that – go in thinking you're going to drive the train or that certain tasks are beneath you – and you're doomed. Embrace that, and you'll be in a position to potentially achieve joy and create wonders.

3.12 Writing versus Narrative Design

Now, there is one distinction that must be made before we go any further, and that is the one between writing and narrative design.

Narrative design is not necessarily something people automatically think of or even recognize as existing. After all, writing is a process people kind of understand. Taking that writing and putting together all the pieces that deliver it to the player? It might as well be magic to a lot of players.

Let me assure you, though, that doing that is a very real job, and it's called narrative design. Furthermore, as games have gotten more technologically advanced, the role of the narrative designer has similarly grown in complexity. That doesn't stop people from getting confused about how narrative design and writing are different, but as a writer, you need to be aware of the real and important distinction between the two.

There is some controversy over the origin of the term "narrative designer," but the truth is that the phrase was coined by Mary DeMarle in the early 2000s at Ubisoft Montreal. Game writing was struggling to get any kind of recognition in those days, and the smart play was to position it as a form of game design. This, theoretically, would cloak it in a vaguely technical context and garner more respect and consideration than it might get otherwise.

Times change, however. Narrative design and game writing have both developed extensively from those halcyon days of yore. They are not the same thing, nor have they been for many years. There is absolutely some overlap between the two, and it is right and appropriate for them to be grouped together on team organizational charts and the like. It is important to remember that they are complementary, not congruent, and mistaking the one for the other can lead to a lot of pain.

In my experience, both narrative design and game writing sit comfortably under the larger umbrella of Narrative. This is to say that both groups, assuming there is a group and not just one person, should be reporting to a Narrative Director who's in charge of getting the most out of them to create and support the game's narrative elements together. Their portfolio covers everything from narrative delivery systems to the actual words. Depending on the size of the narrative team, there should probably be a Lead Writer who takes point on all writing tasks but who reports to the Narrative Director. This is because Narrative is more than just writing, and all aspects have to be taken into account when stuff is getting kicked up to a team leadership level.

Thinking that writing should be in the driver's seat on the Narrative team is wrongheaded and shortsighted. The best words in the world aren't worth a damn if you don't have good systems for getting them in front of players in a way that players can appreciate. Good writing that gets hidden in a bad feature might as well not exist. Instead, it's a collaborative situation, where everyone's pulling together to put the best content out there in the way that players will like best and take advantage of.

There is the key difference, one that is worth exploring.

The way I have always defined it, narrative design is about how the narrative is conveyed to the player, while game writing is what specifically is conveyed to the player.

Narrative design, then, can be a lot more technical than game writing. It encompasses the conception, description, and sometimes the construction of the systems by which narrative is exposed to the player. This does not happen in a vacuum, and the process involves a lot of overlap with engineering and game design. It is all about conceptualizing the *how* of transmitting narrative to players and then formally detailing how the stuff you want to do is going to get done.

This has to happen before any in-game dialog or when text gets written. The shape and need of the narrative systems, ranging from dialog to barks, define the shape and content of writing deliverables. Imagine all you want, but unless you have a specific feature your words can get plugged into, they're not going anywhere, and heaven help you if they don't fit.

That's the narrative designer's role on the front end. On the back end, they're often responsible for implementation of narrative content, getting it in the engine, building string tables, and the like. In other words, they make your words useful. They serve as the bridge between raw imagination and functional implementation, and without robust narrative design, the writing gets lost.

In this context, however, game writing is *writing*. It is the creation of the assets, which happen to be made of words, that the systems created by narrative design will then convey to the player in entertaining and appropriate ways. The game writer feeds the beast with writing in whatever form it is needed. Whether that is team-facing documentation to help others create assets or player-facing writing that gets implemented into the game itself to help create the experience is ultimately a granular distinction.

As a game writer, you want to be friends with narrative design for lots of reasons. They are your closest allies on the team, and they have the best understanding of what you do. Also, you want them to do right by your writing. One of the many ways that game writing gets unfairly slammed is if it is implemented poorly, and that starts with the narrative design of the systems putting it out there. Build a good relationship with narrative design, and you can communicate your wants and needs to them in a way that will get those things heard. Work hand in hand, and you can present a unified front when pitching narrative features to the rest of the possibly skeptical team.

Real issues for writing and for the game arise when there is no dedicated narrative design presence or when narrative-adjacent design tasks get owned by teams that have no understanding of how what they're doing might negatively impact the player's experience of the narrative.

Take, for example, a game where the bark system was designed and written for a certain frequency of lines triggering for certain state changes like "the enemy has detected you" versus "the enemy has gone off alert." Because things were designed for a certain frequency of line calls, that allowed writers to tailor their deliverables – specifically the number of variants for these triggers for each guard – to the expected need. If you only think that five barks are going to be triggered in any given encounter, you don't need to write 50.

So far, so good. However, when a change is made to the detection sensitivity, suddenly those lines start playing a lot more often than planned. More frequent calls mean more lines the player hears in a given encounter, and the faster those pools of variants get emptied. This, in turn, leads to faster repetition of lines, as the various NPCs cycle through their bark pools more quickly than before and then start all over again. The end result is a firefight that sounds like a summer pool game of "Marco Polo," with everyone shouting things out all the time. This, in turn, means the player hears those particular barks way more often than intended, starts to notice repetition, and generally gets annoyed by these lame-brained guards who keep shouting the same things over and over.

All that, from a gap in communications when a narrative-adjacent feature got tweaked.

Is there overlap between narrative design and game writing? Of course. There are some teams where there are no developers explicitly tagged as writers, and the writing workload gets handled by the narrative designers in addition to their other duties. Even on teams where there are both writers and narrative designers, there are times when narrative designers want or need to take a crack at writing tasks to exercise and develop that part of their professional skill set. And they are certainly involved in all sorts of discussions about everything from high-level story stuff to what specific lines might be needed to guide a player through a mission.

By the same token, game writers can sometimes stray into narrative design territory. Reaching out with ideas for ways narrative can be presented and pitching those features should be on the table. Bringing writing expertise to bear on a narrative system design can save painful mistakes and time wasted implementing unworkable solutions.

3.13 Summary

I know. It's a lot. The job often gets discussed as "you write the story and some dialog," and then you can dust your hands and call it a day. The truth of the day-to-day is so far from that it isn't funny, except in an "I'm laughing to keep from crying" sort of way.

To do the job, you must embrace the truth of the job, and that includes every aspect. Understand what you're getting yourself into, and prepare yourself for a dive into the deep end. Dipping your toe in is often a luxury. Far better to be ready for the plunge.

4

The Unique Things That Go into Game Writing and Nothing Else – The Player-Shaped Hole, Barks, and Letting Go

4.1 What Is Unique?

Game writing is a unicorn. It has some familiar shapes to its outline, but there's nothing quite like it, and pinning it down can be quite elusive. This can be attributed to the fact that it is its own form, with specific constraints, demands, deliverables, and limitations that no other form of writing contains. Recognizing and embracing those singular elements of the job are what will allow you to do it well.

There are things you won't do in game writing that you will do in, say, a novel. For example, in my novels, I frequently find myself writing extended passages of description of a location in order to set the mood and tone. I never have to do that in a video game, at least not in anything player-facing. There are artists to take care of that, and audio engineers, and lighting specialists, and all those folks have it as their job to, among other things, set the scene and the mood such that I never need to reach for an adverb angrily. Most of the time there isn't even a place for the adverb to go if I wanted one. As a result, I get to turn that part of my writer brain off.

Similarly, there are things that do happen in games writing that don't happen anywhere else. No other medium, for example, demands barks – systemic dialog used to communicate what's called a state change in the world to the player through a line of dialog. They frequently need to be written in numbers that boggle the mind. At the same time, among those tens of thousands, a single bad or awkward one can turn you into a laughingstock, and they have to be created in concert with engineers who are creating the NPC behaviors your barks will be calling out. There is nothing like this in a movie or a novel, where every line is bespoke and authored, even the improvised ones.

You also have to write to the technical limitations of the game. There is stuff a game cannot do, even if you write it. You cannot call for animations that don't exist, for character or object models that were never made, or for player actions that have never been designed, much less implemented. Your sandbox as a writer has certain mile-high walls, and attempting to scale them is futile.

The point of this chapter, then, is to call out those unique aspects of game writing that you should be aware of going forward. It's not going to be a how-to – there are plenty of books for that that go far deeper than I want to. However, there will be some tips and techniques for mastering this stuff in the next chapter.

You have to understand this stuff first before you can successfully apply it.

DOI: 10.1201/9781003592983-4

4.2 The Three Aspects

Let's start with the big concepts. The way I approach things, there are three aspects to game storytelling. As a writer, you are directly responsible for one of them and indirectly responsible for the other two growing out of that first one. Understanding this is the key to happiness as a game writer. Far too many would-be game writers do not understand the limits of their power in this arena and get themselves lost in the weeds as a result.

The first is what I call Narrative. Other game writers and narrative designers and ludologists and ludo-narrative specialists and whoever else might disagree, but it's my book, and I've been using this model for the better part of two decades, so either skip this chapter or buckle up and come along for the ride.

In my view, Narrative is literally what we as game writers (and our friends the narrative designers) do. It is the deliverables we make, the elements that get turned into a story. It is every line of dialog, every scrap of writing in the world, every name for an item, and more.

It is also emphatically not a story.

It can be plot, absolutely. In a lot of cases, it has to be. You and your teammates need to hammer down the sequence of events so you can lay the track for the player and ready the world for anything they might do. You need to anticipate, you need to steer, and you need to plan for what happens when things go wrong.

This means you prepare the conversations. Prepare the documents they read. Prepare the audio logs they might listen to. Prepare the wanted posters, the graffiti, the ambient background chatter, and everything else that needs words to make it happen. That, my friend, is what I call Narrative – the narrative elements in place in the game.

That's the thing, you see. They're in place. They're there. They're *waiting*.

What they're not doing is . . . doing.

At least, not until the player comes along.

Think of it this way: The stuff we actively create, the deliverables we provide – those are akin to all the elements that are backstage before the curtain goes up on a play. We make the script and all the stuff that, without the actors out there under the lights, is inert. It is nothing but potential.

Waiting.

However, once an actor comes along – or, in our case, a player – everything changes.

Because when a player interacts with the Narrative elements we create, something amazing happens. The moment the player interacts with something we created, it becomes part of the player's linear personal experience through the game. It becomes, in short, part of a Story.

Story, the way I see it, is the linear sequence of events created by the player's act of playing. This is true even if the game itself is resolutely non-linear. The specific and unique way each player moves through it – because no two players are going to play the exact same way at the exact same pace – becomes their story that they have authored. They have put flesh on the bones you crafted, and as a result it has come alive.

Part and parcel of this is instinctively understanding that the story is not yours. It is the player's. The plot may be yours. The individual scripted sequences, certainly. But the pace, the rhythm, the exact sequence of events, and the precise route taken to achieve them – all of this is the player's. If you don't understand this, if you try to exert authorial control in the space that does not belong to you, nobody wins. The player feels constrained. You get frustrated because the player won't do exactly what you want them to do, when you want them to do it, to create the precise effect you imagined. Everybody's unhappy.

Instead, just as you drive the creation of the Narrative aspects, the player drives the creation of the Story second by second. As long as they keep playing, they keep authoring the story. They can take breaks, they can abandon the Golden Path to play fishing minigames, they can play something else for a while and then come back to your game and pick up where they left off. It doesn't matter. It's their story. Your work was building the superstructure.

As much as the publishers of live service games wish, though, no story lasts forever. Sooner or later, there comes an ending. The player runs out of content, or they run out of enjoyment, or the servers go dark. It happens. Alternately, players chop their experiences into smaller chunks, individual play sessions' worth (especially for round-based games like battle royales and extraction shooters). Either way, there comes an ending.

At which point, another miracle happens. The player, who was the author of their story, becomes the editor and teller of what I call their War Story. This consists of the story the player then tells to their audience, whether it be friends or social media followers, of their gameplay experience.

The difference between Story and War Story is simple. Story is everything that happens, built brick by brick in the moment of interaction. War Story comes afterwards, from a place of memory and assessment. It is the edited sequence of events, crafted into a smooth retelling without all the pitfalls and wrong turns and brief failures that make up the results when the player takes the reins. It's like editing an interview to take out all the "umm"s and "you know"s to make everything feel seamless and planned. That is the pure essence of the game writing you did, alchemically transformed by the player twice. The first time is when they first activate the stuff you made, creating Story. The second is when they re-cut the story to be leaner, funnier, cooler, and whatever else they need it to be, as War Story.

One other thing: Damn near every single instance of War Story, whether it is a blog post or a YouTube video or a voiceover on a stream or just a verbal tale told to friends, starts with the same word.

That word is "I." Not Link. Not Lara Croft. Not Ellie or Master Chief or Samus or Batman or even Pac-Man. In that moment, the player's understanding that they are the author of the story is absolute. They are claiming the story as theirs. It's made from the ingredients you in large part created, but you willingly surrendered it the instant the game was released.

Accept this basic truth, and the job gets a whole lot easier and more rewarding. Fight it, and you just create heaping helpings of frustration for everyone involved. This is the crux of the idea of games being interactive entertainment. It is players telling their own stories, gorgeous Frankenstein creatures stitched together second by second from the things you offered them.

4.3 The Player-Shaped Hole

That, more than anything else, is what you must understand without reservation or hindrance in order to achieve your best self as a game writer. You have to recognize that you are building things you must willingly let go. You can plot as intricately as you want, but whatever you come up with has to be able to operate independently of you.

It also needs to be flexible. Linear media depend so much on controlled pacing to achieve maximum effect, but the ability to do that is severely curtailed in games. As a writer of interactive content, you need to tailor your plots to be independent of that tightly prescribed build. Your big moments can and should still be big and impactful. The road to them should be meaningful. With that in mind, firefights are going to take as long as they're going to take. Puzzles are going to get solved on their own schedule. Completists are going to search every inch of every space with methodical, slow precision instead of rushing to the next big moment. Speedrunners are going to blow through your content as quickly as possible without letting any of it sink in because that's not the story they want to create. Players can even tuck their avatars into safe corners to go off and have a sandwich before taking up the quest again. And your writing must contain these multitudes and work for every single one of them simultaneously.

When you think about it that way, it does seem kind of hard and impressive.

I call this "Writing to the Player-Shaped Hole." In linear media, the main character drives the action, meaning writers write to their progress.

In video games, on the other hand, the main character is just the skin-suit (or powered armor, or exoskeleton, or, well, you get the idea) the player slips into to provide context for their actions in the game. The character is absolutely vital, of course – their needs and wants and motivations are adopted by the player as a reason to progress. But they are ultimately hollow. It is only when that void at their center is filled by a player that they come to life and power forward to new experiences.

What that means practically is that you cannot write to the certainty of action. Even if your game is a rail shooter, even if specific puzzles have to be solved in a specific order, there are going to be differences in the way each player approaches the act of playing. And because of that wild card, that inability to pin everything down at a precise moment in a precise sequence, you end up writing to a *possibility space.*

Think about that for a moment. It means everything you create has to be in anticipation of what the player might at any moment do so that when they take that action, it feels like it was right and proper and appropriate all along. What you absolutely don't want is to leave a possibility uncovered such that the player wants to do something that seems logical and appropriate, can't, and then has their disbelief shattered. There's nothing worse than having your badass space marine unable to complete a simple task that a real-world kindergartener could handle with panache.

And I will be honest, that can be incredibly hard, especially if you were trained in writing styles where the author has total control of character action at all times. I confess I was lucky – I came to video games from tabletop RPGs and LARPs, which meant I was used to writing to what the player might do instead of what I wanted them to do. The difference there, though, was that TTRPGs operate on a limitless polygon budget of the imagination so that writing for those games is an exercise in giving people tools to expand their storytelling outward. All a tabletop game master has to do is say, "ten thousand ogres come over the hill," and there they are. Try that in a video game, and it's a question of which explodes first, the GPU or the Art Director's head.

Video games, on the other hand, are all about an approach that directs the player inward to take advantage of the things the game systems are designed to support. Good game writing marries the narrative fantasy – the story the player wants to be the star of – to the gameplay fantasy, which consists of the things the game does well.

4.4 The Writer Is Not the Originator

What else is unique about game writing? How about the fact that, unlike pretty much any other medium, the creative process does not start with the writer? In movies, it's the script. In novels, it's the manuscript. Everything springs from the written word, which is foundational.

In video games, not so much, and being a good game writer means learning to absent yourself from that generative role. That's not to say that some writing doesn't and shouldn't happen early, in conjunction with nailing down the core pillars of the game. The nitty-gritty of game writing, though, is that the bulk of the words you're going to have used by the player come much later. You can't write dialog to lead a player through a mission without that mission being designed first and its needs outlined. You can't write barks until the engineers and designers have hammered out which behaviors and state changes are getting called out and which ones aren't. Everything depends on someone else, and then there are people waiting behind you for your writing in order to do their jobs next.

Without accepting your place in the production cycle and as part of the team, you are going to find yourself thrashing against your own expectations. A ton of game writing is done as support for other departments, as opposed to leading the charge, and that's fine. In the early stages, at least, game writing has the massive advantages of being flexible and fast and easy to change as needed when the elements it is describing themselves change. That's a heck of a lot easier for a team that's trying to build specifics into lines of dialog.

Still, that means game writers must learn to be responsive. There are things you can do to be proactive, but engaging with other departments ahead of senior-level approval only gets you so far. No, many times to be a game writer is to wait for everyone else's stuff to get locked down before you get to paint word pictures of it.

That leads us to the last high-level point: You are part of a team. You may be lucky enough to be on a project big and well-funded enough to have multiple writers. You are going to be a part of a team that could be a few people, could be dozens, could be hundreds, and in rare cases could be thousands. Furthermore, you are going to be interacting with a lot of these people. Sometimes you will collaborate, sometimes you will get mandates, and sometimes you will pass along deliverables. It all varies wildly. What never varies is the fact that you are all the equivalent of individual Lego bricks working in harmony to create a gigantic single model.

This can be a hard transition for writers who are used to flying solo, but it is inescapable and, frankly, kind of cool.

The ability to reach out to artists and collaborate on a character is amazing, as you watch something you helped define come to life in someone else's hands and with their shared vision. The chance to inform others' work and to have yours informed in turn in a way that lets you improve it means your work is only getting better. And interacting with the people who build the walls of your writerly sandbox can provide stability, structure, and focus in a way that a solo writing project often can't.

Game writers can't be solitary creatures, and their work suffers when they try to be. It is far better – and this also gets covered in another chapter – to reach out to peers in other disciplines. This will keep you from getting siloed, wrapped up in your own work without ever making an effort to make it part of the greater whole. That's not to say there aren't times to hang up the "Do Not Disturb – Writer Will Eat

You If You Disturb Them" sign so you can grind out words in uninterrupted solitude, but rather to say that those moments are far from the bulk of the job.

There is more to it, of course, but these are the key understandings you need to absorb to do the job right. Trying to enforce other models on game production, even unintentionally, can lead to a 20-car pileup with your name painted all over it, and you don't want that.

Let go of your need to control every moment and every aspect. Let your fellow developers do their jobs in concert with you, and let the player tell their own story at their own pace. Learn to love the uncertainty and flexibility of writing to the player-shaped hole. Get used to writing in response to specific needs that come from outside of the narrative group but which are themselves vital for narrative. And above all, don't try to tell your story.

Because it's not yours, and it never was.

4.5 Barks: A Unique Specimen by the Thousands

And that brings us the long way around back to barks, one of the hothouse flowers that only grows in the garden provided by games. I'm going to drill down deep here in a way I'm not going to do for other game writing tasks, and I'm going to do it for two reasons.

First, because they are so weird and yet so important, they are a great way in. Come to grips with the awesome power and responsibility of barks, and wrapping your head around a lot of the rest of this stuff gets a lot easier. Barks are the easiest way to understand that not only are you not in Kansas anymore, you're probably not even in the Midwest.

Second, nothing hammers home the strangeness of game writing like barks. Any novel you read is not going to have page after page of listed variants on simple elements in the action. They're going to maybe have one character say something that fits the bill once and then get on to the exploding stuff. A complete shift in mindset is required to produce them because you'll never do this anywhere else.

Ultimately, barks are the writing equivalent of Darwin's Galapagos finches. They are found nowhere else, they have evolved in isolation to be highly specialized, and they are utterly key to the ecosystem they exist in.

Not every game has or needs barks, and this is fine. Barks are designed to handle events that happen frequently in a game in a way that is automatic and thus obviates the need to trigger "He shot me!" manually in a game with thousands of guys to shoot. Games that do not have large-scale repeated events, from adventure games to puzzle games to platformers, tend not to need many barks, if any at all.

But when barks *are* needed, they are needed in hordes that blot out the sky.

Barks add up, you see. Let's say you have a game where there are five things that the guards on a particular level have to convey to players, like "Stop!" and "I see them!" and "I've been shot!" And since there are going to be a lot of fights in your game, you need to write a lot of variants for each of those lines – say, ten apiece. And again, since there are a lot of guards, you'll want to have maybe five distinct guard voices, each saying their own list of those things. To accomplish that, you need to write each of those things five times, once for each voice.

You have now written 10 lines × 5 incidents × 5 guards. Your utterly basic bark system now sits at 250 lines, and you're just getting started. What happens when you start piling on more NPC character classes, each of whom needs their own variants and different voices and stimuli to react to? Maybe you'll have to add enemies from different countries, each of whom has their own way of speaking. And of course, as gameplay progresses toward completion, there are going to be new needs for new barks that have to be met across all these conditions. It's like watching a zombie virus outbreak in a packed arena. Blink, and they're everywhere.

That's OK, though, because barks are really, really important. Players are going to hear them a *lot*, way more than your play-it-once cinematic or bespoke triggered line. And if your bark pools are too shallow such that lines get repeated too early and too often, players are going to call it out.

It is not an exaggeration to say that for certain types of games, barks are the most important writing in the game. After all, they instantly inform the player of what's going on around them in a way that the most elegantly written cutscene can't. The player needs to know, *now*, that the enemy they are fighting is flanking or out of ammo to allow them to react accordingly and *immediately*. The barks are markers for the things the player has to know as they progress and play. They are carefully designed by the engineers to match the features that gameplay is going to support and to reinforce what the player should do to interact with them. They are absolutely vital as sensory information to the player in a way that literally nothing else in games is.

And yet, barks frequently get pushed off onto junior writers because they are seen as easy writing. This is a potential mistake.

What barks are instead is potentially *uninteresting* writing, and that's a different beast.

A memorable bark, for example, is a disaster waiting to happen, a meme waiting to take its arrow to the very public knee. A memorable line is all well and good if the player is only going to hear it once, or at least very rarely. If something witty and memorable and funny goes into a bark pool that's going to get called every time someone draws a weapon, it's going to play a lot, and a lot of different characters are potentially going to say it.

Which is going to sound very weird? What are the odds that this orc and that guy in powered armor and that martial artist and that henchman all independently came up with the same witty turn of phrase? The answer is "pretty damn low."

Which means you have to make your barks informative while also making them anonymous and slippery. They need to convey the information they were built for in a way that often calls no attention to the speaker's personality. Yes, you can write barks that draw on a character's obvious traits and background, but there's a ton of distance between that and trying to make each bark an artisanal masterpiece.

And, oh yes, there have to be a lot of them.

When I teach writing workshops, one of the exercises I give is "Write five variants on 'Arrgh, he shot me!'" Simple, right? Then, halfway through, because I am a monster, I tell them to write five more. Then five more. Then I tell them, many of whom are already at the breaking point because there are not enough reasonable ways available to say "Arrggh, he shot me!" and the variants start getting convoluted and goofy, to change the game context from tactical shooter to high fantasy.

You can hear the groans and the tablets being slammed down in frustration from two states away.

That's the harsh truth of writing barks – they need to be useful but not sticky, and they need to be numerous but not distinctive. And they also need to be short because they need to play, drop their information payload, and go to keep the player from getting distracted.

With all that on your plate and the number of barks you need to write skyrocketing, you still have to keep an eye out for barks that are going to stand out in a bad way when they get played again and again. We had that happen to us on *The Division*, where one bark about someone named Alex being shot got played, for Important Reasons, way too many times in too many early encounters. Fortunately, the fans were feeling generous, and even while they had fun with the idea, they did so with enough good humor that the writing team was able to react, scramble, and pay it off with an NPC exchange in some later conversation.

You're not always that lucky. Sometimes, people twig on a line that sucks. Yeah, it's hard making sure all of the lines are good enough to do the job right, but in this, as in many game writing tasks, failure is not an option.

4.6 Summary

Is this everything? Not by a long shot. That would require a much longer book than this one

It is, however, a good start. Understanding that "game writer" means adapting to a very particular professional environment in a way that asks for very particular things is what will allow you to create those particular things well. Refusing to absorb all of the above, to ignore the absolute necessities, is just setting yourself up for failure.

Open yourself up to the possibilities instead. Be willing to try new forms and expressions. Broaden your palette as a writer, and expand your arsenal to ensure that you're comfortable taking on the game writing space.

The alternative? Let's not talk about that.

5

Tips, Tricks, and Techniques – Things That Will Make You a Better Game Writer

5.1 Introduction

I promised you at the beginning that this book was not going to be about how to do actual game writing, and by and large that's going to be the case. Other people have covered that and covered it well, and there's no need for me to re-plow the old furrowed ground.

On the other hand, I have picked up a few useful techniques that I have found make my writing better over the years. These are ones that might have slipped through the cracks otherwise. I am happy to share them here, as I think they will make your life easier and your writing better going forward. And if they don't, you can always blame me.

Note that these techniques have been developed, tested, honed, and applied for many years to provide optimum effect. Everything here, for lack of a better word, works. That being said, you don't need to follow this stuff to the letter. Figure out what here works for you, pick it up, and adapt it to your needs. It's all free for you to use as you see fit, in whole or in part. That's the great thing about this gig: It's constantly evolving.

5.2 The Ten Words Exercise

The most well-known of the techniques I have authored is the Ten Words Exercise. One of the hardest things to do as a game writer is to establish a consistent character voice, one that serves not only to make the character identifiable but also to flesh them out as an entity. And so, you want to invest time and energy laying out the parameters of a character's voice before you write the first line of dialog.

Here's how it works: Make two lists, each ten words or phrases long. One is for things the character will definitely say – common phrasings, favorite constructions, colloquialisms, and the like. The other ten things they will never, ever say under any circumstances because those words just aren't them.

I created this while I was working on *Splinter Cell: Double Agent*. The baddies in that one were a domestic terrorist cell, and when I came on the project, I was having a hard time getting a grip on who they were or what they wanted, besides nukes. Eventually, I decided the best way in was trying to understand their leader, who didn't feel fully formed at that point. I tried writing his voice, but it just didn't work until I took a step back and made myself write out the building blocks of that dialog, the words he would say and the ones he wouldn't. (I started with five of each, but with experience came

DOI: 10.1201/9781003592983-5

expansion.) I wrote those down, and in the process, I discovered his voice. I learned that he didn't use contractions, making his language seem very formal. That in turn led to the idea that he came from old money and that he'd had an expensive schooling, and it all fell into place from there.

I've used the technique ever since.

I know. It sounds a little contrived. The thing is, though, it works, and it works on multiple levels. By setting the reference points of your character's personal dictionary and style, you are establishing all sorts of things about them. Do they use regional slang? You've nailed down where they're from and possibly their socioeconomic class as well. Do they use big words or small ones? Maybe you've just checked off the "elite education" box next to their character. It goes on and on. There is an entire world of ways those 20 words or phrases can help to define that character. Once you do that, what comes out of their mouth thereafter is unmistakably them from the get-go.

Don't be fooled, by the way. Those lists can be hard to come up with. The further down you go, the more you're defining that character's voice, and the fewer and fewer things will fit cleanly. For me, the cursing usually starts around word seven or eight. It's worth pushing through to the end, though. A lot of times, that's where the real gold is.

Those lists can do double duty as well. You can hand them off to a concept artist who's trying to wrap their head around who that character is and what accoutrements they might have on them. You can bundle it in a package for voice actors to reference as they prepare for a role, giving them insight into who the character is and how they should be played. You can give it to the Marketing department for reference when they're incorporating characters into campaigns or creating taglines. You can even bundle it up and hand it off to other writers as needed because there are times when someone else is going to be in charge of putting words in your creations' mouths.

It's useful, easy, and versatile. The one thing you don't want to do is rush to completion. Doing that tends to result in easy, shallow choices for the lists, and those don't give you as much to work with in the long run. Take it seriously – don't start your "Never" list with "sarsaparilla" or "sesquipedalian" or anything else that nobody in the game was likely to say in any case. The whole point of this is to produce useful guidelines. If you cheat the process, you cheat yourself and just make your work harder down the road.

5.3 Asking the Questions

Sometimes, the Ten Words Exercise isn't quite enough on its own. As a follow-up, I recommend fake interviews.

No, not for you. For your characters.

Take the time to write out four or five questions about things you want to know about the character in question. It doesn't have to be anything earth-shattering or important. All it needs to be is something that they are likely to have an opinion or some information on, so there is an excuse to have them talk.

Then, let them talk.

There is no endgame to this. There is no formal goal. This is stuff that will very rarely see the light of day, and that's perfect.

The one exception from my career was a bit I puzzled out of a character named Victor Coste in *Splinter Cell: Conviction* that started with "The Sam Fisher you knew is dead." I showed that to some other folks to make sure they knew I was indeed working. They ran with it, and in no time flat that was the foundation of a bunch of Marketing stuff and the start of the game. But that was a wild exception. Generally doing this is just an exercise to be kept to yourself, which means you can go absolutely nuts with it.

Because what you want to do here is let the character say anything they want. Let them go wild. The whole point is to provide a space where you can experiment with and refine their voice, so giving them space to expand on their points is exactly what you want to do. The longer the answers they give, the more time you are spending in their voice and the more practice you are getting in refining that voice. That, in turn, is going to make writing dialog and barks for them that much easier in the long run. And if they give short answers, that teaches you something, too.

Who knows, you just might get a tagline out of it.

By the way, don't confuse this with the idea of having your characters talk to you. Some people swear by it, but it's only happened to me once in three decades of professional writing, and I was very heavily medicated at the time. What I do recommend, and this is a part of that, is getting to know your characters well enough that you understand instinctively whether a line of dialog is going to come out of their mouth or not. You may not understand why, at least not at first. If you know a character, really know them, you will know when something hits a wrong note.

5.4 The Kermit Test

With that in mind, there's one more trick for writing dialog that I use a lot. I call it The Kermit Test.

Every game writer should read their written dialog out loud before they dare show it to another human being. It is my experience that the vast majority of clunky, awkward, weird-sounding lines can be prevented by simply speaking them out loud before they get anywhere near an actor.

No, I don't mean have automated text-to-voice read them for you. Computers don't breathe. If there's a line that's too long or that needs pauses, they're going to just steamroll through it where a live actor would be running out of gas or breaking. If you read it yourself, you'll find the places where that happens. If you let HAL 9000 take a crack, you'll be none the wiser.

What I've found over the years is that when an actor bumps on a line – when their rhythm breaks and they hiccup or stop – a huge percentage of the time it's because the line in question is precisely one syllable too long. Reading out loud to yourself, or, if you're feeling sadistic, getting someone else to read them out loud to you. This can let you hear that extraneous syllable letting you spot that stumbling block ahead of time. That way you can remove it before it costs you studio time, money, and goodwill.

Even beyond that, though, it's important to have the experience of hearing the line as well as reading it. What you imagine the line is going to sound like in your head is not always what it sounds like coming out of someone's mouth. Something that looks ornate and elegant on the page can read as marble-mouthed mush when someone tries to speak it. All of us have been guilty at one point or another of being a little writerly and over-clever, of putting words on the screen that, in hindsight, we knew no human being would ever say except at gunpoint.

Reading your stuff aloud cures you of that in a hurry.

That, incidentally, is where The Kermit Test comes in.

You see, one of the defense mechanisms a lot of writers develop is that if they're reading something they know is silly or off, they'll unconsciously try to distance it by reading it in a funny voice. Sometimes they add an accent. Sometimes they slow down or speed up. Sometimes they do it in a character voice.

Me, I find myself slipping into a Kermit the Frog impression when a line announces itself on my tongue as ridiculous. Doing Kermit right, incidentally, is harder than it sounds, which means that if my subconscious takes me all the way there, it's for a damn good reason. And when I hear myself doing Kermit, I stop, mark the line as needing a change, and reset before going onward.

It has saved me dozens and dozens of times. How many? You'll never know, and neither will the producers and actors who never saw the lines that I, upon froggy review, changed. And that's just fine. The last thing you want to do is waste people's time with subpar work that, with a little effort, could have been better.

5.5 And Another Thing

Speaking of things that might surprisingly come out of your mouth, accents are an area to be very cautious. On a base level, you will probably want to avail yourself of a coach who can get your actors' accents right if your team has the budget for such and to help you work in things like local slang and phrasing to add verisimilitude. Even before that, you will need to do research to make sure you are doing the character voice respectfully and well.

With all that being said, one critical lesson that you can learn the hard way is that you never double up on an accent. If you are writing a character with an accent, either put it in the notes for the actor to do that accent or write in the accent so that it shows up on the page. Do not do both, because, even with the best of intentions and skills, you are then tempting fate to give you a double dose of what you think you just ordered one shot of.

This happened to me very early in my career. There was a minor character, a quest giver, and I had written up his description (which was given to the actor) with him having "a bit of a Boston Irish accent."

I also wrote his dialog such that it read like my experience of South Boston Irish neighborhoods I got while living up there for grad school. I lived in Jamaica Plain, about three blocks over from the neighborhoods that gave us the accents in *Good Will Hunting*, and *The Departed, Mystic River*, and a dozen other South Boston-based films, and in my youthful eagerness, I channeled them.

The end result sounded like the character was desperately trying to hide his Lucky Charms cereal from a bunch of annoying kids, but only after guzzling a fifth of Bushmills and snorting six lines of Pop Rocks. That, I swore, I would never do again.

Fast forward to years later and the first recording session for the game *Tom Clancy's H.A.W.X.*, where I was working with a very fine writer and friend I had worked with successfully before. He and I went into the studio for the first day of sessions. As I was looking over the day's recording script, which he had written, I noted a bunch of lines that I thought were likely to change once they made contact with a live actor. He disagreed. I told him to wait, and he would see.

The first actor we recorded was playing a fuel tanker plane pilot. His character bio stated that he was from Alabama. His dialog also made it very clear that he was from Alabama, which meant this very nice, polite actor walked into the booth, warmed up, and then, when the red light went on, launched into the first line of his session.

It came out, roughly, as "HOLEEE KEERAP AHM ON FAHR!!!"

The other writer looked at me. I looked at him. And we said together, "Let's change that line."

5.6 The Writer in the Studio

This opens up the broader topic of what you do in the studio as a writer, because studio preparation and etiquette are something they rarely teach you.

It is, by and large, a good thing for there to be someone from the writing side of things in the recording studio during the sessions. You're on the spot to provide immediate answers to questions about the meaning or context of any given line, allowing the actor to tackle it with the appropriate information and intent. You are a resource in the studio, and approaching a session with that understanding will let you make the biggest impact while causing the fewest issues.

Don't think you're there to run the show. That's the Voice Director's job, and putting too many voices in an actor's ear tends not to go well. Stay in your lane, offer what you can to help, and everything will work out great. It's an important lane. It's just not the passing lane.

In particular, having a writer in the studio allows for on-the-spot rewrites, which can be a godsend. There's something uniquely painful about listening to an actor bump on a line that's just not working for them, again and again and again. Having a writer there to tweak the line to make it more accessible can save immense amounts of time that would otherwise be spent chasing a line reading that is never going to happen, not to mention the frustration for all parties that comes with repeated failed attempts. A graceful offer of a rewrite can be the easiest, fastest, and cheapest solution.

Those are the two obvious reasons a writer should be there. And that should be enough. Being able to answer questions to allow the actors to perform better, passing along key info to the Director to share with the actor, and scribbling changes on the fly in reaction to readings or to take advantage of something the talent is doing – any and all of these are enough to warrant a writer's presence. Otherwise, you either get non-writers attempting to do writer things, which often goes bad, or you have frantic calls to someone on the writing staff because of an in-studio emergency, and that person is inevitably either driving, at the dentist, or in the bathroom when the call comes in.

If you can't be there, do what you can to at least be available and supportive within reason. If you can listen in over a live channel, that's great. If you make sure the folks who are in the studio can reach you to ask questions, that helps a lot, too. If you can anticipate potential issues and have pre-packaged references ready to go, well, you may not need this book.

Within reason, though, can be the sticking point. One game I worked on, the game's producer went out to the recording sessions in L.A. and instructed me to carry the full script of the game with me at all times in case he had a question. Said script was more than 1,200 pages long. I very quickly had some questions of my own. And the one time he called to ask a question, I was driving.

The last reason might actually be the best reason, and that's so the writer can interact with the actor. Writers who guard their lines jealously are missing the point. This stuff is not deathless prose. It can be changed and improved, and possibly the best person to suggest changes, based on their experience at inhabiting the speaking character, is the actor. When an actor offers a good faith suggestion for a line change, it's coming from a place of understanding of the character. That doesn't mean you have to take it unquestioningly, but if it's good, grab it! Just the fact of the suggestion opens up discussion that can lead to a better line. And a better line is, after all, the goal.

5.7 Studio Tips and Tricks

That's the high-level stuff. On a more granular level, there are particular techniques that can come in handy, either in the lead-up to a session or in the studio during the actual recording.

To begin with, once you know who's been cast, do your research. Find footage of their performances, listen to/watch it, and get familiar with any nuances of their performance. This helps in making a connection with them. You can bring up their work, ask questions about it, and demonstrate your interest and respect.

In addition, if they have a distinct rhythm or other trait to their performances that you hear, you can use it to hone the script to make it more natural for them. I did this with the actor we had playing Vic Coste in the last two *Splinter Cell* games, as he had a very clear cadence to his line readings in all the samples I saw. Once I discovered that, I rewrote his dialog so that the emphasized words matched his natural pattern. It worked wonders.

After that but before the session starts, be Proactive about helping the actor. Put together as comprehensive a bundle as you can for them about the character they will be playing. Scripts, bio, concept art, animations if you have them, you name it – gather them all up, bundle them up, and send them along. They may or may not avail themselves of it, but it's better to give them more than they need and let them pick and choose what's useful to them instead of not giving them enough. It definitely beats the hell out of having them come in cold or with a mistaken idea of who a character might be.

Once the session starts, don't be afraid to ask for variants. Just do it politely, do it through the Director, and explain why. "Emphasizing that last word ties it to the next line we're going to record" goes over better than a generic ask without context. At the same time, if a reading is wrong, don't be afraid to call that out as well. The trick is making sure you pick your spots to do these things to make it clear you're being helpful and supportive, not trying to run the session. A few specific asks with clear payoff will make you look good. Asking for alternative takes every third line will make you look . . . less good.

It's always tempting to offer, but never, ever, ever give your own line reading unless you are specifically asked to do so (and they will *never* ask you to do this unless it's a question of pronunciation). The odds are very good that you are not an actor in addition to being a writer. And even if you are an actor, you are not *that* actor. Suggest, describe, do whatever you have to do to get your point across in a way that the actor can pick it up and make it their own. Just don't try to make them do what's in your head instead.

Don't be married to your words. Everything is changeable until it gets locked. Be happy to accept different if different is better. If you have a line reading in your head and the actor gives a different but better one, be happy! Your stuff got better! Don't cling to what isn't; embrace what is. If the actor suggests a word change and it makes sense, take it gracefully and be thankful. That's not to say accept everything without question, as there are often circumstances when you have to gently shoot down a proposed change for plot or character reasons. Still, you should be willing to move on from a stance if a better option is offered.

While you are in the session, listen to what's going on to allow you to anticipate what's coming next. If you pay attention to where an actor bumps on lines and how they improve, you can identify lines coming up that might need tweaks, and you can get ahead of the curve instead of wasting studio time on stuff that won't get used. Don't go nuts, but listen closely and put what you hear to good use. Doing so efficiently and with context – telling the Director why you are proposing changes before a given read and having it clearly come out better can win you a lot of capital – is often a win for everyone.

5.8 Never Mind the Dialog, What about the Plot?

All of that is useful once you've written the nitty-gritty of the game. But what about crafting a plot before you ever imagine a single word of dialog? Are there secrets there?

As far as I am concerned, there are two bits of hidden wisdom. One is simple. One is a little more complicated.

The simple one is, simply, this: Ask why.

The word "why" is one of the most potent tools a writer has in their arsenal. It is fair, it is clean, and it is merciless. That is what makes it effective.

Furthermore, it should be applied universally. Hold up every plot twist and character decision that you have crafted to the searing light of "why," and any weak spots or places where you hoped to just slide something on by get illuminated immediately. Why is this particular plot point happening? Why does the villain do this particular thing? Why does the main character want the MacGuffin? Why is anyone helping the main character when they're clearly a jerk? Why didn't the Fellowship just let the giant eagles take them to Mordor? Ultimately, it's mostly just "why?"

Ask the questions, and then see if you have the answers. If you do have answers, particularly answers that are clean, clear, and crisp, excellent. Your narrative logic is airtight, and you can move on to the next point with peace of mind.

If you ask "why" and the best answer you can provide is complicated and forced, then it's time to perhaps rethink things a little bit. There's probably something in there that can be streamlined in a way that players don't run aground on the logic and get thrown out of the fantasy. Remember, if it takes a long time for you to explain it to yourself, it's probably going to take even longer to explain it to the player, and they're not going to want to stand still for that.

If you ask "why" and you honestly don't know, then it's definitely time to put things into dry dock and see where your narrative logic sprang a leak. If you don't understand why the villain is doing something, then the players won't, either, and you run the risk of lowering the stakes irreparably.

And if you ask "why" and all you've got is "so we can get to the next scene" or "the plot demands it" or "because it's cool," it's time to take a deep breath. There are, in fact, times when, everything else having failed, you need to clothe certain characters in plot armor to allow them to make it through to critical scenes. There are times when simply cool is in fact enough, if it is cool enough and moves fast enough that players don't get bored and start grumbling "wait a minute . . ." and instead hop along for the ride.

If you're going to do this, you need to be conscious of the fact that you are doing the thing and where that might force you into other decisions down the line. Don't automatically shy away from the cool moments. Find a way to see if you can make them make sense first.

The second technique is a little more involved but a little less repetitive. One of the great unspoken difficulties of writing video game plots is the fact that, often, you need to be careful about bringing your big villain onstage. This is because as soon as the player sees the villain, they are going to want to shoot them in the face. If this happens in hour two of a ten-hour campaign, you have a problem. This means game writers and designers have to thread the needle, getting the villain onstage enough that the player hates them and feels good about triumphing over them, but not in such a way that the player can simply blow their head off and go about their business.

This, predictably, produces some strange villain behaviors, including, but not limited to, the hackneyed scene where a major villain kills one of their own henchmen in front of the player character for no other reason than to prove that they are, in fact, evil.

Incidentally, if you ever get asked to write a scene like this, violence may in fact be a reasonable alternative.

More seriously, what you generally get is a lot of very convoluted behavior on the part of the villain to make sure they're not in a position to get taken out until the plot demands it. This isn't necessarily a dealbreaker. At this point, it's a convention a lot of people wearily accept. Still, you can and should want to do better if you can.

What that means is turning the plot around. Map out the sequence of events from the villain's point of view. Make sure that they have a coherent throughput where each decision makes the next seem logical.

And note that "logical" doesn't mean smart. People do dumb things for all sorts of reasons all the time, and that can be okay. The dumb reason just has to seem smart *to them*. It has to be consistent with who they are to keep the player from bumping on it. If the villain is so consumed by the need for vengeance that they overplay their hand as regards the hero, it's good *narrative* logic for that character to do that sort of thing. At that point, real logic can take a coffee break so it can come back, refreshed, later. Because what you want is players' subconscious whispering "I can see them doing that" in the player's ear, and the player accepting it as a logical outgrowth of that particular character's personality.

Therefore, let the villain have an arc, and make sure it holds up to scrutiny, too. Let them react to what the player is theoretically going to be doing in order to advance, and let them do it in a way that makes character sense. The villain's sequence of events has to lead them inevitably to the end as much as the player's sequence leads them there as well.

5.9 Mooks and Sand Guy

On the other hand, minor characters, guards, and the like probably don't deserve full arcs. There isn't the time or the resource to make that happen. There is, however, a real benefit to giving them something to stand out, to help players find an attachment point that can then inform their experience.

And with that in mind, let's talk about Sand Guy, who taught me one of the most important lessons of my game writing career.

Way back in the day, I did a soup-to-nuts rewrite on the script for the original *Far Cry*. One of the things you could do in *Far Cry* was use your acquired super-hearing to eavesdrop on patrolling guards, who would alternately drop game-pertinent info or say things that were hopefully amusing enough that the player didn't feel they had entirely wasted their time listening in.

There were a lot of these guards, and at a certain point my well for witty guard banter ran dry. Meanwhile, I still had a pair of guards on a beach to write for, and, lacking anything better, I decided they were going to talk about sand. Why? Because they were on a beach, and no matter what else might change on that map, there was always going to be sand. It was safe. It was reliable. It was definitely there.

I started writing, and the one guy started complaining about how he hated sand and it always got in his boots and generally being whiny. The other replied that, no, he loved sand because it reminded him of growing up as a kid in Philly and going down to the Jersey Shore during the summer. I had grown up near Philadelphia, and many of my friends made that pilgrimage to Ocean City or Brigantine or wherever every year. I threw that in as a little tip of the cap to them, a throwaway line when I was scraping the bottom of my brain's barrel, and that was all.

Fast forward to E3, where I found myself on a game writing panel back when they did such things. After the panel ended and I got offstage, I got instantly mobbed by a group of students from New Jersey, who all wanted to talk to me about Sand Guy. It seemed one of them had been playing and had been about to pull the trigger on that guard, and then he heard the dialog. In that moment, he had a sudden revelation. He turned to his friends, and he said, "I can't shoot this guy. I know this guy. I *am* this guy!" Because he, too, had gone down the Shore (as we phrased it in those days) as a kid, and so had his friends. They had a connection. And as a result, he and all his classmates changed their play style to spare this one guard, no matter how much more challenging it made the encounter.

Was there a deep and detailed backstory for Sand Guy? No. There was a single detail, conveyed in a way that implied there was perhaps more to him than being there to catch a bullet. That one light bit of dialog provided an impactful, emotional experience for these players, one I never could have anticipated from a source that I didn't think much of at the time.

The lesson there is simple. If you give a little TLC to your minor characters here and there – give them specific details of their interests or backgrounds to share without going whole hog – you can reap a tremendous reward. You don't need to write up a complicated backstory for everyone, but a single hook to hang things on, the hint that there's more, or the suggestion that they and the player have common ground can pay you back a hundredfold.

5.10 Tell One Story

Finally, there is one general rule that applies to pretty much any player-facing non-dialog task, ranging from character bios to item write-ups to spell descriptions.

And that is Tell One Story.

Each thing or character you write about should have one story attached to them for players to read and get involved with. You want a simple throughput, a sequence of events that explains who they are or why they are the way they are without getting overly complicated. Clean basics are what is called for, and singular vision.

Too often, these innocent write-ups become victims of a writer's fear that they're not doing enough. There is the temptation to try to cram in all the things, to overload something that should be accessible with mood-inducing adjectives that add nothing except foreboding. There is the urge to tell too big a story for a short write-up or to try to marry various plot elements together without seeing if they are compatible or if they fight against one another instead.

Descriptions like that are failures. They don't convey the what or who of what is being described in a way that produces an easy understanding. They obscure the facts the player might want in order to get excited about something. They eat word count that is needed to tell the item's story. Worst of all, they often produce stories with mismatched elements that end up going nowhere useful. Players notice this, even if they can't put their finger on what exactly it is, and they often don't like it. They don't attach to it. In many cases, they ultimately reject it, and nobody wants that.

Far better, then, to tell one story. If you've got a cursed sword, lay out who cursed it, why, and how, and then top it off with a hook that links to the current gameplay. If you've got a character history to explore, their growth should flow naturally from one event to the next to lead them to where they are at the start of the game. Trying to give too many aspects to a character instead yields a disjointed, self-contradictory mess who can't function well in your plot. You have limited time and bandwidth to present a character, and while real people are complicated, made-up people should be a little easier to understand.

Take the time, then, to examine all the things you think are key to a character's backstory, and see if it sounds like the same person doing all of them; if it feels like one thing led to the next; and if there are elements that come flying in out of nowhere, disrupting what is already established before vanishing back into the ether of random coolness.

Just tell that one singular story, and tell it in a way that is easily understood and appreciated. Do that, whether it be for a demon lord or a type of gun or an eager young space cadet or a mythic empire, and you have who or what they are available in a way that brings players in.

Which, to be fair, is pretty much the point of the exercise.

6

Dansky's Three Laws of Game Writing

6.1 Introduction

There are three rules – laws, really – that I have found hold true over the years, regardless of the size, scope, genre, or other details of the project at hand. While they are broad by nature, they are a useful lodestone in the vast majority of my experience.

Yes, there are always edge cases, but the sorts of people who deliberately seek out anomalous edge cases just to assume a position of superiority are mainly an obstacle to getting stuff done. A hammer isn't the best tool for absolutely every situation, but it works for an awful lot of them, and the odds are you'll get pretty good mileage out of reaching for a hammer to solve problems that are blunt force-shaped.

Here they are, Dansky's Three Laws of Game Writing.

6.2 The First Law

> *Dansky's First Law of Game Writing: Words are always the cheapest solution until they are suddenly the most expensive.*

This one comes into play a lot. Inevitably, during development, there is a moment when wires get crossed and miscommunication happens. And when it does, a department – be it art or level design or whoever – generates assets that are not in line with what may have been agreed on previously. Now, when I say this, I don't mean "art ignored the narrative docs and did their own thing," though that is certainly something that happens. I mean more that, for whatever reason, there is deviation from the planned, scheduled, outlined, and tasked setup for deliverables that has been agreed upon and that everyone across the team is supposed to be working toward.

Sometimes, it's a result of inspiration – someone came up with a great idea that made things better but failed to communicate it through proper channels to propagate the new information across the team. Sometimes it's a result of people not reading the documentation closely or even choosing to ignore it. Sometimes the planned outcome doesn't work or doesn't work well and needs to be changed. And sometimes there's an accidental oversight or a mistake that needs fixing.

What happens next is like the tides in its inevitability: Team leadership is presented with a variety of options. They can have the modeler or animator or level builder or whoever roll back the new stuff and

DOI: 10.1201/9781003592983-6

course correct to what was originally planned. This takes time and money. The work they have done is skilled and delicate. Reversing it, fixing it, or replacing it is not cheap and easy.

Or they can have writing paper over the new reality by altering what is sometimes erroneously referred to as "the narrative wrapper." This, on the other hand, is in fact cheap, if not quite as easy as folks might think. Up to a certain point in production, deleting old words and inserting new ones in their place costs a lot less and takes a lot less time than redoing a model or an animation set. It's plain easier.

In that case, yes, words are the cheapest fix, and experienced game writers know it and prepare for this sort of thing. It happens a lot, and it often happens last minute and in an emergency, which makes it even more likely that the quick fix – write something new – will get selected instead of the longer, more time-consuming one.

Now, there are drawbacks to this reliance on the sudden rewrite. In cases like this, there is often no time for iteration and feedback to make sure the new narrative elements are as strong as the ones they're replacing. There are even a lot of moments when what is being asked is to paint over the welding marks where something new is awkwardly jammed into the game for other reasons, ranging from the good (improved gameplay) to the not as good (someone thought it was cool and won't let go). In cases like that, it's hard to make the fit clean and seamless because this is an outside element being introduced late and suddenly instead of being organically developed in conjunction with the rest of the design.

And then there are times when stuff gets cut, when missions go away, and key narrative elements go with them. In moments like that, writing becomes the duct tape that binds the whole thing together, finding new places to stick the vital content under the new, stressed constraints.

With any of these situations, the content is often not as good as it once was. Seasoned professionals who have been through the fire previously develop a sense for when something like this is likely to come down the pike. They can often turn around pretty good content on demand and under the gun, but it's highly unlikely that it will be as good as something that's gotten full developmental attention and polish instead of a sudden "fix this!" As I have said many a time in my career, I write a pretty mean first draft, but it's still a first draft.

And all of that holds true as long as it's only words that are being altered, words in the original language of the game. The math changes, however, when you start bringing other elements into the equation.

That's the second part of the law. As soon as you start talking about localization or voice, then it is a whole other ballgame. Now bear in mind a good writer can do good work up to and literally including the last minute. I have written extensive amounts of scripts – the entire tutorial for *Splinter Cell: Double Agent*, for example – while sitting in the studio while other content was recorded. But even stuff like that was still functionally cheap. Yes, the scripts handed to the actors had to be exported and printed out and whatnot in a hurry, but the cost of that was peanuts. They were still just words *until they got spoken*.

Take a step back and consider what it takes to get a line of dialog into a game. You need to hire a studio (expensive). You need a recording engineer and a Voice Director (also expensive). You need actors (definitely expensive). You need to potentially send someone – say, the writer – to the shoot to help get things as good as possible. (Did I mention expensive, especially in these days of multi-continental co-development?) You need the audio team to process the files from the recordings and then get the files implemented in the game (time-consuming and expensive both). You get the idea – the investment in time and money piles up rapidly.

All of that is well and good, but what happens if someone else changes something that obviates the recorded dialog? Suddenly, changing the writing gets very expensive indeed. The words are still cheap, but changing the way they have been expressed? That's where the cash registers start going berserk, the producers start tearing their hair out, and wacky hijinks ensue. Throw in additional complications like actor availability – the voice talent may well have lined up other jobs and thus be unavailable, or if you're dealing with celebrity talent, there may be a certain number of sessions allowed locked into the contract and no more – and it becomes clear: Revising writing after the recording session happens is a very expensive tall order, to be avoided at all – dare I say it? – costs.

Now, well-organized projects will have foreseen some of this and likely budgeted and scheduled for what are called pickup sessions, catchall recording sessions late in the project where mistakes can be corrected and new material can be added to cover the gaps that have been exposed in the interim. It's not a perfect fix, however. No matter how late you try to go with your pickup sessions, there has to be a cutoff point so the files can be worked with and localization can do their thing.

You also have to plan your pickups very carefully when you start looking at what you're fixing. You can't bring an actor in to do one line, pay them for ten minutes, and have done with it. Actors are talented and deserve to get paid for their talent. It's not worth their time to commute 45 minutes each way to a recording studio, work for ten minutes, get paid for ten minutes, and then take 45 more minutes going home.

As such, you hire them in multi-hour blocks. This protects them, but it also turns your recording schedule into a giant game of *Blokus* as you try to figure out which characters are vital to do pickups with, when you can do them, and how many lines you can put in front of them to make the session worthwhile. Yes, that one line you want to change may be key, but do you really want to book a four-hour session for the sake of eight whole words? Can the session wait until any other possible changes are discovered? How many lines are enough to justify putting the machine into motion?

And no, I'm not forgetting localization. Localization is often the caboose on the development train because they can't do their job until everyone else has done theirs. They are in charge of taking the original script and all other writing, from UI text strings to in-game artifacts, and translating it into however many languages the game is going to be published in. This can range from three or four to well over a dozen, and every single written and spoken word in the game needs to go through the process.

Needless to say, this takes time. There's organization time, and there's translation time, and there's communication time when the localization team reaches out with questions about the text they are translating.

Be aware, incidentally, that slang does *not* travel well. Jokes also do not travel well. Idioms? Forget about it. Be prepared to explain the spirit of the line in these cases rather than the actual phrasing. The sooner you accept this reality, the less time you spend banging your head against a wall trying to communicate literal verbiage instead of the much more flexible idea of a line. This has the added benefit of letting the folks doing the translation get a little creative, which means they might be a little more invested in what they are doing. That's rarely a bad thing.

In short, localization, if it is to be done well, requires time, and the sooner you can get finalized material to them, the better. The last thing anyone wants is a bad or awkward translation that turns your game into a punchline or makes it seem like you don't care about a particular market. While smart producers try to build a cushion in for localization in case of emergencies, the truth is there are *always* emergencies and slippages. As a result, that cushion gets rapidly devoured. But there is a line beyond which localization cannot go, and asking for last minute high priority translations is awkward, expensive, and not always possible.

As a result, the law stands. Words are the cheapest fix until they're suddenly the most expensive. There are times when a team has to bite the bullet and shell out, say, when a feature is cut or redesigned after recording has happened, but this is the sort of thing you want to avoid if at all possible.

6.3 The Second Law

Then there's Dansky's Second Law of Game Writing:

More detailed exposition is never the answer.

I mean, okay, maybe it was the answer once, possibly twice, but the odds are good that it is not in fact the answer in any circumstance you're likely to run across.

Anyway.

There is a stubbornly held belief in certain decision-making circles of some game studios that every player must understand everything intimately, or the narrative is a failure. As a result, what they press for is a minutely detailed, lengthy explanation of every aspect of the story, including motivations, history, backstory, and consequence that is presented inescapably. And if a single player in a playtest session says they don't get it, the response is often to press for even more exposition.

This approach is flawed on several levels. At its base, it's a case of targeting the least engaged users, the ones who probably care least about story, and directing the bulk of the narrative resources at them. Which is a strategy, I suppose, but it comes with an unintended consequence: It turns off the players who are more likely to be involved in narrative content. The players who are able to put things together for themselves, draw inferences, and make logical connections are instead getting spoon-fed everything, and there's no way to do that without basically bludgeoning the player over the head with lengthy exposition.

That approach turns off players who normally would be interested in narrative because all the flavor and tension has been drowned in a sea of verbiage. The spicy fun of discovery, of anticipation, and of putting the pieces together to figure out things for themselves gets turned into bland paste. The reward for sudden understanding and then finding renewed purpose in acting on that understanding in the game evaporates. A chunk of the fun, a core feature for a segment of players, is gone as a result.

Those people who otherwise would have gloried in discovery – seriously, there's a whole class of lore interpreters that sprung up around the Souls games because the narrative content is so dense and occulted and yet so essential – find less for them to enjoy. Some of them leave bad reviews or slowly drift away. This is most certainly not the desired effect.

The numbers will be hard to come by, but I have a sneaky suspicion that for every fan gained from the pablumization of the narrative at one end, someone with a more refined narrative palate is pulling the ripcord on the other.

Ultimately, it's a failure to trust the majority of players to understand what they are playing. People are afraid that players are going to miss something, so they slap training wheels on the writing. This stabilizes things, but it also removes any thrill or sense of accomplishment the player might feel from figuring things out for themselves. It makes the writing worse, and as a result, it makes the game experience worse.

Long ago, I worked on a game that had no in-mission narrative. There was just a set-up briefing in the beginning of a mission before play started and a short debrief at the end after play had concluded. The pre-mission stuff had to cover a lot of territory: Where the mission was, what was going on, what the player characters had to do, and a little bit of context as for bad guy motivations and the consequences of failure.

This was a lot to pack into a few paragraphs. In order to achieve this and to keep the briefing from droning on too long when the player wanted to get started playing, I wrote those briefings in a specific way. I trusted the player to figure out the enemy motivations and understand why and how to stop them. This both showed respect for the players and kept the briefings to a manageable length.

Unfortunately, the feedback on those briefings from the Powers That Were was that they didn't quite understand. They wanted all those motivations and connections spelled out. Dutifully, I did this, only to be told that this round of explanations had raised more questions and that now those needed to be answered. Lather, rinse, repeat.

In their final form, those mission briefings were detailed, thorough, monstrous, and boring as hell. They went on for ages, frustrating players who wanted to play and filling their ears with information that was not directly pertinent to what they would be doing in the actual mission. Making the receipt of this information mandatory may have answered all the questions, but many of those questions didn't need to be answered in the first place. The players simply didn't care, and that exposition got shoved in between them and the experience of play.

That's another key point: Exposition, unless you're going to go full *Game of Thrones* and only provide it in conjunction with frequent nudity, gets really dull really fast. Yes, there are nerds out there, myself included, who pored through the various appendices to *The Lord of the Rings*, but even we did that with the awareness that we were largely reading a textbook that just happened to have sections in Elvish. Dropping massive exposition bombs into gameplay is a losing proposition. It interrupts the player's fun to lecture to them, often at great length and with references to names and places that they probably won't remember. It is boring, especially if delivered as a single monologue. It wrecks pace, it saps tension, and it fights against interactivity.

And yet, there's always the cry to do more of it, to eradicate that slight sliver of uncertainty that someone might have. To stamp out the fear of the one bad review that says, "I didn't get it," never mind that you're inviting all the bad reviews that say "overwritten and boring."

Trust me. It's not worth it.

And let's circle back for a minute. More exposition is, quite literally, more work. It's more stuff to write, revise, polish, record, localize, and generally make. It takes more time. It takes more money. It takes focus away from other tasks in a way that generally can't be pulled from elsewhere and replaced.

It is cutting the good stuff with oregano. Going back again and again to make the infodumps longer and longer is time that's not being spent on other deliverables, time when they're not getting the attention they need. The negative effects ripple across the entire set of writing tasks, the work isn't as good, and the fans notice.

There are also the aesthetic drawbacks to loading on more exposition. Unless someone is a gifted storyteller, most of the time their audience is not going to sit still for an in-depth explanation of, well, anything. They'll get restless and bored. They'll call, "Cut to the chase!" They'll look for ways to skip that infodump and get right to the shooty McBangbang, or whatever your core mechanic is.

Even among professional writers, not everyone is a storyteller to the degree where they can get an audience to hunker down in rapt attention to what is essentially a high school-level social studies lecture. The fully armed and operational infodump, evolved into its final form, is an impenetrable monster. It is a behemoth who must be endured in order to get to the good stuff (the gameplay) it stands gatekeeper over.

Not all characters are good storytellers, either. Even the best writer cramming words into the mouth of someone the player does not want to listen to is going to have an uphill boulder push ahead of them. Long bits of exposition coming from otherwise unimportant and/or uninteresting characters – especially from those who serve specifically or even exclusively as vehicles for exposition – are like listening to your drunk uncle talk about the local sports team at a family gathering. The material might be interesting in another context, but nobody wants to hear it now, in that way, from them.

Here's another harsh truth. No matter how good your lore or your worldbuilding is, most players are not going to absorb all of it at first contact. That's what lore videos and fan wikis are for, for the curious to come back and catch up on the nuances they know they missed along the way. At first encounter, though, very few survive a blizzard of names and dates and motivations with perfect retention. The information, the very reason all this was insisted upon, is lost.

More accurately, it is never found in the first place. All the player is getting, if you're lucky, is delayed. The wall of text stands between the player and the play, the medicine before they can go for their spoonful of sugar. Most of it won't affect the action in the slightest, nor will plugging the tiniest air leaks in a narrative with vast swathes of verbiage bring much return on investment. It's a solution in search of a problem that doesn't exist.

Now, the cynic will say, "If the players don't like the exposition, write it better. You made the world and the story, give it to them so it's detailed and interesting." And there is something to that, but less than you'd think.

Obviously, a writer who can't communicate the core aspects of their world in a concise and digestible fashion might need to rethink things. Worldbuilding that is too dense and character motivations that are too heavily obscured do nobody any good. Instead, there is much to be said for trusting the player to, having inhabited the skin and the headspace of their character, draw their own conclusions. To let them fill in the blanks instead of doing "Here comes the airplane!" with every bite of world logic and character motivation.

That's not to say that you shouldn't answer obvious and glaring questions or that you don't need to plug gaping holes that break suspension of disbelief badly enough that everyone starts demanding the equivalent of the giant eagles flying the Fellowship straight to Mordor. If there's stuff that people genuinely aren't getting, if there are motivations that a sizable chunk of the playtesters are unclear on, that's a clear signal to apply some spackle. This can be done efficiently and judiciously, and as a writer, you should be thankful for the opportunity to make the fix before your work hits the street. It's when the demands for more and more are endless, when there's more spackle than wall, that you know you have a problem.

6.4 The Third Law

Finally, there's Dansky's Third Law of Game Writing:

> *There are a limited number of miracles that can fit in any given ass to be pulled out at any moment, and they are not necessarily a renewable resource.*

Yes, I know it's crude, but that kind of helps make the point.

Every experienced writer has stories of the time they produced a miracle, fully formed and fresh, under an impossible deadline and with panache and style. These are the tales those writers trade back and forth, the epics of compositional heroism and triumph over kaiju-sized hostile circumstances. It's fun to *have done* something like that as opposed to actively having to do it all over again. It's good to have it in your back pocket and as part of your track record as proof of what you can do when circumstances are dire. It's less good to have it as the regular first item on your to-do list.

The problem comes, however, when various folks look at a situation where a writer or a writing team burned the midnight oil, put the hammer down, and ingested enough energy drinks to light up Toledo (Ohio, not Spain) in order to meet a deadline and decide, yup, that's repeatable. That can become the expected new norm faster than you can blink. The miraculous and the damaging can be framed as the baseline instead of recognized as a prodigious effort, and what that means for deadlines and feedback going forward, you don't want to know.

This is a very bad idea.

It comes from not understanding that writing is work like anything else, that it takes time, and that it has its own processes and requirements in order to get done right. All that gets looked at is the end result, and if the end result happens fast once, the logic goes, why can't it happen fast all the time?

Well, it can't, even in the industry of mandatory crunch and idiot geek macho over who worked the most hours and who got the least sleep. The well of creativity is not bottomless. Sooner or later it gets tapped out, at least temporarily. It needs time to recharge. It needs fuel to reload. It needs, in short, to be treated like a valuable and precious resource and not like a six-year-old's vision of their mom's endless time and attention. There are only so many words you can write before you start slowing down.

Before you start writing crap.

Before you stop writing at all.

Some writers hit that wall sooner than others. Some claim they never hit it at all, though I remain a little dubious. The fact is, as a game writer, you cannot be operating with the needle buried 24/7 without eventually burning out and producing inferior work on your way to crashing. It's too easy to break yourself, especially by saying, "Yes, I can do that" to an ever-more insane list of deliverable demands because you don't want to be seen as "not a team player" or lazy or unwilling to put in the same 120% that everyone else on the team is being asked to do.

I have been on projects where crunch was exactly that – pedal-to-the-metal work for 60, 80, or even more hours a week where everyone was watching everyone else to see who would be the first to crack because they didn't want it to be them. These projects generally saw short-term productivity gains, rapidly offset by long-term declines, massive upticks in bugs introduced by exhausted devs that then needed even more time to fix, and less productive per-minute deliveries. It was not worth it.

I have also been on projects where crunch was declared; people would stick around after regular hours to eat dinner on the company nickel, goof around for a bit, do maybe an extra hour or two of work, and then head home feeling both virtuous and well-fed. To no one's surprise, this didn't achieve the desired result, either.

The hard and simple truth is that miracles need to be saved for special moments. They should be called on to meet special challenges in times of crisis and to be appreciated as, well, special. To quote *The Princess Bride*, you rush a miracle man, you get rotten miracles.

Instead, there needs to be recognition that these moments of effort above and beyond are exactly that. The wise producer keeps their powder dry and picks their spots. They save those herculean efforts for when they are most needed instead of squandering them on stuff that frankly should have been planned better. They understand the innate truth of Dansky's Third Law.

My advice is to heed that law. Don't sign up for self-destruction. Make it clear that you have reasonable limits and that pushing beyond them will cost more than it will gain. Be willing to stretch sometimes. It's part of the biz, honestly, and the dirty secret is that every once in a while it's fun to start writing like your hair's on fire, riding adrenaline down the line count at ramming speed in order to have that story to tell friends later. Just don't let it be established as the baseline. You have to set reasonable expectations for how fast you can work, how long you can work, and how much good work you can produce. Doing this means that realistic, achievable schedules can be made and appropriate resources (read: enough writers) can be assigned. You have to make it clear that you can, in fact, only pull a limited number of miracles out of your ass in any given timeframe, and expecting more is wishful thinking.

Don't be a jerk about it, but do be clear, be honest, and be forthright. The desire to say yes to anything you are asked to do in order to demonstrate value is strong, but ultimately that way lies destruction. It's better to head off the unreasonable expectations at the beginning, establish a reasonable delivery schedule, and then amaze them all when you go into beast mode when the chips are down.

6.5 Conclusion

Thus, I present to you Dansky's Three Laws of Game Writing. Apply them sensibly and consistently, and they will save you heartache, late nights, and agony. Fail to heed them, and there's a too-good chance you'll find yourself slamming your sixth energy drink of the night at 3:00 am for the fifth time this month because you failed to set boundaries, and now the shit is hitting the fan from every direction all at once.

Let's be real. Nobody wants that. Ultimately, even the people flinging the poo don't want it; they just don't know it yet. Take these three laws and educate those people before things get messy.

For everyone.

7

The Game Writer on the Team – What You Actually Do versus What They Think You Do

7.1 Introduction

Your role can vary wildly depending on whether you are the only writer on the team or part of a larger writing team. The latter further breaks down into what position you hold among writers. Being a junior is very different from being a lead. And then there is the question of on-site versus remote, with all the questions that swirl around that.

7.2 The Lone Writer

Let's start with the lone writer versus team of writers dynamic. If you are the only writer on the project, you are also automatically the sole champion for writing on that project. It is your responsibility to stand up for and explain the value of the writing that you are doing such that others can learn to value and support it. There is no one else but you.

Certain other things fall out of that status. If you are the lone writer, then you are responsible for *all* the writing. There is no one else to pick up the slack. This means you need to be even more careful than you might be otherwise about scoping tasks, agreeing to schedules, and accepting additional responsibilities. You also need to make sure you are balancing your writing time with maintaining contact with other departments because there is literally no one else who will do that for you.

Being the sole writer means that you probably will have a lot of trouble finding someone to talk through craft issues with. The odds are low that anyone else on the team will be conversant with professional writing enough to understand and help with your problems on that level. It will be more difficult finding good readers and good feedback for your drafts. And, if you run into trouble, there's no backup coming.

All of this means you have to approach things with the understanding that you must be self-contained and self-sufficient. Be prepared to do everything related to writing because even if they tell you it's not going to be that way, there's always a good chance it's going to be that way.

This, incidentally, is when having a broader network of fellow game writers can be vital. Even if you can't share specifics with friends and peers for obvious legal reasons, you can at least talk in generalities and maybe get some help that way. You can also draw upon their experience and advice for dealing with work situations. The chances are good that someone out there has seen it before, whatever "it" is, because these things do indeed repeat themselves.

So even if you are alone, remember you're not entirely alone, and use that to your best advantage.

DOI: 10.1201/9781003592983-7

7.3 Lead Writer

If you are leading a team of writers, then you have certain additional responsibilities that come along with it. You may (should) be tasked with fewer actual writing deliverables, but other tasks will fill up your schedule handily.

Part of your task is to help the other writers on the team, and most specifically the junior writers, get better. This is true whether it is officially part of your job description or not. To begin with, it's the right thing to do. If you've got experience and knowledge to share to help people who report to you, you have something of a moral and professional obligation to share it and help them advance in their careers.

On a strictly functional level, the better your juniors get, the less time you will have to spend explaining where and how they made mistakes, asking them to correct those mistakes, possibly arguing with them if they don't think they made mistakes, and sometimes giving up and correcting their mistakes yourself.

It's a matter of survival for the juniors as well. A junior who constantly fights against feedback and fails to understand that they are on the receiving end of the decision-making process is a junior who is wasting your time. A junior who needs very specific instructions as to what to write and cannot take feedback and run with it is a junior who is not saving you any time, because in writing that level of instruction, you're basically writing it yourself anyway. Juniors who waste seniors' time without showing improvement don't necessarily last. It really is in everyone's best interest for you to help everyone else get steadily better.

Methods for training up juniors vary. It can be as simple as offering steady, constructive feedback and giving positive reinforcement when they do something well. It can be more formal, with you giving out exercises that the junior needs to do and that hopefully they will learn from. It can take the form of professional development. You can get them to watch videos or read books that are useful in improving their craft, or introduce them to members of the broader game writing community, or get them conference passes so they can learn firsthand out of the crucible of production.

All of these things add up, and all of them help make the writing on the project better. A small investment of time at the beginning of a series of dialog tasks where you explain the basics of character voice can save you a ton of rewriting time on the back end if that message was never conveyed and all the characters sound the same. A little here and a little there and a little time to let it all grow, and you can see massive improvements in quality and speed as the project develops.

Something you must avoid, however, is setting juniors, or anyone on the team, up to fail. Every writer has stuff they are good at and stuff they are less good at. Maybe someone who can knock it out of the park on weapon descriptions can't tell a good origin story. If that's the case, it is criminally negligent to assign character bios to that writer. What you'll get will be subpar. It will require additional effort to correct it, which means additional time, which means additional money spent. And it will produce negative emotions both on your part and on the other writer's.

Try a different path instead. If you've got any say in assigning tasks, make sure that people are shunted onto ones they can excel at instead of ones that will result in crushing failure. Once they're settled in a successful place professionally, then you can start to stretch them safely and help them conquer other tasks. Starting with a double-barreled shot of "do the thing you suck at" is a loser from the get-go.

Beyond that, you have a responsibility to the entire writing team, and also to the project as a whole, to set direction and guidelines in order to maintain a uniform level of quality. It is up to you to make sure there is consistency across the writing and that character voices are unique, appropriate, and internally consistent. You need to make sure everyone has access to all the lore they need to do the job, and you need to serve as a bridge between them and other departments if they have questions and things have to go through channels.

As part and parcel of all this, you generally have to read and give feedback on pretty much everything. Yours is the authoritative voice in the group. You have the mandate to say whatever needs to be said before stuff gets shared out, to make sure that it's in the right shape to get shared out. That takes time and focus, but it's a force multiplier. The more tools you give the writers through actionable feedback, the better their writing is going to be, the more they can work on their own, and the more confident you can be turning their work loose in the wider team space.

On top of that, you sometimes have to stand between your team and the angry gods of Olympus. If they're not happy with a piece of writing, ultimately, that's on you because you let it escape into the wild. As such, you need to accept the responsibility for it, take the negativity, and put a plan into place to make sure it doesn't happen again. It even holds true when the wrath is undeserved or about things your people can't control.

At moments like that, I refer to my job as being a "shit umbrella," keeping the badness off my team so they don't start worrying or spiraling or otherwise getting knocked off their pins. As a lead or a senior, you should be more secure in your career, in your role, and in your work such that you can take a barrage or two in stride and keep on going. That's when the scar tissue that we all build up over the years from countless crises and shenanigans gone wrong can, in fact, be useful.

One last non-writing thing you have to do is set an example beyond writing. You need to set a professional example as well. That means teaching them how to meet deadlines and how to comport themselves in meetings with decision makers. It means helping them develop pitch presentations and guiding them to a place where they're the ones owning the meeting and driving the agenda. It means showing off how to collaborate and how to give and take feedback inside and outside your group. And perhaps most of all, you need to show them how to survive. You need to demonstrate how to pace yourself so that when the inevitable crisis hits, you're able to rise to the occasion instead of already running on empty. You need to take a vacation yourself, so they see it is OK to take a vacation and they won't be thought less of for doing it. In short, you need to get to the end of the project, no matter what comes your way, in such a fashion that they learn how to do it in one piece, too, and they're better prepared for the next one.

7.4 What about the Writing?

You may have noticed that I have not mentioned actual writing thus far. That is because, believe it or not, as a lead, you will probably be doing less of it. The other tasks (and the meetings that go with them) add up. There is less time than you'd think available to settle in and write. As such, I have found that when I am in a leadership role, I tend not to schedule myself for many deliverables at all. What that does is it keeps me from biting off more than I can chew, and it also leaves me available as a writing reserve for when things get tight. (News flash: They always get tight.) Sometimes being a game writer means not writing . . . until you suddenly have to.

7.5 Just a Writer

If you're on a team but not the lead, things shift. You will be getting handed tasks of various lengths and flavors. These will often involve working with folks in other disciplines. The authority is less, but so is the workload. What you need to do then is establish yourself as reliable. Accept your deliverables, make sure you have the information you need to achieve your deliverables (both in terms of the technical side, like word count, and the content you're working on), and produce your deliverables. Don't be afraid to speak up and suggest stuff you think you'd be good for. Just be prepared to deal with it if you don't get that particular slice of verbiage. A lot of times leads will ask who wants what, but sometimes you have to play the hand you are dealt. Do that well, prove your worth, and you might get something more to your liking the next go-round.

Being part of a writing team carries with it a few extras. The fact is, if you're part of a team of writers, you are each other's best resources on the project. You speak each other's language, you know each other's hardships, and you're in the best position to offer feedback, suggestions, and encouragement before anyone at a higher level sees word one. Make yourself available if others need an ear or an eye or someone to talk something through with. Brainstorm together. Share your research, whether it be what the fans are saying about your work online or subject matter stuff that might be cool to add into the game. Be a teammate as well as a writer, and you'll get what you give back and more.

That's all focused on the writing team. Bear in mind, there is a project team as well, and where you fit into all that is maybe even more important.

7.6 Eyes on You

Very few people on the outside know how the game writing process works on the day to day. There is an assumption instead that writing is a constant head-down, nose-to-the-grindstone activity whereby the keys are constantly clacking and the words are constantly flowing. Either that, or it is a job where you basically do nothing because words are magical and not hard at all.

Anyone who has done the job for any length of time knows that this is not how it works. There are long periods of research in order to prepare to write. There are moments of inactivity when you're thinking with your brain, instead of your fingers, and all the hard work is going on inside your head where no one else can see it. There can be moments of silence and then sudden, furious bursts of activity.

The content of any given moment does not, in fact, matter in the grand scheme of things. What matters is that at the end, the deliverable is done, and if you spent a minute or an hour or a shift staring at the ceiling while your subconscious went to work on it, it shouldn't matter.

That's the view from the inside. The view from the outside is considerably different. These are folks charged with tracking productivity who don't understand how writers might operate day to day, or what a writer's process might manifest. Instead, they look over when there's two days left before the deliverable and see a writer staring off into space, and they take this to mean that someone might be slacking. This, as you might expect, is a problem.

Writers who are not constantly hunched over their keyboards are seen as less than dedicated or productive, never mind what the end result is. Writers who are not constantly squeezing out words are seen as either lazy or less productive than they could be. After all, if you can punch out a cinematic script in a couple of days, including those daydreaming breaks, you should be able to eliminate those breaks and extrude twice as much. Thus, the logic goes from those who have never had to let a script marinate in their brain juices long enough to be ready to emerge into the light of day.

The truth of the matter is that this is not the way things work. Sometimes the brain is engaged in preparatory work behind the eyeballs. Sometimes it is engaging the fingers to type. Sometimes it is urging you to get up and walk around so you're not staring at a screen that's resisting your best efforts, with the understanding that a change of scenery will enable you to get out of a mental rut. This is all part of the writing process, and it all leads to the desired result in the end.

If you want to survive, you have to get the people with oversight over you to understand this. If they think you're relaxing when your brain is actually hard at work getting you comfortable enough with the material to be able to give it form, then you are going to be penalized for it. You will be called lazy or a slacker or something even worse. You will get marked down in performance reviews because you won't be seen as giving Omega-level effort at all times. You will, ultimately, get cut no slack.

That, incidentally, is for writers who are at a desk on-site. Writers working remotely have it even worse, as there's no nuanced way to track their productivity minute to minute. At best, they have keystroke trackers, or they check the activity light on your Teams account, or something to that effect. "People won't work" was always the big pre-COVID argument against remote work. That fear remains today, even while many people find themselves more productive than ever when able to work in their own environment and at their own pace. Regardless, though, there is always the possibility that unless a remote writer is constantly generating keystrokes, someone is going to think they are off napping instead.

All of which means that you need to head this discussion off before it has time to establish itself. That means getting buy-in for what you do before someone gets the wrong idea and uses it to spike a raise or a promotion. The best thing you can do is keep someone aware of your workflow and prepare them for when stuff is going to arrive, making sure they don't get antsy, check in on you, and get the entirely wrong idea. Sadly, saying, "Look, sometimes I have to stare off into space or watch cat videos for a bit while my brain sorts it out without me in the room" doesn't play with the schedule-oriented types. Nothing is going to convince those folks who think that creativity happens like clockwork and that writers are like vending machines.

Those who are not creative often do not understand the creative process and look down on what does not match their idea of maximum efficiency as a result. All you can do in the end is deliver, and if your moment-to-moment workflow gets challenged, keep the conversation focused on results.

What you can do, however, is get Proactive in a way that they don't feel the need to look at you in the first place. Announce progress as it happens. Share small deliverables to help create a genuine sense of forward motion. Do this, and you build up trust that you are being productive and an asset to the team. The more trust you earn, the more you can push to do other stuff to make the writing even better. It starts, though, at the beginning.

7.7 Joining the Team

Speaking of beginnings, when you come onto a team can dictate how you come onto a team.

It's one thing if you're there from the early stages or even the beginning and have a hand in cultivating the content as it develops from nothing. This can make for relatively smooth relations, as you're part of the blossoming whole, and your contribution is more or less organic. You are a part of the existing team, and other devs will have a certain comfort level with that.

The same even goes for planned roll-ons. No game is ready for a full writing team on day one. The work just isn't there. Instead, it's better to have planned additions to the writing team such that there is staff available and up to speed who, when a foreseen need arises, can hop on board and make an immediate impact. Because their presence was anticipated and needed, the onboarding is generally pretty smooth, and if everyone in the hiring process did their jobs right, the fit is good. The work gets done, the force gets multiplied, and everyone is happy.

On the other hand, if you get dropped onto an existing team mid-cycle, it's probably not because things are going well. Perhaps the writing is perceived as lacking, or the team isn't keeping up with production demands and needs help. Either way, if this is your fate, you're there because things could be better.

Now, when you walk into the room as the living embodiment of that idea, it can get tricky. Yes, there are certainly teams that welcome fresh bandwidth, talent, and ideas in the interest of making their game better. Integrating with these teams is by and large pleasant, as they are eager to share their ideas, get you up to speed, and work with you to reach that next level they understand might be out of reach without you.

There are also teams who view a new addition, particularly one imposed from, say, a publisher, as a judgment directed at them that their work isn't good enough. That can lead to resentment, and that leads to resistance, and that leads to trouble for the work. If a team thinks their writing is perfect as is while everyone around them agrees that it's not, you have every right and reason to be there. You're dealing with the additional hurdle of working with people who don't want you there and who may not have an interest in making your life easier.

I've gone multiple routes with this, to the point where I once gave a conference talk on how to be a video game script doctor. I've joined teams that knew they were in trouble and were grateful for help to get them out of what they knew was a hole. I've joined teams that were doing fine but were open to additional assistance, and I felt I could bring a positive to the work. I've also been assigned to teams that fought tooth and nail to preserve every last line of a script that had been deemed by all other parties to be unusable. I even had one project where I would get flown across the Atlantic to work with a team that routinely froze me out of all meetings while I was there, wasting time and money, so they could then complain that I wasn't doing anything. Your mileage, as they say, varies.

If you are brought onto an existing team, there are things you can do to make your transition smoother and your work more warmly received. For one thing, familiarize yourself with what has already been done. This is as true for joining a live services game team mid-lifespan as it is for joining a one-off project before recording. Get to know what has been created and give it a clear look to allow you to understand the strengths and weaknesses.

Then and only then, communicate with the team members responsible for it. Be sure to point out the good stuff. When you bring up what needs work, do this in a way that is not accusatory, contemptuous, or dismissive. Even if it's total crap, someone worked hard on it and is probably attached to it, and you're not going to make friends by heaping abuse on it. Put the concerns in context and offer a path to making things better together. Do not come in like a kaiju and stomp the city flat, even if you have a mandate to do precisely that. This makes enemies, and the industry is small, and people have long memories.

I have been informed by reliable sources that in some other media, it is customary for the rewriter or script doctor or whoever to come in and aggressively trash everything that has been done before, regardless of quality. This is done to make them look good and to remove any points of comparison to other stuff that might, in hindsight, make them look bad. And if their stuff doesn't work, hey, it was on fire when they got there.

I don't believe in this model. I believe in working with the team, not against it, and salvaging anything that can be salvaged as a way to support them and earn goodwill. I believe in offering things to the team instead of taking things away from them. As much as I love cryptozoology, I refuse to come in and Bigfoot all over things. Even if the team doesn't want me there, I want to make their work better, not heedlessly overwrite it with my own.

7.8 The Teardown

There are absolutely times when you do need to tear stuff down and rebuild because things just aren't working.

If you're forced into a position to do that, give context and explanation before you fire up the wrecking ball. Lay the groundwork for your efforts and set up a clear plan for what needs fixing, why it needs fixing, and how you're going to fix it. Get buy-in on that instead of resistance, and your job gets much easier.

Once you do start cutting, cut ruthlessly. Trying to save stuff that isn't good enough to protect someone's feelings will come back to bite you later. Leaving stuff in that's not strong enough to be load-bearing for sentimental reasons invites having the whole thing crash down on you later. Better to act like a surgeon and cut the whole thing out. Then, with a clean slate, you can start on something better, and if the others are still on the team, you can bring them with you on the journey.

If there is resistance, active or passive, you have to get past it as quickly as possible. If you are there in the first place, you are there to do a job, which is to make the writing better. If you are working with professionals, once they see the end product, they will understand and appreciate what you did. If you are not, odds are good you won't have to worry about working with them again.

7.9 When a Writer Has to Go

This leads us to a real downer: What to do about a writer who can't do the job.

I have stated bluntly in a couple of places in this book that not every would-be game writer can do the job. Corollary to that is the idea that the writer who cannot do a job should not have a job. A great fiction author or screenwriter who can't handle writing for an interactive medium is not an asset to your team. A game writer who is not up to snuff and shows no signs of improving or who requires so much hand-holding and rewriting that they hinder other writers from doing their tasks is not helping you. They are instead actively dragging you and your fellow writers down by producing subpar work, taking up your time, potentially clogging up meetings, and generally not helping get things done.

As harsh as it seems, a writer like that needs to go. There is an unspoken bond of solidarity, a "we're all in this together" spirit that infuses many writing teams that makes cutting out one of your own seem unthinkable. In order to save yourself, you have to be able to do it. You can like the person while still understanding that the work is insufficient and below acceptable standards.

Now, this has to be tempered with logic, compassion, and good-faith efforts to put someone in a position where they can succeed. If you've got a writer who excels at dialog but who sucks rocks through a straw at character bios, don't ask them to write character bios and assign them dialog instead. You can then start giving them exercises on the side to help expand their skill set, but handing a plumber a scalpel and telling them to go operate never ends well.

Also, if someone has never been trained in a task, it makes sense to at least attempt to train them before blowing them out the door and embarking on the difficult, expensive, and time-consuming process of hiring. One of the things this industry is absolutely terrible at is providing career growth for writers and narrative types in general. There is no clear career path for writers except maybe "bigger writer." There is almost never any resource or time allotted to professional development and training, as time spent working on craft doesn't knock out Jira tickets and show up in velocity tracking. Again, this means it devolves on you, if you are senior, to do the work, thankless though it may be.

Which means if they've never been asked to write barks, show them sample barks. Then assign them a small deliverable and go over it with them, letting them incorporate your feedback and take another swing. If you get lucky and the training takes, congratulations, you've improved the team. If it doesn't, then you at least did your due diligence and can proceed with the knowledge you tried your best.

If you do have to go forward with a firing (words like "separation" are bloodless nonsense that people use to convince themselves their hands aren't dirty), do it cleanly, quickly, and fairly. Make sure you know what you legally can and cannot say, and if the person getting canned asks for a reference or a letter, what you can or cannot do for them. Don't lie, don't soft-pedal, but don't be cruel, either. Even if it's someone you actively wanted gone, there's no percentage in rejoicing in someone else's pain. That stuff gets noticed, and it might be your turn next if it does.

Hopefully, it will never come to that. Removing someone from the team, even if it's someone who doesn't deserve a place, is almost always hard. To quote the guy who wrote that Keanu Reeves dialog I discussed earlier, "If it were done when 'tis done, then 'twere well it were done quickly."

7.10 In-House versus Freelance

On a happier note, let's talk about forms of employment. Some writers are full-time employees who work directly for the studio and are part of the team. Others are contractors, freelance workers who are often on time-limited contracts and whose tenures are likely to be tied to the needs of a specific project. You will hear a lot of debate about which is better, but the truth is that both sides have their pluses and minuses, and what is right for one writer may not be particularly good for another.

My experience has almost exclusively been as an in-house writer, albeit with the caveat that I was basically deployed as an internal freelancer by Ubisoft for two decades. This gave me a lot of benefits of the freelance life, such as the ability to work on a wide range of projects, while also providing the stability (and health insurance) of being a full-time employee. My perspective is admittedly rare, in that my role was so odd that I heard peers at other companies referring to similar positions as "the Rich Dansky job." In that time, however, I got to work with in-house teams, short-term contractors, long-term contractors, narrative consultants who dropped in for short periods of very well compensated time, and everyone in between. As a result, I like to think that I do have at least a little perspective on the topic.

The benefits of being in-house are obvious. They include professional stability and removing the necessity to constantly hustle for your next gig. Things like benefits, bonus plans, regular paychecks, and establishing strong relationships with your teammates in a way that allows you to operate at high efficiency are all good to have. Plus, as a writer, if you are in-house, there is a very good chance you will be brought on early in a project and be able to contribute to the development in a meaningful way all along.

On the downside, very few studios know what to do with writers long-term. As I briefly noted earlier, professional development is almost nonexistent because there aren't enough senior writers to go around to train up juniors, and those seniors are almost certainly tasked to the point where aiding in professional development isn't on the production schedule. Studios are tightfisted in general when it comes to employee development, and there are few proven out-of-the-box solutions for developing writers for them to turn to.

Hand in hand with this is the lack of clear career paths for writers. The ladder of titles to climb is short, at best, and the guidelines for ascending to the next rung are frequently unclear. Get a job at a studio, and that may be your job for a very long time because they may not have any structure in place for you to achieve promotion. After all, the title might not exist for you to be promoted to.

The other caveat is that if you are in-house, most likely you will be told exactly what you are going to be working on come hell or high water. Very few studios afford their writers the chance to pick and choose what they'd prefer to do. Instead, you get assigned where there is a need. If that means you get plugged in on a game you don't personally like, you may not have any recourse. It's part of the deal.

Freelance life, on the other hand, can be more exciting in good and bad ways. On the positive side, you get to work with a wide range of people on a wide range of products. You get to decide what you apply for and what you work on by and large, and you have a large degree of professional freedom. It's also easier to work remotely as a freelancer instead of having to relocate on-site. And you get to pitch your own salary and contract terms, setting you outside a studio's usual pay structure, which might dole out raises only in geologic time.

On the downside, there is the lack of security and the need to constantly hustle for the next gig. Insurance can be a real issue, and a lot of contracts are written in a way to end a contractor's time on a project before bonuses get calculated and paid out.

Freelancers also can come onto a project much later, often when there is suddenly a perceived emergency. This can force them to hit the ground running without the benefit of the institutional knowledge an in-house writer might have. Some teams might appreciate the new perspective an outsider joining them might bring, but too frequently it can boil down to being told to grab a bucket and start bailing.

Ultimately, which one works better for you can be determined by a lot of factors, including your appetite for risk. Folks have carved out successful careers on one side of the aisle or the other or done both at different points in their professional journeys. Just be aware of what you're getting into before you sign on the dotted line.

8

Breaking In and Finding the Next Gig

8.1 Introduction

There are certain questions I get asked a lot when I tell people that I write for video games. The most common one is "So, you code?," but there are others that come up frequently as well, and most of them revolve around the idea of getting hired.

Let's be clear about one thing: There is no foolproof way to get hired as a game writer. For the longest time, game writing was the Wild West when it came to professional pathways in. Some folks started as designers or in QA and moved over to writing tasks. Some came in from other media. Me, I came in from tabletop RPG/LARP design and writing, thanks to a friend in the industry who convinced me to apply to Red Storm Entertainment, and I initially got hired as a game designer for a game that was going to be writing-heavy as a result.

That, however, was 25 years ago, and things have changed a little bit since then. Now, we have something faintly approaching a talent pipeline for junior game developers, though the path for writers is still muddy and largely unmarked. We also have an established professional community and a body of work, online and in print, to guide people on their way in.

Bear in mind, too, that every studio's wants and needs are going to be different. What I'm going to do here is give some broad-stroke advice that can then be customized to suit an approach to a particular studio. Yes, a studio that's making dating sims is going to want something very different from one making tactical shooters, and both of them are miles away from a team that wants a narrative wrapper for a hidden object or match 3 game, but still, there are some ground rules.

8.2 The Basic Skill and the Portfolio

The first thing you have to do to get hired as a game writer, broadly speaking, is demonstrate that you want to, know how to, and can write specifically for games. Unless you have a big name in another medium and there's Marketing value attached to you getting hired, you need to show up front that you can do the job that you're applying for. Other writing credits can be very helpful, particularly if there are people on the team who are fans of your work, but your 700-page fantasy novel is not going to help you when it comes time to write barks, and your tight screenplay is not going to prove conclusively that you know how to write for an interactive medium.

DOI: 10.1201/9781003592983-8

Instead, show that you understand what game writing is and that you want to and know how to do it. This leads to stocking your portfolio appropriately with game writing-appropriate samples.

Do put in short scripts and character designs, and maybe some worldbuilding, and a bark sheet. Some item descriptions might be useful as well. Make sure all this stuff is targeted at being useful to a game development team. If you're doing a character write-up, make sure it calls out the key details that a concept artist might need, and don't spend 5,000 words on a detailed history that a player will never see or care about. If you're writing dialog, do it in a way that shows an understanding of how it fits into a game.

Over the years I have gotten wonderful portfolios that clearly demonstrated the person applying had the skills and talent that were wanted. I have also gotten fanfic for IPs that I was not hiring for, lengthy transcriptions of the applicant's *Dungeons & Dragons* campaign, and multiple instances of soft-core pornography. None of these helped someone get a job. Focus, be appropriate, and make sure you're presenting yourself as in tune with the job.

If you already have a body of work, pointing to clips on YouTube is an easy and fast way to demonstrate your bona fides. This also helps you get around the issue of not being able to provide script documents if they belong to a former employer. If you don't have a track record, though, you will want to construct one however you can as fast as possible.

There are a couple of ways to do this. One is to get your hands on an engine and start making your own games. This is useful on a couple of different levels. For one thing, you build actual, viewable content for your portfolio. For another, you get experience and confidence working with a tool set. And for a third, you get to hear how your writing comes across when played, not read. Trust me when I say there is a world of difference between the reader and the player. The reader wants to savor the words, and the player wants them to help them play. The most mellifluous writing imaginable will bomb as game writing if it prevents the player from engaging in the act of play, and this is a first step in teaching yourself that lesson.

In addition to that, seek out game jams where you can and offer your services as a wordsmith. A lot of these teams will say they don't need any writing; many of them will realize their folly when they get bogged down trying to come up with names for stuff for their UI to no avail. Be polite but persistent, and by doing this, you will build up a body of actual games for your portfolio.

I do not recommend getting involved in "for the love" projects or ones that promise to pay in "exposure." As a wise writer once said, people *die* of exposure. Investing a couple of days in a game jam is one thing. Investing months for no money is very much another, especially since there is a non-zero chance that someone else *is* making money off that game and your work.

Don't think your portfolio has to be monolithic and static, either. You should tailor your portfolio to the job you are applying for, putting in the work that shows your skills to best effect. Don't keep old stuff in there because it's there. If you've got newer, better work that is more likely to get you hired, it's replacement time.

8.3 Networking

Beyond that, networking matters.

I don't have the numbers, but I do know that a fair number of writing jobs get filled through the recommendation network before they ever get posted. That means you need to get to a place where, when a job opens up, your name gets brought up as a possibility.

The noble first instinct on hearing that is "That's cheating! My writing speaks for itself!" The sad truth is that noble instinct is not your friend. There is absolutely nothing immoral, sneaky, or underhanded about building a reputation for yourself as someone people want to work with. That is what we are talking about here. Your writing may be Virginia Woolf on sliced bread levels of awesome, but if it never gets to a hiring manager's desktop, it doesn't do you any good. Knowing people and having them think your work is worth passing along gets you on that desktop where your writing will then have that chance to shine (or at least get to the next person in the hiring process).

You have to make yourself known, and there are ways to do that without being a pushy, over-eager jerk. That means networking in a way that lets you come across as smart, interested, and serious. Going all fannish is generally a turn-off, as is trying to neg the experienced folks whose attention you want to get. I've seen a lot of writers walk into the industry saying "Let me show you how you suck," and I've seen most of them walk right back out.

That means attending conferences, real or virtual, if you can, and reaching out to speakers and pros you meet there. If you're going to a conference like the Game Narrative Summit, check the speaker list beforehand, see who's interesting to you, and do a little research on their work. Then, when you do engage with them after their talk, you can present yourself as serious and interested. Ask good questions when you talk, instead of trying to overwrite what you might have just heard. Ask if you can connect on social media, and if the answer is yes, absolutely follow up after the conference.

Opportunities to engage like this are valuable and rare. If someone says "talk to me," they mean it, so talk to them. If they offer to introduce you to someone for your benefit, follow up on that introduction and build a bridge of your own. If someone wants to give you a stage, seize it. Never be embarrassed or say you don't want to be a bother, or tell yourself you're not worthy. If the offer is being made, someone clearly thinks you are worthy. But those efforts put forth by others are not infinite. Sooner or later, they dry up, leaving you regretting the lost opportunities that may never come again. Don't do that.

On social media, engage positively. If there's a conversation in the comments of a post, get involved in a way that shows you've thought about the issue at hand. Feel free to repost something you like, but don't auto-repost everything. Post your own thoughts on game writing, and engage with the people who like or comment on them. Streaming about game writing or videos? Bring them on. In short, be someone people want to talk to, and be that person consistently to keep from vanishing from view. Eventually this can get you on people's radar, and *that* means when there are openings and they are thinking of who to recommend, your name comes to mind.

8.4 Accepting the Opportunity

It is unlikely that you will get hired for your dream project right off the bat. To build a track record, you will need to cast your net wide. Sometimes that means working on an IP or a game that isn't your favorite thing. That's OK. It's still going to be a paying gig, it's still going to be a credit, it's still going to teach you something, and who knows, you may find yourself changing your mind.

Don't turn your nose up at stuff because it's not your kind of game. Be willing to at least try. If it doesn't work out and you're emotionally unsuited to writing high fantasy dialog, great, move on with the knowledge, and there you go. But if you can find a way in that lets you find enjoyment in the project where you didn't think you'd find any, that's a much better outcome.

For example, when I got tapped for a racing game, I knew absolutely nothing about the subject matter and was actively afraid of motor oil. Having the gig, though, goosed me to go learn. A nigh-infinite number of YouTube videos and books and magazines and rewatches of the *Fast and the Furious* movies later, I found myself at parties talking about how an electric vehicle can totally dust you off the line in a drag race because of torque, and, well, it was a long time ago, and I've forgotten most of it, but it sure made writing that game a lot more engaging.

8.5 Writing Tests: Threat or Menace?

One controversial subject in the hiring process is writing tests. A studio has every right to ask you to provide a sample of your work. This allows them to make an informed, evidence-based decision as to whether you are a good fit for the project and the team. If you're in an interview process and you get asked to take a writing test, the answer should always be yes *if the test itself is reasonable.*

Sadly, not every test is. There are studios that genuinely want to see if you can write what they need. There are also ones that will force you to jump through hoops, demanding an impossible amount of work for free in a very short time to see if they can crunch you from the get-go. And there are those who are unscrupulously looking for you to generate a raft of free material for them that, since they own the results of the test, they can then use without paying you.

Being asked to take a writing test can be great. It can mean you are under serious consideration. Just make sure to look carefully at the parameters of the test to make sure they're not trying to take advantage of you.

If they are, walk away. They're not people you want to work with anyway.

8.6 Generative AI and Juniors

And speaking of people, that leads us to the elephant in the room: Generative Artificial Intelligence (AI).

It is a given that a lot of companies are going to seek to replace writing roles with generative AI. I feel this is a mistake on several levels. Leaving aside the wild immorality of the model generative AI was built on and the massive resource cost that sustains it, there are practical reasons not to use it.

For one thing, it's frequently inaccurate. For another, the quality generally isn't terribly good. And for another, you will never get something original out of a generative AI. Literally all it can do is spit out a variant of the stuff it's taken in.

I won't go into the stark ethical concerns with using technology that was admittedly based on stolen content, or the massive environmental costs of generative AI, or all the other badness that goes with it.

You see, the bottom line doesn't care about any of that. It sees a way to cut costs in the short term by axing writers and their low (for the industry) salaries. It sees a way to check a box cheaply and quickly. Plus, there is the added feature that generative AI will never look at a prompt and immediately explain why it's a bad idea based on actual reasons. The depressing truth is that while generative AI stuff isn't going to be good, for some folks it's going to be good enough, at least in the short term.

Right now, generative AI is largely being used to replace juniors and entry-level positions, and that is a tragedy. The long-term consequences, in my opinion, are going to be dire.

Simply put, companies are unwilling to invest in junior writers for what can only be described as bad reasons. They view juniors as an unnecessary expense because they're not contributing as much as seniors, they think their tasks can easily be picked up by other members of the team or by generative AI, and they do not want to invest the time and resources necessary to turn a green newbie into a functional professional.

All of this logic is shoddy. Of course, juniors are not contributing as much as seniors. That's because they're not seniors. At the same time, they're not being paid as much as seniors, which means it evens out. Furthermore, the tasks commonly assigned to juniors are the sorts of things that seniors either do not want to or should not be doing. If you can have a low-cost junior write barks or wrangle text strings, why on earth would you want to tie up your high-powered, high-salary senior who could be doing other things that they are uniquely suited for instead? Letting juniors do junior tasks as part of their professional development benefits the team short- and long-term. It matches people with appropriate tasks, keeps them busy and productive, and helps develop professionalism and skills in juniors.

Then there's the other issue: Investing in your juniors. As noted earlier, many studios do not want to spend the time and therefore the money it takes to have seniors mentor and train juniors. Everyone wants a writer who works perfectly out of the box and can hit the ground running on day one, in a way that no one would expect of an artist, engineer, or, dare I say it, producer. The thing is, there are only so many of these unicorns to go around, and that means they're expensive. Furthermore, we are at a point in the industry's history where the first wave of seniors is starting to age out, retire, be frozen out, or otherwise leave the business. Guess what? If you stop hiring juniors, investing in their development, and helping them grow into seniors, the flow of talent to replace those seniors is going to dry up permanently.

Unless you're targeting an industry leader to join your team to put out a fire, it is often more sensible and cost-effective to hire a junior or mid-level writer and take a few months to train them up ahead of a looming need. The cost will be comparable to, if not less than, what it will take to bring a rock star in six months down the road when everything is on fire. And if you go the latter route, hiring only when there is a crisis, you will then have to pull your seniors out of production to do interviews and read samples and resumes precisely when you need them working the most. That, in case you were wondering, also costs money. In the long run, it's inefficient, and it's bad business for the project, the company, and the industry as a whole.

Now, I can sympathize with producers to a certain point. They no doubt have hard head-count limits to hew to, and their concern is not the future of the industry or even the viability of the next project. It's hitting that next milestone as efficiently as possible. However, what is cost-effective in the short term is often more expensive in the long term, and the costs only go up when you start looking at the long term effects of not having home-grown talent that knows your system and your process available at all times to pick up slack and move forward. Waiting for the (often foreseen) crisis to hit six months down the road may make for a couple of sunnier quarterly progress reports for a little while, but the bill inevitably comes due, and the payment for rush shipping is not cheap.

And there's one more point to consider here: Entry level is where the new voices come from. Newer and different voices are going to tell newer and different stories, which is going to be vital to the industry's success once everyone finally gets tired once and for all of Ye Olde Stubbly Grizzled Space Marine. Telling more stories also appeals to the audiences who aren't being served now and who aren't playing and buying games as a result. Getting a broader array of skills and talent on your team can only be a plus.

Not investing in juniors, then, means slamming the door on this talent pool. It means cutting the industry off from expansion to new audiences that would come when these juniors became seniors and started doing more and more creative things. It means throttling the talent pipeline in a way that will be hard to recover from for years.

8.7 The Bad News

Where does all of that leave the next generation of people wanting to be game writers?

I'm not going to lie to you. It's not a great place. There are a whole lot of people vying for jobs. There is a whole lot of static to cut through to get your voice heard. Rich people are looking to cut back on hiring. It's hard, and it stands a very good chance of being harder.

Faced with this, a lot of folks I know are no longer comfortable encouraging people to get into game writing and narrative. They feel it's not a positive to lead people toward something that stands a good chance of not panning out and that offers nothing in the way of long-term security.

They have a very good point.

It's not the only point.

I have thought long and hard about the issue, and the conclusion I came to is that it is never my place to tell someone not to follow their dream.

What I *can* do is this: I can warn them that the road ahead is rockier and more dangerous than the nameless, washed-out, one-lane dirt track I took on a Bigfoot expedition in Georgia one time. I can prepare them for potential disappointment and temper expectations. I can provide tools that will help them give it their best shot and give them a better chance to succeed. And I can be there as a resource, whether here or on social media or at conferences, to provide assistance along the way.

Even for the best of the best, it's going to be hard. Think about whether you want to commit to this before you make the leap. If you do, then it's absolutely worth your shot, knowing nothing is guaranteed. You won't know if you don't try.

8.8 Finding the Next Gig

So much for the good and the bad of getting in. Now, what about staying in?

On one level, having credits on a shipped game or even a project that reached a reasonable stage of development before getting shut down helps you find the next gig and the next one after that. Make no mistake, you will need to find another gig. My personal experience, where I spent 23 years at one studio, is an extreme outlier, and even then, it's a bit misleading. Sure, I was based out of Red Storm, but the vast majority of my work for a solid 15 years was for Ubi Montreal or Massive or Ubi Toronto or wherever. I was functionally switching jobs on the regular, but with the benefit of not having to fill out paperwork every time.

Therefore, prepare yourself to find the next opportunity, and always be prepared to do it at a moment's notice. Projects get abruptly canceled. Layoffs happen. A senior-level team member could decide they don't like you and that your days are numbered. Or maybe the project reaches a stage where fewer writers are needed and there's no other work on site for you to transition over to.

Plus, there are times when you want to get the hell out of Dodge. This can be a perfectly reasonable reaction. If you or your work aren't getting respect or support, if your day to day has you dreading every online meeting, if you're being asked to do stuff you are not comfortable doing, if the money isn't enough for what you are doing and there's no redress in sight, then look for the exits with a clear conscience. Self-preservation is not a crime, and if you find yourself in an untenable situation, you owe it to yourself to get someplace better to make sure you don't damage yourself or your career.

In any case, there will always be a time when you need to move along to something new. On rare occasions, it will come looking for you. You cannot count on this. It's great when it happens, when a fan of your work on a previous title comes calling with an offer, but it is not a reliable source of employment. Instead, you are going to have to hunt.

This is another place the networking I mentioned earlier comes in handy. Knowing professional peers and having a good relationship with them means you can reach out in a non-slimy way to ask if they know if anyone is hiring. It means you can ask them to amplify the signal on your job search (if it is public, which is not always the case) or pass it along through the whisper network. It means that you can ask for a reference. All of these go a long way.

You also will want to get your samples in place. If the separation is amicable, you can ask if you can use writing samples from a game as part of your portfolio. Some studios are OK with this, some want you to replace the names and proper nouns on the script before they will let you, and some studios say no. It's always worth checking, though, and you might get a pleasant surprise.

The dirty secret here is that you need to prepare before the last gig ends, not after. That means being careful, because you don't want to give the impression (whether it's true or not) that you're looking to jump ship. If you're in a situation where you're contracted for a particular project that has an end date in sight, you can generally get away with asking questions about stuff for your portfolio ahead of time. After all, everyone knows the end is coming. If you're in a more fluid situation, it gets tougher.

Incidentally, the last thing you want to do is check out before you leave. Your current team deserves your best effort as long as you are on board. Furthermore, it's always better to leave on good terms. Cruise to the finish line and slack along the way, and word might get around. As noted elsewhere in this book, it's a small industry and people talk, and that same network you have worked to be a part of can also communicate warnings if you've mandated them.

Above all, though, when looking for a new role, you have to be persistent and flexible. Be prepared to knock on a lot of doors, because the numbers are big and the competition is fierce. Be flexible in what you are willing to do and in framing your prior experience as pertinent to the job you are gunning for.

8.9 Interviews

Finally, there's the question of the interview. Obviously you want to present yourself at your best. That means doing research on the studio that you're looking to get hired at, and if their project is public, on that as well. Do fact-check before you say anything silly that will mark you as an unserious or sloppy person; I lost track of the number of candidates who wanted to get jobs at Red Storm because of how much they loved *Splinter Cell*, which was made at Ubisoft Montreal. (Note: Red Storm did contribute substantially to *Splinter Cell: Blacklist,* the sixth main game in the franchise, but these candidates generally came along well before then. Timing matters.)

Do what you can to make yourself look smart. Often times, companies will send you a list of whom you will be interviewing with. Take that list and run with it. Look up credits, look for interviews with them online, and figure out what you can talk about with these people that shows you do your homework.

Do not, under any circumstances, even if they ask you to, trash the work of the studio or previous iterations of the IP in question. This holds true no matter what, even if you hated it or even if it sucked. Go constructive instead. Talk about places where you think certain improvements could have been made or elements that didn't quite work for you for reasons. You shouldn't be phony and pretend to like something you don't, because that sort of thing is obvious and a red flag. With that in mind, turning on the flamethrower immediately is always a losing tactic.

Don't trash your previous/current employer, either. If you slag them, it's not a stretch for a potential employer to think you're going to slag your next stop on the way out the door as well. Grumble privately as much as you need to preserve your sanity, but do not toss grenades behind you in order to walk away from a metaphorical exploding building in slo-mo. Be graceful, suggest that goals no longer align or something similar, and leave it be.

When asked to talk, don't ramble. Answer questions efficiently. If it's a complicated question, you can give a complicated answer, but you don't need ten minutes' worth of backstory and edge cases. Use examples, but don't dissect them down to the cellular level. If you can't be clear and direct in an interview, you're not going to be clear and direct in a meeting, and you're sunk.

And when it's your turn, have good questions prepared. Ask about writing and process. I once turned down a job because when I asked every writer I talked to about their team's process, they all responded with the same single expletive. Ask about what your interviewers like and don't like in other games, and see if there is common ground. Try to build a couple of your questions off ones you were asked to demonstrate you were in fact paying attention. And be appreciative of the answers.

Remember, you're interviewing them as much as they're interviewing you. You want to make sure the thing you go to is a good fit and that you're not going to be chewing on the furniture in frustration after two weeks. Don't be afraid to ask hard questions if the answers matter to you. Just be prepared for those answers when they come, and if you don't like them, have the strength to walk away.

8.10 Saying No, or Not Right Now

You may not have the luxury of being able to say no to a job. If that's the case, do what you can to make a less than ideal situation work for you. Go in with your eyes open, and if necessary, keep your eyes open for a better possibility. Do what you must to keep the lights on and food on the table, but do so fully aware, and don't resign yourself to it as inevitable.

There will also be times when you need a lifeline out of a bad situation. If that's the case and one comes along, you should grab it. What you shouldn't do is mistake the improvement from your current situation for something that is objectively good or stable or long-term. It might be all of these things; it might not. Either way, don't fall in love with the rebound gig because it's there. Be willing and able to move on if it doesn't fit your needs either.

If you can afford to be choosy, however, you owe it to yourself to do so. If possible, you want to be going to something good, not just away from something bad. Make sure before you sign the dotted line that if you don't have to do it, you still want to do it. Confirm for yourself that the IP is interesting, and the team seems cool, and the work model seems good for the way you do things. Look toward your career as a whole if you can, and seek out gigs that will bring you new challenges, greater opportunities, and a chance to do good work that people will appreciate.

In the end, always do the best for yourself that you can. It may not always be kittens and rainbows, but that doesn't mean you shouldn't at least try for the occasional kitten. You owe that to the people who will play your work, and you owe it to yourself.

9

Working with Other Disciplines

9.1 Introduction

The absolute worst place to be in game development is in a silo.

Yes, I know, it sounds grand to be locked away in your own space that you control while no one is interfering with your art as you create 30 new variants on "Flanking!"

In reality, it sucks. It makes you look weird and unapproachable. It cuts off needed communication that can provide you with the information that your writing needs. Ultimately, it makes your work worse, it makes other people's work worse, and it makes the game worse.

Rather, you need to learn to communicate with other disciplines across the team in beneficial, appropriate ways. You need to start a process of synergy and cross-pollination, where your stuff informs theirs and theirs informs yours. You need to keep the lines of discussion open to prevent suddenly getting surprised by a changed feature or a new level. You need, most of all, to be able to work in harmony, sharing and receiving information so that you are all rowing in the same direction. Otherwise, you will find gaps on the back end that can only be filled by herculean expenditures of effort and money, if at all.

9.2 Baby Steps

The first thing you need to do when talking with members of another discipline is to be open. Don't sit around waiting for them to talk to you. Reach out. Ask if you can set up syncs where you can show each other your work. Ask if there are tasks on their plate that could benefit from some verbiage. Tell them if you could maybe use even a rough piece of concept art to help you visualize what you are writing. Build a bridge of communication where you feel comfortable talking with them.

Something else that's useful is to learn to speak their professional language, at least a little bit. Or, to put it another way, you present in words. Artists present in images. Engineers are present in code. If you are trying to communicate your writing ideas to an artist by gifting them with a Borg Cube of text, you are going to be sadly disappointed because they are not going to read or absorb it. Your time, and theirs, will have been wasted, and the work will remain where it was before you started.

What that means for you is changing the way you tell your stories to other teams. This is not a betrayal of the sacred text. This is lateral thinking, a slicing of the Gordian Knot of misunderstanding. If you want to get your point across to an artist, spice up your document or your board with images and

DOI: 10.1201/9781003592983-9

video clips. Don't make them read when they're not wired to; present it in a way that they resonate with. If you're going to do a slide deck for, well, for anyone who isn't a writer, keep the text lean. Three bullet points per slide in a pitch, maximum, is a good rule of thumb. Give enough for someone to understand. Save the dense, deep dive for later once you've hooked them and they want to know more.

Beyond that, you should learn a bit about how artists and engineers operate. Get the definitions of the stuff they're talking about. Learn the terms and how those aspects implement your work. Be willing to listen when engineers talk about how they need the barks to work and what they can and can't give you in a cinematic.

Doing this offers multiple benefits. Understanding how other disciplines work helps you write more in line with what is doable, instead of throwing verbal pasta at the wall and seeing what sticks. Understanding terms and concepts means you can have more in-depth conversations about what works and what doesn't. This in turn leads to tighter and more ambitious collaboration because you can wade into deep waters together instead of messing around in the shallows. The cherry on top is that if you demonstrably take the time and effort to learn a little about how another discipline works, they're going to notice. They're going to appreciate the good-faith effort, and that's going to win you some goodwill. You can always use more of that.

One early game I worked on, I wrote a script that had two characters embrace. The Lead Engineer immediately flagged it as impossible because of issues with character collision. I said, "A hug?" "No." "A handshake?" "No." "What can I get?" His answer was "A curt nod."

We ultimately went in another direction, but it was an eye-opener.

This is not to say that you should run off into the weeds with, say, the animation group in slow motion while string arpeggios swell behind you. Yes, there should be free and easy communication – within bounds. Make sure that anything you discuss is within the limits set by production. Don't decide to do work that isn't scheduled or wanted – some of the worst blowups I've ever seen on a team came when a small cell of folks had a Brilliant Idea (™) and went nuts working on that instead of their tasks. Then, when they presented their foundling idea and it got shot down, they got resentful that no one appreciated they had put in all this work that no one had wanted them to do in the first place.

Keep your powder dry. Keep talking and sharing and keeping each other informed, but don't take it too far without a mandate from above.

9.3 Beyond the Words

One of the interesting places the idea of collaboration leads is to storytelling beyond dialog. There are plenty of games that do a wonderful job of expressing writing either without dialog or by using non-verbal means of expression alongside spoken ones.

As a writer, you should be actively involved in this sort of non-verbal writing as well as writing dialog and everything else. That means collaborating with other departments to achieve this aim. The first thing to do is to reach out (or be receptive if they reach out first) about putting effort into this sort of thing. Define how it might work. What are the benefits, and what are the costs? Who's taking point? Can you put together a fast prototype to show off your intent to the powers that be? You have to nail all that on your own before you move forward with intent.

There's a wide spectrum of this sort of thing you can be a part of. The most obvious is what's called environmental storytelling, where the elements of the game world – architecture, props, color palette, lighting, and more – tell the story of what happened there. This can be a full-blown tableau, or it could be a single graceful note that only the most carefully observant few will find.

Mind you, one of those observant few will then blast their discovery all over social media as soon as they can so shortly everyone can find it, but you know what? That's a feature, not a bug. You *want* people to see this.

Elements like this are created largely by art and related disciplines, but they're derived from the game's world and plot as written. They're expressions of writing through other forms, passed through others' creativity and given life beyond what you wrote. And as such, they tell the story of the game and the world in a way that players who maybe don't want to read lore blogs or listen to dialog can appreciate. They can add deeper understanding, illuminating little corners of the world that would be distractions if they were forced onto the Golden Path for everyone to forcibly experience. They are voluntary, to be explored or ignored at the player's whim. Ultimately, they can add a remarkable amount of content and feeling to your game, a manifestation of game writing that leaves the words behind.

9.4 Working with Audio

Another way to do storytelling beyond explicit verbiage is to collaborate with audio. There are a ton of ways you can get added impact by getting on board with the audio team and working with them to elevate or complement your writing.

This collaboration can work on various levels. The most basic is in adding effects and context to lines of dialog. A hint of distortion to a line can infuse the player with unspoken dread. A bit of static on a VO line coming over a radio can hint at trouble ahead. These aren't words, but they are ways of presenting words, and if you have a good rapport with audio and can demonstrate the value of what you are proposing, there's every chance they will listen.

There is also every chance that they have thought of this stuff already and are way ahead of you, but that's a good problem to have. Working with a smart, proactive audio team is one of the dreams that every game writer should have.

There's also world-based storytelling you can do in collaboration with audio. Sound is a powerful invoker of emotion. It's how we are wired, because once upon a time being able to act on the snap of a distant twig was the difference between survival and becoming a short-faced bear's lunch. Working with audio to tell the story of a place through sound as well as visuals and words is something you should look to do. Ask for those snapping twigs or groaning timbers or ghostly footsteps or distant howls. The rumble of distant artillery or the scream of jets overhead can express how the world is progressing far more elegantly than a lengthy infodump from a commanding officer. The slow creak of an opening door tells a different story than the slam of that same door against a wall as it is kicked in. Take advantage of this to give your writing another form of manifesting itself through the expression of others' skill.

9.5 Scrawl on the Wall

Sometimes, it doesn't even need to be big. Consider signage and graffiti.

Game maps can be big. They can have lots of buildings in them. Gates, too, and cave walls, and all sorts of flat surfaces for people to scribble things on. If they're left blank, you are missing an opportunity to tell the story of that space through the signs left by those who had been there before.

Those markings, whether they be formal signs of a business or cave paintings or words spray-painted in desperation, can all illuminate the story of the space. This is the perfect place to bang heads with art and level design in order to bring some specifics and hint at unwritten tales. Working with these two groups to determine what sort of signage is needed lays the groundwork for you to get creative. Sometimes you'll be asked to come up with a company name for a building to hang off a sign up front. Sometimes it will be a sign found inside a building – ironic safety instructions in a post-apocalyptic world, perhaps, or a listing of the former inhabitants of the stalls in a barn that can provoke a sense of loss. Sometimes it will be scrawled, improvised messaging, warnings, or final defiant cries.

The range is broad. What matters is getting on the same page in order to write appropriately for this manifestation of another discipline. If all they need is a sign to hang out in front of a deserted pharmacy, then be brief. If you're asked for something more substantive, then stretch your wings.

Attached to this sort of writing are what I call in-game artifacts, bits of diegetic writing or voice that the player encounters in the world. Audio logs are perhaps the most prominent expression of this sort of collaboration, but there are also in-game books, diary entries (video, audio, or written) available on a computer in the vast majority of science fiction horror games, flashback cinematics that suddenly manifest, and more.

These represent a tremendous opportunity, either to dive deeper into the main narrative of the game or to tell small, self-contained side stories that nevertheless provide depth and breadth to the world. These assets can absolutely be resource- and work-intensive, which means they have to be planned for well in advance. Even a simple text-only "book" may contain hidden nightmares of needed UI features, meaning it's best to ask about this sort of thing well in advance.

Once you get the green light, though, then you can go nuts (within reason). These sorts of deliverables let you tell small stories. If your game is an AAA monster with a world-shattering plot, it can be refreshing and important to take five minutes of a player's time in four separate audio chunks to show how things are going on the ground level and how people other than big damn heroes are being affected. People build surprising connections to that sort of thing, often spinning off entire narratives about these mayfly characters and turning them into genuine phenomena.

One of my favorite moments from my entire career came on *Tom Clancy's The Division*. The writing team on that project was scattered across two continents, three countries, and four time zones, so we came together for a week-long summit at Red Storm, which had the advantage of being both centrally located and close to my extensive collection of single malt scotches. We would spend all day in a conference room, writing together, reading each other's work, critiquing, and building working relationships and feedback loops that would let us continue to operate with high efficiency once we all went back home.

On the fourth day of the summit, a couple of folks who were working on the Dark Zone – the free-for-all, no plot or dialog allowed extraction shooter aspect of the game – came down to visit us.

What they wanted was simple. They wanted to tell stories in their world. They also knew they couldn't tell stories the way we could in single player, with dialog and cut scenes and triggered lines and audio logs. What they asked us for was a list of 20 stories they could instead tell visually that would explain how the Dark Zone got that way. They asked the writers to help them tell stories without words.

We loved it and leaped on it instantly. Everyone started brainstorming, then we shared our lists and built on each other's ideas, and the magic happened. By the end of maybe two hours, we had a list of 20 strong concepts for them to pick and choose from. The Dark Zone folks took the list and ran with it. Everyone loved how it came out. It was a perfect example of cross-discipline collaboration and inspiration.

And the only thing about it I still question is why, in that initial brainstorm, did everyone's list start with the words "Dead Santas?"

9.6 The Tricky Bits

What's the downside, then, of working with other departments?

To be honest, there isn't much of one, as long as they respect your work as much as you respect theirs. When it goes well, everyone's work is better. Your work helps inform other people's. Their work inspires and guides you. The free exchange of ideas opens up new possibilities and approaches. Everyone wins.

That's when it works, though. Never forget that collaboration has to come from both sides. Where problems for writers arise is in an imbalanced relationship, where other disciplines expect writing to support their decisions, but they treat agreed-upon writing as optional. This slides a little bit into the territory of Dansky's First Law of Game Writing, where writing is expected to paper over gaps other people create, but it can go beyond that. An art team that takes an agreed-on and approved write-up and delivers something that ignores key described aspects should not be allowed to simply shrug, say, "Oh well, too late to change it," and move on. If that happens once, it can be corrected. If it happens repeatedly, something's got to change.

The same holds for writers, of course. Any writer who expects to steer the ship is deluded. There are areas where writing helps drive the direction, absolutely, but treating other disciplines like they are there to manifest a writerly vision is a horrific blunder. The conversation from your side should always be open and respectful. If you have to say no, say why and offer alternatives. Just don't try to establish "my way or the highway" authority, because unless you are also the Creative Director, and possibly the studio head to boot, you're asking for it.

The other place where collaboration with other disciplines gets tricky is when they decide that they are within their rights to annex writing authority. It's cool that people from other disciplines want to get involved. It's great that they have ideas and feedback. However, they should never be encouraged to think they can slide into the driver's seat on this stuff. That sort of thing needs to be nipped in the bud. That's where you need to draw a line and get backup to enforce it. It may get painted that you don't want to collaborate or that you're being a bad teammate, but there is a world of difference between being open to collaboration and rolling over. To quote the great Mary DeMarle, who when faced with other leads on her project trying to tell her how to do her job, she said, "If you had half the faith in me to do my job that I do in you to do yours, we wouldn't be having this conversation."

Truer words, my friend, were never spoken.

10

What Is It Good for – Teaching Others the Value of Game Writing

10.1 Introduction

What is game writing good for?

That's a question that gets asked a lot. The good news is that there are multiple answers that cover the various angles and levels. The even better news is that one of those answers is couched in the language of the folks who don't understand storytelling and who particularly don't understand how storytelling ultimately pays into the bottom line.

Make no mistake, there will come a time when you have to defend the resources spent on game writing. Too many people in positions of authority in game dev honestly think that you can push the Writing Button and have it magically spew out giant gobs of money. That's not the way this works, and it never has been.

They can, however, invest in storytelling in a way that then leads to sustainable, ongoing, long-term sources of revenue. While this sounds like it's a long way from the nuts and bolts of game writing, trust me – being able to explain to the people who sign checks how your work is going to more than pay for itself down the line is in fact vital. You need to be able to make it clear that you understand that for all that you want to do good writing for good writing's sake, you understand that the bills have to get paid and that you can be a big part of paying them.

10.2 Attachment, Anticipation, Identification, and Investment

The first thing you have to get across is that this stuff works on an emotional level. It takes time and resources to come to fruition and skill to do it effectively. Its purpose, beyond the specific content, is to drive four things: Attachment, Anticipation, Identification, and Investment. If you create strong storytelling content, your chances are good to produce these desired results. If you don't, there's a good chance your content will be forgettable and thus eventually forgotten.

Let's walk through those four concepts, one at a time, to spell out how each is important, necessary, and beneficial.

First, we have Attachment. Good storytelling content gets people attached to your game. As human beings, we learn through stories, and we connect with characters. We crave meeting people who will have adventures we will never have but who let us step into their shoes for the duration of the experience.

DOI: 10.1201/9781003592983-10

For all that great gameplay is invaluable, for most franchises it is the characters that people get attached to and want to see and get more of. That's why many franchises endure and cross genre boundaries even as gameplay evolves and changes.

This extends beyond the character name to the very expression of the character itself. When, on *Splinter Cell: Blacklist,* we cast a new and very talented actor to take up the role of Sam Fisher, there was massive outcry from the fanbase that it wasn't Michael Ironside any longer. This was because of attachment. The match of Ironside's voice and performance with dialog crafted to work with his delivery created an iconic concept of Sam Fisher that was intrinsic to the franchise. That's what the fans expected because that's what the fans had built their attachment to. Losing that, no matter what the reason, broke that attachment. Negative sentiment and backlash were the result, despite the fact that we got a great performance.

Do this sort of thing right, and people will return the energy you put into it in a way that produces real benefits for the game. Strong attachment is what encourages people to turn around and share that attachment with others, building communities and spreading the word. Fans don't do cosplay for features, and they don't write fanfic for UI, as key as those elements are to a good and successful game. It's in large part the writing that people latch onto, adopt, and then transform into their own work for the world to see, incidentally giving the game free advertising in the process.

And yes, creating stuff that builds attachment is not a writing task – it involves collaboration with art and audio and the rest of the usual suspects. Writing is still what's at the heart of it, and building that attachment is key.

Next comes Anticipation. By providing interesting storytelling content and reinforcing it with regular follow-ups, you get the player to look forward to what's coming down the pipeline next. You build the habit of them wanting more and of them being excited about the next thing to come along. And if they're excited about the next thing you're doing, they're not bailing from your game to go play Fortnite instead.

This requires time and investment of resources to build. It does not manifest, fully formed, overnight. Instead, content like this needs to be teased, then provided, then followed up on via a regular schedule to build the habit of waiting for the next shot. The audience needs to know it's there, they need to know it's going to keep coming, and that it's OK for them to surrender themselves to it without fear that the rug is suddenly going to get pulled out from under them. That in turn means getting the powers that be to commit to producing the content, exposing the content to the fans, and continuing to publish the content in a way that players are going to overcome their reservations about possibly getting burned by another premature cancellation.

To take a page from the fiction market, all of us fantasy nerds – and I include myself among those ranks – have friends and loved ones who have categorically stated that they will never buy a fantasy series again until the last book comes out. This is because they've been waiting for that next George R. R. Martin book since approximately the end of the Bronze Age. That's the fear you have to overcome, and the only way to do it is to give the fans what they want, frequently and consistently and over an extended period of time so that they trust you to give them more. If you can get to that place and keep giving them good writing that they like and want more of, you've built a link to an audience that's going to stick around. And if they're going to stick around, there's a very good chance they're going to spend money, which is, after all, what the suits want.

Up third is Identification. Strong and unique characters drive Identification – the moment when a fan says "I am" about one of your characters and integrates it into their identity. That fan is then going to follow that character from that point forward. If you continue to keep the character interesting and consistent, they will most likely spend money on stuff that feeds that identification.

When I was at White Wolf Game Studios back in the day, we had a literal bulletin board of pictures fans had sent us of tattoos they'd gotten of the various *Vampire* clan symbols or *Werewolf* tribe symbols and suchlike. They identified. They said "I am" to specific pieces of that storytelling content. They made it, for lack of a better way of putting it, part of their identity, and if something is part of your identity, you're going to stick with it. Again, that's character, and at the core, that's writing. Good characters can extend a franchise far beyond a single iteration of a game, into downloadable content (DLC), sequels, transmedia, merch, and more. Bad ones can kill it. The much-anticipated *Concord*, dead in less than a month, stands as a monument to this truth.

Finally, there is Investment. Give players the good stuff, the stuff that makes them want to put time and effort in, and they will feel invested in the experience they create with your material. They will keep coming back because it matters to them. They will spread the word because they want to share what they like. If they feel invested in what they have played so far, they're that much less likely to abandon that investment and leave for another game.

And all of this, if you do it right and support it and give it time, leads to ongoing participation in those precious revenue streams. That's how writing more than pays for itself.

It seems pretty cut and dried, but there are, of course, catches.

10.3 The Catches

The first thing is understanding and communicating that there is not a direct correlation between writing and cash return. You cannot monetize dialog on a per-line basis. Yes, I know, there are tie-in novels that serve as a form of writing being directly transformed into money, but they're a small piece of the larger picture. I once had "collectible writing" seriously proposed to me as a model to drive sales for a tabletop roleplaying game, and I had to bite my tongue nearly to the point of drawing blood to keep from laughing. The short, straight line between writing deliverables and dollars simply does not exist.

What does exist, however, is a longer, less direct connection. No, the odds are not good that fans are going to help you straight up monetize the vast majority of your writing, be it character histories or lore blog posts or whatever. Where the magic happens is in creating the four elements listed earlier to produce invested, loyal fans who love your characters, your world, and your story, and who want more across all the parameters. Create your characters well and give them time to demonstrate their unique and appealing awesomeness, and you will make fans that will be with you for the long haul.

Once you have them, you can then sell them more content, either DLC or new games, sequels or prequels, or spin-offs. You can sell them new avatars and skins and weapons and mounts that match the character's fictional adventures. You can tempt them with t-shirts and jewelry and action figures and board games and belt buckles and Lord knows what else. Make them well and make them worth fans' while, and everyone goes home happy.

Furthermore, as a bonus, they're going to preach the word of the stuff they enjoy to others. They're going to do lore videos and gameplay breakdowns on social media. They're going to stream gameplay. They're going to argue on your behalf on Reddit, and they're going to give you strong user reviews on Amazon and Rotten Tomatoes and wherever else. The crafty-minded among them are even going to cosplay and be walking billboards for the characters they love enough and identify enough with to want to be.

All of that gets noticed. All of that drives discourse. All of that brings eyeballs, and then hopefully players, and then hopefully players' wallets to the game you're writing on.

That, then, is how game writing drives revenue. Not directly, no, but it is the guiding principle behind a whole lot of indirect spending that never happens without the storytelling that people latch on to. Nobody buys action figures of characters they don't care about, not even the completists. They're completists because they love the world as written and illustrated and experienced, and thus want to drain it down to the very dregs rather than miss something you put in it.

10.4 Quality and Support

All of that also depends on two things: Quality and support.

The quality issue is obvious. The writing has to be good. The characters have to be interesting and relatable. They have to do and say things that people like and cheer on and want more of. Half-ass it with yet another grizzled former space marine who grunts monosyllables and who will inevitably get betrayed by his mentor in the third act, and you're wasting everyone's time. Shamelessly copycat what worked for someone else, and the fans are absolutely going to notice, and if they notice, they are going to mock you. Mockery is the kiss of death for this sort of thing. Once your work becomes a meme, it's time for the Viking funeral.

Here's where the support has to come in. It starts with supporting the effort to create the writing. There needs to be time and care and feedback given in order to allow you to write something good. First draft and slam it out there is never good enough. You'll want responses and maybe audience testing for big concepts, and generally the time and tools to polish so that you're putting your best material in front of the paying customers.

That's the beginning. It's a long play, and if you try to rush it or expect too much too soon, you risk presenting something undercooked to a skeptical audience. That is a recipe for failure.

Now let's be clear. A character by and large needs to make a splash right out of the gate. Yes, we are all familiar with the narrative that starts with the humble villager/space colonist/anthropomorphic critter gazing off into the distance and yearning for something more exciting, but even then, there has to be a reason to care about them. There has to be something about them in particular that makes the player want to follow them out into the wider world and see what happens to them next. Sometimes, it's a line of dialog, an unforgettable quip that establishes character right off the bat and invites connection. Maybe it's a cool landspeeder. The specifics are yours to create.

Sometimes, it's the scenario that piques interest. Maybe the character crash-lands on an alien planet and now must struggle to survive. Maybe there's a shock interaction with the villain of the piece, which the character somehow survives and which promises a payoff down the road.

And sometimes, it's the hint of deeper secrets. A character who appears onstage with the whiff of mystery to be explored and who offers the tiniest hint of what else there is to discover can be irresistible. What's a Gandalf? We don't know when he first knocks on Bilbo Baggins' door, but we sure as hell want to find out, and that holds absolutely true for game characters as well. There are secrets to the worlds we create, with the characters often holding the keys, but the trap must be baited from the get-go to lure the curious in.

All of these, however, have one thing in common: They hit at the beginning. The hook needs to be set, gently in many cases, but still firmly. That's on you as a writer. You need to tell a story and build characters that are instantly interesting enough to make people willing to accept more. Slow burn is a wonderful literary technique, but game audiences tend not to appreciate it. That means that even if you have a long build planned, there still needs to be something announcing points of interest at the beginning.

Like I said, that's on you, the writer. You have to make it good, for a broad range of possible definitions of "it," and you have to make it compelling, and you have to make it accessible. The connection needs to happen immediately. Think of it as speed dating with a character or scenario. If it's not clear or doesn't click in a metaphorical 30 seconds, they're going to move on. Don't make the player have to work to find something to like or want to know more about. Make it easy for them. Seductive, even. You want them to enter into a relationship with your work freely and of their own will.

10.5 Settling in for the Long Haul

And then, if the connection happens, to make this work, you absolutely need a license and support to reinforce it. You cannot expect to throw a character out there once and expect never-ending fan loyalty immediately. Real attachment builds from repetition and reinforcement. It's not a one-night stand; it's a long-term relationship.

In practical terms, this means you need the resources and the platform to build a habit in your players. This is not something you can do alone. You can write all you want but unless people with the power to make and enforce decisions greenlight the means to get that writing in front of people in whatever medium works best at the moment, you're out of luck. It doesn't matter how good your start is or how many people quoted a key line on Reddit or how many (positive) GIFs got made out of that killer first impression you made. If there is no second impression, the impact fades and is forgotten.

That means you have to make the case for more. You have to get the decision makers to understand that it's not one and done. You don't need a cameo; you need a platform to bring your magic to the audience again and again and again in a way that trains them to anxiously await the next installment.

Which, in turn, means they have to commit to a few things. They have to commit to that platform. It might be in-game content or DLC featuring a specific character or plot point or bit of lore. It might be a series of blog posts. It might be short animated sequences. Team Fortress made absolute gold out of these for a game that had no intrinsic narrative element. It might be transmedia content, where character stories that don't fit in a game can be told for audiences who want to know more. Hell, they can be on funny t-shirts or memes or in ads. On a certain level, it absolutely does not matter *as long as they are out there*.

Why? Because presence matters. And while the preference is for that presence to be full and deep, sometimes a small reminder is enough. As long as that presence is steady and repeated, as long as you remind the players why they thought this character or this world or this battle or this monster was cool, it works. You want to make sure they are getting regular hits of content in a way that gives them a little more each time. That way, they feel like they're getting something of value instead of being asked to view or even pay for something that doesn't do anything to advance their knowledge or attachment.

This works better if it is planned and reinforced. You need to get a commitment that the character you want everyone to fall in love with will, in fact, be in a public-facing position on a regular basis. Ideally, you get a commitment for a series of things. The easiest and cheapest is something like blog posts.

10.6 The Pitch for Writing

Digression time: Writing is something that, frankly, Production and Marketing should both love. It is the easiest, cheapest, and fastest way to generate content to slam into various media going. For relative peanuts, you can have a writer or team of writers generate reams of material that can be iterated on, polished, adjusted to various departments' needs, and ready to go in a very small window. Compare that to the amount of time and money it takes to do a trailer or make a character model, and writing offers some definite benefits. Of course, those other approaches offer unique benefits that are well worth pursuing, but A) some of those benefits are derived from writing, and B) purely written content has its unique charms as well.

As such, it makes sense for those other departments to lean on and value writing as something that can support their efforts in a way that is cost-effective, fast, and flexible. They may or may not recognize this, meaning it is up to you to make and reinforce the point until they see value and start taking advantage of it. That, in turn, leads to more written content, which leads not only to reinforcing the stuff I was talking about earlier but also to a greater need for writers, which is never a bad thing.

In any case, an ongoing, consistent, formal series of blog posts, for example, is a great low-level way to start. If someone's feeling ambitious, you can even pitch something like an ongoing narrative through a series of audio diaries or trailers or short video sequences, among other things.

Something with, say, a frame story, be it a storyteller character or a conceit that this is someone's diary or sworn testimony, or maybe even a fiction of a fictionalized account that supports multiple chapters, gets the audience into a rhythm. They know what to expect and begin to anticipate it. They start speculating about what's going to be in the next one publicly, which sparks discussion, which sparks engagement.

And every dose they get – assuming it's good and aligned with what they want to get from that element – builds that emotional bond more and more. It sets them up to want the next one, and the next one, to stick around. Plus, while they're sticking around, the better the odds they're going to buy the stuff you mention in those content drops. They're also going to talk about this thing they like online. Maybe in a stream, maybe in a YouTube or TikTok video, maybe in a Reddit post – again, the details matter less than the fact that they are putting it out there on your behalf, which is good for you and your work and ultimately the game.

10.7 What It Means

Don't, incidentally, walk away from this thinking, "If I write a bunch of blog posts, everyone will love my character and we'll all make lots of money." That is most emphatically not what I am saying here. What I am saying is that if you create something good and formulate a well-supported plan to get it in front of people regularly as content they deem worthwhile, then you will build attachment to and investment in your game, and that will ultimately be turned into money from players who will want a steady stream of 19 different flavors of more.

What does that mean for you as a game writer? It means you have to be Proactive. This stuff is not going to happen without a lot of sweat and effort. Angels will not descend from on high, granting you carte blanche to write wildly and without restriction. You need to produce a concrete plan for this stuff, present it to potential allies, and, with their support, get the people in charge of the schedules to agree. Get it in writing, and even more importantly, get it assigned in your task-tracking software. That transforms it into something real and tangible and there to hold up when people maybe start to slide away from their part of the bargain.

Because if you don't, what will happen is sad, predictable, and unpleasant. If you do not aggressively move to establish places where writing needs to go – and you do this in large part by taking all the stuff I just said and cramming it into a slide deck with a few pictures with humorous captions to keep people involved – no one else is going to think to do this. They're not wired that way. They don't think about the value of this stuff because it's not immediately quantifiable. You must make the case in terms they understand so that they will give you what you need to ultimately produce what they want.

A fashionable counterargument is to reference a game like *Fortnite*, where the characters are largely borrowed and out of context, and gameplay is absolutely king.

You know what? That's cool. And kudos to the team for making something that people love and come back to and spend a ton of money on.

Hang on, though.

Let's think about those characters, those out-of-context characters, for a moment. Why do people buy those skins? Despite the skill of the modelers and texture artists and animators who make stuff that does indeed look awesome, there is a reason that they're specifically licensing Goku or Ezio di Auditore or Peter Griffin or whoever. It is because those are strong characters that have been repeatedly and consistently used elsewhere in a way that fans build identification with and attachment to them. There is absolutely a reason why they shelled out for Ezio instead of making Oddly Familiar Knockoff Dude In A Hoodie Named Ozio. There is a reason they went above 9,000 for Goku instead of Generic Spiky-Haired Anime Guy. It is precisely because they have been written, and written appealingly, and written extensively so that fans could learn to love them enough to want to be them in this game (and to make them dance, and on and on).

It's the same equation, at one step removed. Is it all of *Fortnite*? Of course not. I never said it was. But it's certainly a big enough part of it for it to be prominent, enough so that it can't be summarily dismissed.

10.8 Making the Case for Writing

You have to make the case for writing, not as artistically necessary, but as a cold-blooded, relentless, cheap, indirect profit-generating machine that happens to be also artistically fulfilling and interesting and challenging and cool.

And no, I am absolutely not saying to shove all concerns of craft and art aside in the sole pursuit of the almighty dollar. You can do that, sure, but fans sniff it out fast, and when they do, they generally note that it stinks.

What I am saying is that by making the very real, very cogent business case for writing, you are winning yourself the time, space, and resources you need to do all the cool stuff. To write the unique and fascinating characters with potential for growth and then to allow them to grow in front of the fans who love them. To build and show off the interesting world and get enough fans clamoring for more of what you do to get to show off more. To tell the interesting, extended stories with time to grow and develop and do unexpected things that get talked about instead of stampeding to the grand finale and the inevitable explosions contained therein.

Your work has value. You also must internalize, accept, and then spread the word that it has value to the bottom line as well. You need to champion it, call out the benefits, and dispel the myths in order to give yourself the best chance to succeed. If you sit back and let the myths endure, hoping that your work will speak for itself without advocacy, it won't get used to best effect. That, in turn, means that the Attachment and the Identification maybe don't happen, which can lead to less Investment on the part of players, which leads, with grim resolution, to less revenue.

And when you put it that way, talking about how writing can make money down the road makes a whole lot of sense.

10.9 The Long-Suffering Creative Side: Games as Art

That's the business case. Now let's take a moment to talk about the merit of the creative side of things, which I have skimped on a bit here because that, frankly, isn't what this book is largely about. That doesn't mean, however, that it isn't worth considering.

The question gets brought up whenever someone needs a lot of clicks: Is game writing art?

The answer, as far as I am concerned, is "That depends."

The whole "Are video games art?" debate has been raging for at least as long as I have been in the industry. Back in the day, I would attend GDC with a mental "time until Floyd" counter in my head, the death of Floyd the robot in the legendary game *Planetfall* being the first go-to example of games being able to generate more refined emotions and thus being art. I did not disagree; I just wanted people to call out more examples so as to prove the point by overwhelming evidence that I thought then and still think exists.

The arguments against games, and specifically game writing being seen as art seem to fall into a pair of basic categories. The first is that lots of games are about shooting lots and lots of things, which means they're not art. The second is that games aren't movies and thus don't provoke the same response movies do, which is apparently a dealbreaker.

Both of these are nonsense. Yes, there are a lot of games with a lot of shooting. There are also a lot of books with a lot of shooting and a lot of movies with a lot of shooting. The existence of Jason Statham's entire body of work does not negate, devalue, or preclude the existence of *Casablanca*, Cocteau's *Beauty and the Beast*, or *Moonlight*. A medium of expression can and should contain multitudes. Not everyone wants the same thing from any given piece of media, and the same consumer can want different things at different times. This is understood and accepted in other media, and to use this canard against video games is cheap and lazy thinking. Of course, battle royale shooters probably aren't "art," whatever that may be, but they are not the only games out there, and they are absolutely not archetypal or representative of absolutely every game everywhere.

10.10 The Ebert Debate

The other argument, that games don't make you feel the way movies do, was famously advanced by the late movie critic Roger Ebert, who was, of course, dead wrong. Of course games don't make you feel the way movies do. That's because they're not movies. Games are by definition interactive entertainment, and as such provide very different emotional responses than the passive media of movies or television.

Those emotional responses, however, are no less valid for having come from a place of interactivity. For years, the knock on games was that they could only provoke basic emotional responses along the fight-or-flight adrenaline axis. This is demonstrably not true. One has only to look around to see evocations of love, heartbreak, tragedy, despair, altruism, and everything else on the emotional spectrum. So-called higher emotions are in ample evidence, and some games are specifically designed to provoke those responses. Some games have even redefined the marketplace definitions to stand as icons, emotional touchstones that stand years later.

Are we not still referencing *Final Fantasy VII*? *Papers, Please*? *Life Is Strange*? Many, many others? Their endurance is evidence that this argument is weak sauce.

As a result, my feeling is that games, and game writing, can absolutely be art. Is every game art? No, but neither is every book or movie or poem or play. I'm not a fan of setting out explicitly to create art. I feel that sort of self-centered ambition often reduces your chances to create something genuinely great. At the same time, I also believe that, whether solo or in collaboration with other developers, a game writer can be part of something that rises up in a way that makes a genuine statement, challenging the player far beyond the immediate puzzle or combat to be resolved.

That, I would submit, is art.

10.11 Where Does the Writer Fit In?

Where does that leave the game writer, then? Writing is often a lightning rod for this particular debate. The best and worst lines of dialog, the most impactful scenes, and the most ridiculous – those are the things that get rolled out in an endless game of missing middle arguments for or against. Because writing has a connection to other "respectable" media that goes back decades or centuries in a way that other aspects of games perhaps do not, the writing is often in the forefront of the debate. That, in turn, can be felt as pressure to carry the banner for games' "worthiness" as art, often to an uncomfortable degree.

I have always maintained that as game writers, we are honorable practitioners of a craft. Our goal should always be to produce the best work possible, based on the parameters we are presented with. At the very least, what we do should get the job done. It should define a character or inform a player of something they just accomplished, or, perhaps inevitably, it should warn of that incoming grenade. It should do all of this with grace and style, with an appropriate voice in a way that supports the player experience.

In short, we should approach our work the same way a master woodworker approaches making, say, a chair: The goal is to combine the functional and the aesthetic, but first and foremost, make sure the chair isn't going to collapse the first time someone sits in it.

However, that's the floor. Let's talk about the ceiling.

10.12 When Magic Happens

Because sometimes, art happens. Sometimes when you do your best and the design comes together a certain way and the art is just right and the gameplay brings it all into a unified experience that transcends the bounds of the controller and the screen, you find you have made art. Sometimes this happens in small games, like the desperation and utter heartbreak of the aforementioned *Papers, Please.* Sometimes it's splashed across a big canvas in the AAA space, like *The Last of Us*. Sometimes it's individual encounters that rise above the rest of the game they are in, provoking awe and wonder and pity in a place you'd never expect to find it. It emerges in all sorts of places and all sorts of ways, and an awful lot of the time, you only realize what you've done in hindsight.

My advice to you, then, when it comes to art, is simply to do your best and let it happen as it may. It may happen your first time out. It may never happen. All you can do is do your best to create the things the game you are working on demands and let the player response to the finished product make the decision on whether or not it is art. Actively chasing "art" through forced complexity or elements that fight against gameplay and the overall experience in an attempt to be the game equivalent of Oscar bait. It doesn't get you any closer to creating something that will endure. Do your best work. The rest, ultimately, has to take care of itself.

10.13 And One Last Thing . . .

Good writing doesn't always get praised or called out. A lot of it doesn't even get noticed. Good barks, for example, fade into the background of the player experience seamlessly. They're audio wallpaper, there to be unremarkable and not get called out as ugly. Like a baseball umpire, some writing is only noticed if there's an obvious screw-up.

That is fine. Sometimes silence is the highest praise you could ask for when it comes to game writing. It is utterly delightful to have people get hooked by a line you wrote and start repeating it, but those moments when your stuff does exactly what it's supposed to do and no one is nitpicking or complaining or saying they could have done it better are wins, too. It is, of course, nicer to hear your work actively praised, but sometimes it's good to realize that everything is humming along the way it should without reason for anyone to complain.

Take that as a win. Because every single one, even the quiet ones, counts.

11

The Value of Internal PR and Techniques for Doing It

11.1 Introduction

It would be easy to look at the title of this book and decide that game writers are passive victims in all this nonsense, and that is all they will ever be. This is, to quote the legendary dev team t-shirts printed for *Rainbow Six: Vegas*, based on a false premise. The fact that the industry does indeed hate game writers does not in any way absolve you as a game writer from taking action to improve your lot, confront that hatred, and ultimately help to move the industry past this illogical reaction.

Let us be honest here – there is no one out there who is going to reliably advocate for us, or at least not with the intensity, knowledge, and stakes that we have ourselves. It's kind and good of other folks to sing writing's praises now and again, but it's not their responsibility (with the possible exception of a producer whose bailiwick includes writing) to do this on a regular and persistent basis. Thus, the task falls to us as writers to toot our own horns, elevate our virtues, and enlighten the rest of the team one developer at a time as to why it's a good thing to have writers around.

11.2 Internal PR: The Basics

This approach is referred to as "internal PR," and that's about the best name possible for it. You simply cannot sit there and expect team members from other disciplines to pick up on sheer damn awesome writerliness through osmosis. Your team members do not instinctively know how to value writing, and there's no one else out there who's going to tell them how to do it if you don't. You cannot expect them to automatically understand why your work is valuable because, odds are, they may never have been exposed to that perspective. That doesn't mean you should get mad at them for not knowing, at least not at first. It does mean, however, that you need to step up and do that educating, both for your benefit and for the benefit of the game that you are working on. The more your peers and leads understand the value writing brings to a game, the more they will feel good about supporting in ways across the board. In turn, the more they support it, the easier your job will be and the clearer the path to best outcomes will become.

PR, like ground warfare, is waged in campaigns. The best and most successful ones are well planned and executed, with clear goals set beforehand. Random and intermittent attempts, on the other hand, are likely to result in failure, or at least not in sustained success. If you want to get your teammates on

DOI: 10.1201/9781003592983-11

board with game writing, you need to plot out your actual goals and how you intend to achieve them. Once that is in place, you then need to initiate a persistent, organized campaign to reach those goals and to do so with consistency and clarity.

The why of an internal PR campaign, as noted earlier, is simple: To educate your fellow game developers who might otherwise not know better about your work – its value, its requirements, and its role. By extension, you are at the same time educating them about you – what you do on a daily basis, how it impacts the team, and what value comes out of it.

As noted previously, writing is too often seen as this mysterious, magical art whereby a writer (or a writing team) disappears into a dark room with an unlabeled bottle of something that's probably north of a hundred proof, only to slide a pile of pages underneath the door six hours later for others to use. If that's honestly what people think, or more accurately don't think, then they're not going to be able to make well-informed decisions when it comes to your work. And if they're not in a position to make well-informed decisions, odds are they're not going to default to the positive.

Therefore, it behooves you as a game writer to mount a polite but aggressive charm offensive to share the necessary knowledge. This does not mean one and done. It does not mean trying for a little while and then throwing up your hands because the results weren't miraculous immediately. It means understanding that there are attitudes and assumptions that have been hard-wired into this industry for 50 years that are going to take time to erode and turn around. If you're doing it right, you'll see a slow blossoming of understanding that eventually proves to be beneficial. Road to Damascus moments of conversion to the love of writing in all its forms are much rarer and should absolutely not be expected.

11.3 Setting Up the Campaign

Now, an internal PR campaign is exactly that: Internal. It is specifically directed at other members of your team to get them aligned with you and your work. It should also illuminate the nature and content of your work, making them feel in the loop, and they can then integrate what you're doing with their work. It also cuts down remarkably on the number of unpleasant surprises at the end of the development cycle.

In order for it to be successful, you need to make sure it fulfills certain requirements. It has to be clear and focused. It needs to be digestible. It needs to be available as a resource when you aren't in the room. And it needs to be presented as inviting, a space where others can play and collaborate.

The last thing you want to do is to drown, say, artists, with an infinitely granular breakdown of one aspect of your worldbuilding. That's because those artists will almost certainly not care, and they will zone out by line three of the giant avalanche of text you are presenting. It won't matter how well thought out or crafted your pitch is at that point or how much work you've put into it. If you haven't created something that will teach people where they learn best, you're wasting time. Visual learners don't like to read. If you make them read, and read a lot, you are setting yourself up for endless disappointment.

11.4 First Steps and Missteps

What do you do? You start by setting up lines of communication. They can't hear you if you're not talking with them, and by talking I mean real face-to-face (or at least Zoom-to-Zoom) encounters. Just sending out documents for people to read or the equivalent does not get the job done because, given a choice, people generally don't read stuff like that. It gets received when people are busy, which means it gets back-burnered, and back burner means "no burner" way too much of the time.

Furthermore, the odds are that a significant portion of your team members are going to be visual or auditory learners, not readers, which means you're not putting your best foot forward by compiling a massive document and setting it loose on them. Also, you cannot ever rely on team members reading stuff that you post to a central document site, be it a SharePoint or a wiki or whatever, because, to be blunt, they won't. Even if mandated to do so by the powers that be, the vast majority of team members will find a way not to do extensive reading of this sort of thing because it isn't a priority over concrete tasks in their wheelhouse and because it's not presented as being of interest or importance.

That's if it's made available at all. Too often, writing gets siloed off in every way possible. Scripts are never shown to other team members. Story documents stay locked down unless absolutely necessary, and sometimes not even then. Writing too often operates in mysterious isolation, with the rest of the team walled off from the juicy bits for no good reason whatsoever. When this happens, the rest of the team does their work without integrating what the writing is doing, and what you inevitably get is divergence, which will then be either repaired with time and cost or allowed to stand and weaken the game.

A lot of the time, this comes from above, from Director-level folks who don't want their departments distracted or who fear sharing the writing so that it's understood across the team. This, they fear, limits their ability to exert control over it and make sudden, unilateral changes. That they shouldn't be doing that except in the most dire emergencies in the first place never enters into the discussion.

Too often, though, it's the writers themselves who do the hoarding. On a certain level it's sort of understandable. When you put your work out there, you invite commentary on it, and since everyone thinks they're a writer, you run the risk of getting flooded with suggestions that, to be charitable, may not be useful. And if you don't implement those solutions, a small but statistically significant portion of the folks providing suggestions will get *very* upset, regardless of the quality and fit of the suggestions in question. Nobody wants or needs to deal with that. Viewing things strictly from that perspective, it is a little understandable why game writers don't always rush to share.

However, there's a dark side to this logic: The fear of making any changes at all. The simple truth is that nobody's writing is perfect. We do not deal in deathless, immortal prose. Interaction with other members of the team and their feedback grants new insight as to how it can best fit into the game as a whole. Adopting the mindset that your writing is an untouchable crystal chandelier that the slightest breeze will shatter irreparably is a bad look, counterproductive, and instrumental in reinforcing bad stereotypes about writers. You can't keep it to yourself forever, so why not get it out there in a way that does you some good?

11.5 Give a Damn about Your Bad Reputation

The reputation of writers as aloof and unwilling to collaborate makes problems in all sorts of ways. If people default to the demonstrably false notion that writers don't want to talk to anyone, they won't talk to writers. They won't seek out their opinions, they won't offer opportunities to collaborate, and they won't ask questions, because they already "know" they're not going to get answers. If writers are seen as standoffish, this reinforces the bad idea that writing is separate from gameplay, a coat of paint to be slapped on at the end and not something that's collectively worked into the player experience from the get-go.

If people think writers would rather not work with them, they won't want to work with you. And if they don't want to work with you, they won't support writing initiatives in high-level discussions about where resources and time get allocated. They won't be there for you in peer reviews and salary reviews and all the stuff that everyone hates but that impacts you directly. And, God forbid, they won't be there for you when it's time for cuts, either content or jobs.

That is why you need to break down the borders and get in their faces, at least as a first step. Set up a meeting with another group in the team, preferably a small, discrete one. For that meeting, put together a focused presentation on an aspect of the writing. It can be the overall story. It can be a particular character or two. It can be the story of a specific mission or quest. It can be a bit of item lore, though this is generally something to be saved for later on in the process. What it is matters less than the fact that it is self-contained, easily digestible, and interesting.

You absolutely do not want to walk into that meeting behind a wall of words. Walls are there to keep people out, and that's exactly what a wall of text, an imposing, unbroken stream of verbiage, does. Instead, tell a story. Tell all of the story, but make it one single story with a beginning, middle, and end that people can absorb and understand in a single sitting. Don't be too long; don't be too detailed. There may be grace notes of writing that you are thrilled about that you want to share, but save them for the Q&A afterwards, if at all. Now is not the time to drown people in details. Now is the time to talk about bold themes and big ideas and to get them excited.

For a first step, that's all you need to do. Get in, get out, answer a few questions, get them excited, and leave them wanting more. Don't overdo it, and don't overstay your welcome. It's as simple as that.

And when you're done with one group, move on to the next. Then the one after that, and the one after that, and the one after that. Yes, this takes time. Yes, it takes coordination with other groups on the team. Yes, you are almost certainly going to need help from your producer to coordinate with the producers of other groups to carve out the time necessary to do this.

11.6 Baby Steps Are Good Steps

All of that is all right. You're taking steps, not leaping to the finish line. The cumulative effect is positive. Making sure that people on the team know about what you're writing and why you're excited about it lets them get on board and get excited about it. If they're excited about it, a couple of other good things are going to happen. One, they're going to talk about it among themselves and with other people on the team, thus doing your work for you.

Two, they're going to want to find ways to integrate it into their work. That means the writing is that much more integrally woven into their game as a whole, opening up new avenues of collaboration. And three, they're going to have ideas they're going to want to share with you. Some will be good. Some will be bad. Some will be, frankly, bizarre. Still, the odds are good you'll find yourself using at least a couple, and it gets people excited when their ideas get picked up and run with.

There's another benefit to this as well. By reaching out and talking with your teammates, many of whom might not have ever met you or have reason to interact with you at all during day-to-day production, you suddenly manifest as an actual, honest-to-God person. You become more than letters in a chat message. You become approachable.

This, in turn, adds heft to what you are saying. When an idea comes from a document or an email, it's functionally anonymous and autonomous, detached from a human connection. That makes it easier to dismiss. By planting yourself in front of people as a living, breathing advocate for the writing, you suddenly put a face on your words. You give your stuff a source and a connection, and that makes it resonate more strongly with your internal audience.

11.7 Bring Them All In

Depending on the size of your team, you may even want to skip to addressing the entire team at once. On *Assassin's Creed: Nexus*, I coordinated with the Creative Director to carve out a space for story during our regularly scheduled team meetings. During each of these meetings, I would get ten minutes, which I dubbed (and called out in the meeting agenda as) Storytime. For Storytime, I would put on a silly hat – a cheap knockoff fez with a picture of Bigfoot on it I had won at a horror writers' convention years prior as a result of pranking a bestselling author with $60 worth of ice cream sandwiches – in order to make myself less threatening as a Director and more approachable as "a guy in a silly hat." Then I would take those ten minutes to tell the story of one of our missions. It did a lot of good getting people engaged with the story and making the writing seem less mysterious and more approachable.

Key to note here is that it wasn't a one-off. We did Storytime at every team meeting until we ran out of that sort of story to tell and were deep enough into production that the benefit had dropped off. It rapidly became something that people looked forward to and engaged with, to the point of making memes in anticipation. It very much did what it was supposed to do.

This is not the only thing to do to keep the positive pressure on. You want to provide constant reminders of cool story elements to the team. This is where more collaboration, with art and with production, comes in handy. See if you can get posters made of your characters and put them up where the team can see them. Post cool quotes from the dialog that folks like and maybe even repeat. If there's a map to your game, get that printed out and posted prominently. All of these tie into story and writing, and having them omnipresent keeps writing in people's minds.

11.8 Changing Up

As the development cycle progresses, you'll want to change tactics to keep things current and pertinent. As deliverables get approved, look to share them with team members, maybe key ones, maybe the team as a whole. Again, this does not mean dumping all the scripts on everyone, but rather judiciously going through and finding highlights that will get people psyched up. If your game is doing voiced dialog, see if you can share some of the cool bits when they come in. Keep it up and keep the excitement high. Always have something new to share to keep from getting forgotten or relegated to the back burner.

One particularly effective method of down-the-road engagement is with table reads. If you can and you feel comfortable that the scripts are in good enough shape to stand up to an audience, invite team members to a table read. Maybe they're there as audience, maybe they're even reading and taking part, but either way, that sense of being allowed behind the curtain really does build a connection. Once that connection is there, they're more likely to support you and your work within the team. And having those allies on board for when things get sticky can be invaluable.

11.9 Targets Outside Production

Bear in mind, you don't want to limit your attention to your fellow developers. Include the Marketing and Communications teams in your charm offensive as well. These are folks who can benefit from your expertise and who can use your work in theirs. By all means, keep them in the loop about where the story is going and the cool writing deliverables you're turning in. They should have their own schedules as to when things are going to be shared with the audience, but you can and should keep them updated as to spicy bits they can use.

In the larger picture, it is vital to keep Marketing engaged with writing. Time and again, I have seen Marketing deliverables go out that brutally misrepresented the story, character, and setting of a game. The one thing all of these had in common was that the writing team was not consulted for a fact check before the deliverable went out. But go out they did, and the results were predictable. Audience expectations were created that the game had never been set up to meet, and the mismatch caused all sorts of problems. Naturally, the writing got blamed.

These are things you want to avoid, and you avoid them by being proactive in promoting your work to the people in question. Eliminate the excuse of "We never saw that" by keeping them updated in your best bright-eyed, bushy-tailed fashion. Don't present it as preventing disaster (even if it is); present it as getting ahead of the curve and giving them the best and freshest material to work with. And actively put it in their hands, because you cannot know for sure they will seek it out. Doing this will get you a reputation as a good team player and an asset and may even lead to more interesting writing tasks. That, in my opinion, is a whole lot of wins.

Some of this may come across as a little cynical, but I would disagree. The simple fact is that by letting your coworkers know who you are and what you do, and maybe even a little of why you are doing it, you protect and enable yourself. You get more respect for and interest in your work, you make allies for confrontations that inevitably arise, and you make yourself a better and more accessible member of the team. It is not cynical to say that you need to do this for your own benefit. It is not cynical to say that no one else is going to do it for you. It is not even cynical to suggest that if you don't do it, there are negative impacts that you will feel in a variety of ways. And nobody wants that. Or at least, nobody you want to work with.

12

Idea Generation and Narrative Integrity

12.1 Introduction

You can never assume that anyone knows anything about what you do or why you do it. To do otherwise is to invite endless surprise and frustration when somebody asks a question (or worse, makes a decision) based on ignoring something that is as basic as oxygen to your understanding.

Now I understand that talking about writing to a writer is like talking about water to a mantis shrimp. It's a constant and unquestioned part of the environment, as is everything that goes along with it. Just because it's instinctive to you, the writer, who has hundreds if not thousands if not tens of thousands of hours spent soaking in this stuff, does not mean it is instinctive or even apparent to someone else. This means you have to frame your proposals carefully when you present them, and you have to frame your critiques even more carefully when you have to give them.

This holds even more true when someone outside of the writing team comes up with a proposal they expect you to accept and implement unquestioningly. If it's a fellow laborer in the digital trenches, then it might not be too bad to say no, though it always makes sense to offer a gentle "why" as opposed to a flat-out rejection. Even the phrasing of the disagreement can be important. I had a designer working under me at one point whose reaction to every proposal he disagreed with was "No," then a pause, followed by a thoughtful, rational explanation of why the idea couldn't work in the proposed context. Unfortunately for him, everyone shut off after hearing the brusque "No," and he got a reputation as a dictator. It wasn't until after he had left the company that people realized what he had been trying to say, but by then it was far too late.

Things get more interesting, and you have to be more delicate, if you have to shoot down an idea coming from an elevated position. These are people you literally cannot say "No" to. You need to walk them to a place where they understand and accept, at least grudgingly, your professional diagnosis. Often, you will have to dig deep to figure out why they thought the idea was a good one or to explain why it isn't.

A good chunk of the time, the idea in question is something that came out of the wild blue, and as such, doesn't fit with any of the long-established writing that is already in the game or is planned. The idea may not necessarily be bad in a vacuum, but the writing isn't happening in a vacuum. It is happening as part of a detailed, intricate development process where one deliverable is dependent on the contents of the last, and trying to bolt the equivalent of an outboard motor onto a bathtub won't help either the boating or the bathing experience.

DOI: 10.1201/9781003592983-12

Case in point: One game I was working on, the Creative Director heard a song that they thought would be a great addition to the game, especially if a particular character quoted lyrics from it. Leaving aside the niceties of licensing songs and song lyrics and the basilosaurus-sized hole doing this can punch in your budget, it was still a very bad idea, and I recoiled against it instantly. Why? Because the song was 40 years old in a particular musical subgenre that the character in question, who was supposed to be in their mid-twenties and forward-focused, would have been utterly unfamiliar with. It would have come across as someone on the development team sock puppeting the character in order to reference one of their favorites, not an organic and appropriate thing for the character to say. Those lyrics were words that would never come out of that character's mouth, not in the way that they had already been established, signed off on, and written for.

Even then, I had to phrase my disagreement in a way that would educate, preventing negative emotion up front and repeat performances on the back end. With this in mind, I tried to explain why those particular words were a bad fit for that character. That they would never say such a thing. That those lines didn't sound like anything else we had them saying in the game before, during, or after. That it didn't match their character voice.

At which point, I discovered that the Creative Director did not, in fact, know what character voice was.

This allowed me to take the discussion to a positive place where I could explain what character voice was, how we could use it to our advantage, and how it was a useful editing tool for cutting lines that didn't match it. It was still touch and go for a while after that, but the explanation at least bought me the space to write alternate lines for the scene that were more in line with the character's voice. Those were what we ended up using in the end.

But that example illustrates the larger point that even the most well-meaning of outside suggestions often come from a place of lack of knowledge. It's exactly the same as if someone comes into a restaurant kitchen and starts getting nutty with the spices based on their personal preference, without knowledge of what the chef's intended flavor profile is or how any given dish fits into the progression of the entire meal.

Be prepared to educate if you can, starting from the beginning.

12.2 Basics: The Plot

The first task a game writer has on a project is frequently coming up with the plot.

This starts with the flow of the action of the game, with occasional side trips to major character definitions and arcs, and possibly worldbuilding as well.

To build this stuff effectively, in a way that benefits the game and gets buy-in from the powers that be on the team, you need to understand what the rest of the team wants, needs, and is mandated to do. What are the key features of the game that need to be shown off? What settings is the art team keen to build? What's our narrative genre, and what tropes do we need to observe or avoid as a result? Are we using characters that already exist, or is the slate blank? These are the bedrock the plot gets built on, the key elements without which your work will get dismissed out of hand.

My approach is to absorb all of this and then do a series of short pitches. These pitches are generally a single paragraph, a high-level overview of the action, and I will bundle roughly five for the first pass. You do not want to overwhelm people with too much reading or too many choices. You want to give them a range of distinct options instead. This is why, when I send along that list of pitches, I also send along the explicit statement that these are ideas, that I am not married to any of them, and that what I want is information on what people liked and didn't like. I can then take that feedback and produce a second, more tightly focused, round of pitches. It is vital at this point in the process to present yourself as flexible and open to ideas.

Sometimes, this yields a clear winner off the bat. Sometimes, people like bits of one and bits of another, and the task is then to find a way to fit them all together into a new, coherent whole. And sometimes, nothing's going to resonate, so it's back to the blank page in order to come up with something different instead. I've worked on games where I nailed it with the first pitch I made. I've worked on games where I produced two dozen pitches and had them all get turned down. Your mileage does indeed vary, but regardless, it's all feedback you can use to make the next one better and keep moving forward.

The next step is to iterate. Then, you iterate some more, and some more, and some more, and maybe some more on top of that.

Also, bear in mind that even if something is agreed on, approved, and locked, that doesn't mean it can't and won't change. The realities of production have a way of intruding on even the most tightly sealed chambers. Maybe there's been a sudden mandate from the studio or the publisher to make certain changes. You're not going to be in a position to say no. Maybe something wildly unexpected happens, like a celebrity signing on to be a part of the game with all the strings that come attached. And maybe, and most often, there will be cuts.

12.3 Cuts

There are times – lots and lots of times – when a game is scoped too ambitiously, and things have to get cut midstream as a result. Entire game modes, features, characters, maps, and missions can go away in an instant because there simply isn't the time and money to make them happen. One game I was on literally had its main campaign cut in half over several rounds of cuts, but in the end, the team still needed to produce something complete in a way that the players would never know anything was missing.

When it does happen, writing is often the weapon of first resort in dealing with the damage that has been caused. Sometimes this works, sometimes it doesn't, and if you want to do it well, you need to dig deep. Figure out what has been cut: What character beats, what information drops, what encounters that were supposed to pay off later, and make a list. Next, figure out which bits you need to transplant elsewhere and which ones you can let go. If a character is getting cut, lay out what purpose that character was supposed to serve in the narrative and then figure out where you can reassign the important aspects and lines. Save what you can, bid farewell to the non-essential, and remember, the player should never know this happened in the first place.

Frankly, they won't care. Either you're giving them a good experience or you aren't, and if you aren't, then "it was better before the cuts" isn't going to fly. They didn't get the game before the cuts. They got what was released. Furthermore, they paid their hard-earned money for it, and they don't care about why it is the way it is. They know what they've experienced, and they're not shy about letting you hear about it.

This is a reality of the business. With that awareness, it's best to take steps to pre-empt that where you can.

One of the nasty secrets of the role is that everyone past a certain experience level knows that cuts are going to happen. Maybe not this week, maybe not this particular project, but there are always cuts. The only thing you can do is prepare.

My preparation is doing what I call "ablative writing." Basically, anything I produce, I build in potential fallbacks and write content in chunks that can be cut discretely, leaving as few jagged edges as possible. If stuff's inevitably going to go, I want it to go as cleanly and neatly as possible, and I want the hole left behind to be one I have already planned on how to fix. I always know where the easiest cuts might be, which gaps will be easiest to bridge, where the key bits of information or items are going to go after their original home does a full Numenor, and who's going to pick up the slack if a character goes bye-bye. Planning ahead of the curve lets me be prepared to offer quick, efficient responses to what is generally a traumatic event.

12.4 How to Win Fights, or at Least Not Lose Them

Knowing how to do that implies knowing the whole plot and keeping it in your head at all times. This is vital information. It lets you answer questions about what's going on, why things are needed, etc. It also gives you evidence to push back against ideas that may seem great in isolation but that will cause more problems cascading down the line. "We can't have the main character say the thing, because doing *that* would mean re-designing a questline and possibly rebuilding a quarter of the map" is a powerful argument. This is because it uses production realities, not artistic sensibilities, to support writing best practices. As such, it's the sort of argument you need to be able to make, and make convincingly.

You cannot expect to win debates based on what is best for the writing alone. You might win some of those discussions, you might lose some, but in the end they all boil down to matters of opinion. There is no absolute arbiter, which means that your only weapon is the combination of your experience and your skill. That, as noted elsewhere, is not always enough.

If, however, you buttress your assessment of a proposed idea or change with the hard facts about how it will impact production, then you've acquired the ability to counterpunch. If you can respond to the next round of out-of-nowhere "You know it would be cool?" with "That will cost us this many person-hours to implement, costing us this much money and delaying these other deliverables, which puts the next milestone at risk," you're getting your point across in a way that reads as thinking of the project. You are not, on the other hand, coming across as being precious and trying to protect your work at all costs, not if you can hang real numbers on the cost of the suggestion.

Be aware there are times when there is, in fact, nothing you can do, that a higher-up has their mind set on something that you disagree with, and your job is going to be to make it work. This is when knowing that a battle has been lost comes in handy. If it is clear that the boss wants a certain thing, come hell, high water, or losing two points off the Metacritic score.

Continuing to fight at this point is counterproductive, for you and for the game. If the thing that is being suggested is honestly something you can't live with, then you have to reconsider your employment. If, however, it's an aesthetic or artistic decision, fighting against it is trying to hold back an avalanche. All this can do is hurt you, as you waste valuable time, energy, and capital on a fight you cannot win, and you do it in a way that brings you into direct conflict with the person or people who make decisions about your work and employment.

This is rarely a good idea.

Instead, take a deep breath, look at what is being foisted on you, and then make it yours if you can. Take a deep look into what is being asked and try to discover something, anything there that you can latch onto and use as a launching pad for your own letter-of-the-law implementation. Who knows, even the craziest idea could be what a former coworker named Kathleen Ryan once called "the grit in the creative oyster." Even the most nonsensical idea can spark good responses, and then you can encyst the bad spark in shining nacre.

Go with the flow until you can direct the current, giving everyone what they need – including you.

12.5 Worldbuilding from the Ground Up

Something to bear in mind is that every game needs a world to ground the plot. This can be a version of the real world with greater or lesser fidelity, or it can be something utterly fantastical. I got my start in games working on a setting that was the real world, but with vampires, werewolves, and other unsavory supernatural types running around, and then I spent the next two decades-plus working largely on hyper-realistic technothrillers that required deep dives into geopolitical minutiae. I have also, on the other hand, helped craft fantasy and horror settings, and pretty much everything in between.

Worldbuilding provides the foundation for everything you write. It's where the characters come from, what they do and what they want, and more. It's their history, their culture, their clothing and their gear, and the source of their motivation. Every game character has to come from somewhere, and as a worldbuilder, you're establishing where.

On the surface, worldbuilding seems like a glorious, easy task. It's anything but. Yes, there is magic in the act of creation and pride and joy in being able to say, "That was my idea!" when someone grooves on something in public. The truth is, it's a lot of hard, detailed work. Consistency may be misquoted as the hobgoblin of small minds, but it's absolutely a thing in worldbuilding. You're going to be ideating, concepting, fleshing out, and naming literally everything in the world, and any mistake you make in the process is going to put you under a microscope.

I'm not going to get into the nitty-gritty of worldbuilding here. Honestly, I could probably write a book on that topic alone. Instead, I want to offer some basic guidelines that have produced success in the past.

Let's start with a warning: Worldbuilding is dangerously addictive.

If you get on a roll while crafting your world, you can find yourself diving down holes no self-respecting rabbit would lay claim to. Yes, you want the world you build to be as detailed and interesting as possible, but for many folks engaged in the task, forms of obsession can emerge that render your efforts suboptimal and, at times, wasteful and useless.

The most important descriptor for any aspect of a world that you create for a game is "useful." Is the specific thing you are creating going to be useful to someone – the current team, Marketing, the player, someone writing transmedia content, or even someone two sequels and a half dozen DLC drops down the road? This is a trickier question than it might seem at first blush. The temptation is there to always say that something is useful, because if you don't know X, you can't understand Y, and if you can't understand Y, then Z will be totally incomprehensible . . . except it won't be. As fun and as exciting as it can be to flesh out your world to the nth degree of lore only you know right off the bat, by doing it you are making multiple mistakes.

For one thing, you're wasting time. If you keep building crenellations and epicycles and deferents and who knows what else onto basic world structure that other team members need, you are chewing up their valuable time. Far better to put the basics in people's hands and have them ask questions about what needs to be clarified and thus give more detail as they work with the stuff they already need and have.

For another, if you get too detailed too quickly, you're hogging the creative space. The more tiny details you write down, the less room there is for others to bring their creativity and vision to bear on the project. You run the risk of reducing everyone else involved to a pair of hands, making them feel creatively unfulfilled and demotivating them as a result. And I don't care if you were the Narrative Director on God's own blueprint for Heaven, you will always benefit from having voices that aren't yours involved in the creative process.

And for a third, you risk making your work unreadable and thus unusable. The more detail you lay out, the less your work is lore and the more it's a textbook, a dry, dusty textbook. Handing people who are visual learners a world write-up slightly shorter than your average Brandon Sanderson novel ensures one thing: It's not going to get read. At least, not in any useful, measurable way by the most important people – the team.

Beyond that, the most important thing is to make the world feel lived in, that the player is coming into a space that is already vibrant and established. This helps set the stakes by showing what could be lost, and it grounds the writing in a way that lends it weight. If your world feels like you just took it out of the plastic, you need to rethink. A too-shiny, too-clean, too-perfect world is too slick for players to attach to. Something with some character, that feels like it's already been broken in, is much more accessible.

12.6 New World versus Existing IP

Not every game you work on will be starting from narrative scratch. Franchises and licensed intellectual properties are everywhere, from free-to-play phone games to AAA titans. That means if you're going to write for games, you need to learn to write for IPs and potentially the people and companies who own those IPs.

Writing for an IP is not as simple as simply slapping a Batman skin on your existing idea. If you're going to be working in an established world, you need to know that world. You need to know the lore – characters, world, history, monsters, you name it – and that means doing research. No, you don't instantly have to become the world's greatest expert on whatever IP you're attached to. You do, however, have to know at least enough to be able to understand what the hell the rest of the team is talking about and to avoid obvious howling blunders.

Like I said, that means research. You don't have to read every single issue of every Spider-Man comic book ever if you're going to be working on a Spider-Man game, but at the very least read some, watch some lore videos, play previous iterations of the franchise if there are any, and get yourself up to speed. Also, this is an ongoing process. The knowledge you need at the start of your adventure is significantly less than the knowledge you will need for more granular work later on.

Hand in hand with knowing the IP is respecting the IP. You don't have to like the IP. If we only had to work on games we liked, the landscape of games would be very different. Even if you don't particularly enjoy the game you're helping make, you have to understand that there are people that love it and people who are willing to pay you to make it. Therefore, figure out for yourself what there is in the IP that commands your respect and appreciation. It could be a particular character or setting, or an aspect of the lore, or the basic fact that millions and millions of people love the game in question. The details are less important than the fact that you treat the material professionally when it is in your hands. Half-assing it because you're not a fan is not going to slip by unnoticed, nor is contempt for the material you're working on.

This extends particularly to the misbegotten notion that some writers coddle that they are going to "fix" a favorite franchise if they get to work on it. This is the fastest way known to humanity to get yourself fired off a project, short of throwing an uppercut at a senior producer. You are not there to "fix" the IP. Many, many people have worked to make that IP successful enough to have a game that you're writing on made out of it. The people who own the IP presumably like it the way it is. The idea of coming along and trying to overwrite everything according to your particular tastes is both arrogant and disrespectful. Unless you are given a specific mandate for a hard or soft reboot, you are there to extend and build on what has gone before.

If an IP is significant, there is almost certainly going to be some sort of formal continuity guideline as to what you can and cannot do with the characters and world. Often this takes the form of an individual whose job is literally to be the lore-keeper. And just as often, these people work in tandem with the IP owner's legal department. The lines they lay down, you cannot and should not even try to cross. Their job is to protect the IP and keep it viable. Even if you disagree with their approach, it's theirs to approach as they will. Get the guidelines before you start writing. Follow them. Ask before you wander into gray areas. Don't break rules for the sake of breaking rules. And understand that you are playing with their toys, and they can take them away at any time.

Working with an external IP often means approvals are written into the contract. Sometimes these are quick and easy, and the IP holder loves what you have done. Sometimes they take forever and can gum up the works mightily. There's not much you as a writer can do to push the IP owner to go faster, but you can and should build time for this into your writing schedule with your producer.

The actual writing of something in an existing IP can be described as a long series of asking two questions: "What did they miss?" (meaning what gaps are left in the existing continuity that you might squeeze your work into) and "What happens next?" (which is extrapolating existing lore forward, creating new content, and potentially extending the continuity as you go). The latter can be particularly tricky if you are working on a licensed IP that got its start in movies or television. There is a non-zero chance that there are sequels or spinoffs or next seasons in the works, which means some stuff is going to be off-limits to you. This is because the owners of the IP do not want to deal with a fannish firestorm of "In the game you said X, but in the movie you said Y!" or have you preempted stuff they were planning to film? To avoid that, they will simply set certain characters, storylines, locations, and other bits and bobs off limits to you, and you will have to deal.

There's no point in fretting over what you can't use, so commit fully to exploring what you can instead. Who knows, you may make a contribution to the lore canon spectacular enough that your work will get picked up and run with in a way that thrills millions beyond the confines of your game.

12.7 What's in a Name?

Then there's the theoretically easy, fun stuff. Naming things in a game is a task that gets yo-yoed in front of game writers a lot. It makes sense to get the people who are good with words involved. However, there are other considerations in coming up with the name of a game or a DLC. Marketing is certainly going to want to get involved. Outside consulting firms may be, well, consulted. And everyone from studio heads and Creative Directors down through the most junior team member is going to have an idea.

If you're lucky, the loop gets closed, and so does the meeting room door (or the Teams channel – you get the idea). Next, a core group of stakeholders sits down to hammer out the name. The best way to approach a meeting like that is with an open mind and a prepared list of suggestions. Come in ready to drive the conversation if the option presents itself, and do it with a variety of options. Once the conversation starts and you can read the room, you will have a good sense of which ideas to propose and which ones to quietly bury.

At the same time, be willing to listen to what other people come up with and work with those ideas. This is a perfect place for the improv comedy technique "Yes, and . . ." where you take the last suggestion and build on it directly. It makes people feel heard and appreciated, and if you riff off something that someone else in the room likes, you've upped your chances of buy-in.

There are usually one or two bad ideas that you have to nip in the bud before they acquire momentum. It is industry legend how placeholder names for products like the Xbox, the Wii, and *Assassin's Creed*: *Nexus* were working placeholders that people got used to. If something comes down the pike that might be a problem if it catches on, there is no shame in moving quickly to redirect the conversation elsewhere.

Naming can also get more granular. Names for characters, items, powers, skill tree elements, and world locations can be part of the writing workload. These frequently come with a fast turnaround time, especially if you are producing live content. As a result, you will want to hammer out ironclad approval processes ahead of time and then make sure you have backup on them when the rubber hits the road.

It's generally a bad idea to get cute with this sort of thing, even if the urge is strong. In-jokes can be fun, and so can references to friends, favorite bands, etc., but when they take priority over the integrity of the game world, you have a problem. It's OK to indulge every once in a while, but on one condition: It does not distract from the game. A reference that makes people who get it nod their heads and feel smart without breaking the narrative flow can be a positive, the sort of Easter egg that people go nuts for. It's just that a constant barrage of Rush lyrics or character names ripped bleeding from your favorite anime crosses a line. Use references sparingly and don't call attention to them. Let them be a natural part of the game writing, not a flag awkwardly planted on top of it.

13

Feedback – Giving It, Taking It, Training Others to Do It Right

13.1 Introduction

It's time to talk about feedback: Giving it, taking it, acting on it, and training other people to do it in a way that is helpful. This is a complicated and delicate subject, and it needs to be approached from multiple angles. Bear with me. I'll get to it all in time.

A writer cannot function at optimum levels without good feedback. I don't care how talented you are, how well you know the subject matter, or how much you're getting paid; your work is always made better by informed, actionable feedback. Having other eyes on your work can reveal something you missed. You may have known exactly what you meant when you typed it, but the reader – who becomes the player down the road – didn't. You're not psychic, and you're not going to be bundled up with every download to explain to every player what you meant, so you have to listen when the gaps get pointed out.

In truth, any game writer who fights the concept of feedback is being foolish and unprofessional. Nobody in this industry is writing deathless prose in words of gossamer and crystal that emerge unsullied from the depths of their genius. We are working writers adapting to constantly changing situations in ways that are equal parts functional and creative. While we may, with luck and inspiration and encouragement and collaboration, create genuinely great work, we are not going to Robin Hood the bullseye with unrevised first drafts. We're certainly not going to do it every time.

Instead, a game writer should welcome informed and actionable feedback to address concerns and improve their work in multiple iterations. Good feedback makes work better. It's that simple. The trick is not all feedback is good or appropriate or actionable.

13.2 The Method of Feedback

Feedback can arrive in different ways.

It can come in a meeting or a video call, delivered directly and vocally. It can be written directly into a manuscript as comments, rewrites, or parentheticals. It can be dropped into a chat channel if inspiration strikes quickly and a full conversation is not warranted. It can be sent as its own document, bullet-pointed and organized. Or it can be put into visual form on a Miro or whiteboard.

All of these are valid forms, but they all convey information differently. You have to be able to adapt to these different types of feedback and be able to use them all, drawing on their strengths and being ready to counter their weaknesses.

DOI: 10.1201/9781003592983-13

Direct feedback can be the hardest to work with. Many times it is an immediate reaction to something said in a meeting or a line reading or a quick skim, and as such it is perhaps less grounded than it might be with more reflection. This is both good and bad. The good is that you know immediately if something landed. If it provokes this kind of response, it probably didn't. Also, this sort of feedback readily lends itself to real-time iteration and collaboration, where everyone in the meeting can build on the initial note. You have to be careful it doesn't spin into a positive feedback loop between a subset of the attendees who keep egging each other on.

Verbal feedback can also be uninformed, and it can be difficult to wrangle the conversation back to a place where the gaps can be filled in. Furthermore, unless the meeting is being transcribed or recorded, or someone is taking notes, there is no record of that feedback. That can make it hard later when there are different recollections of what was agreed on at the time. I recall one particular project where the entire team leadership would be gathered expensively for an hour on end to hash through every single beat of a given mission until we were all in agreement, and then ten minutes after we walked out of the conference room there would be an email saying something that completely contradicted what had just been agreed on.

Written feedback generally has more thought behind it and can go into greater depth. It's also best for suggesting alternate phrasings and for spelling out why a particular criticism or concern has been levied. Also, those notes are there in black and white and can be referenced or debated at leisure, or at least with some time to calm down before you respond if you see one that gets your hackles up.

This goes double for distinct feedback, incidentally. If someone has taken the time to write, organize, and format their notes, it seems likely they have given it some thought. The difficult part there can be extracting the actionable bits from the larger statements and making sure that what you're getting is directive, not prescriptive.

Then there's visual feedback, which is often how folks like artists best communicate. Such input can be shocking and difficult to handle for someone who is used to dealing exclusively in words, but if it helps them get their points across most effectively, you have to learn to deal with it. The advantage here is that a medium like this tends to be mutable. With that in mind, you can do things like move story beats around on a board, virtual or otherwise, in response to feedback. You can get your hands dirty moment to moment in a way that other forms don't allow.

These days, every team uses most, if not all, of these approaches. Being able to be receptive to any and all of them is a professional necessity, but doing this lets you extract maximum value from what the rest of the team is telling you.

13.3 The Three Types of Feedback

There are three main types of feedback for video game writers. I break them down into Peer feedback, Approval feedback, and Collaborator feedback. I'm going to tackle each of them in turn, but we'll start with the easiest, Collaborator feedback.

Collaborator feedback comes from other members of the team, and it is vital. Writers basically have carte blanche on a blank screen when working in a vacuum. We can write an alien death fleet coming out of the sky or a guy reaching into his pocket to pull out a money clip and riff off a few bills or anything in between, but there is a vast gulf between what we can imagine and what the game is capable of. As a result, other departments should get the opportunity to weigh in on our ideas to make sure they can be achieved within time, within budget, and within technological constraints.

What that means in practical terms is that they know how their stuff works, and they should be in a position to tell you in a way that lets you write appropriate content. They can tell you how many characters can appear in a single scene, so you're not wasting time polishing stuff that's too overcrowded to live. One of the most useful bits of non-writer feedback I ever got was from an audio designer, who advised me that the tech we were using only allowed for three voices to be active in a given mission at any given time. That led to a hasty rewrite of a game's worth of cutscenes, but if I hadn't gone outside the writing group for feedback, I never would have known about this limitation until it was far too late. I can provide similar examples from Art, from Animation, from Engineering, and from every other discipline out there.

You get the idea. Writing needs to show what they've come up with to their collaborative disciplines to make sure they are creating things that can be realized, and those disciplines need to provide firm feedback that serves as the walls of the sandbox writing is working in. Those other disciplines need to communicate clearly what they can and cannot achieve with reasonable investment. Having those conversations early can save a lot of heartache and late nights.

Now, let's talk about Peer feedback in a game writing context.

When I use this term, I mean feedback from other team members whose focus, role, and experience are primarily in the narrative or writing realm. These are the people who are the true and closest professional peers of any given writer. They are the ones who have faced the same challenges, speak the same professional language, and understand the craft of creating words for games as a specialty. They are the ones best equipped in many ways to give granular on-the-ground feedback *to* a writer because they understand how the writer does their job.

This is not to say that feedback from folks who are fellow developers below the approval level but who aren't narrative professionals should not be sought out. Good feedback comes from anywhere and should be actively encouraged from other disciplines. But just as I think we'd all agree that engineers are best equipped to critique code on a certain level and artists are best equipped to critique art, so too are writer types best equipped to critique writing. It's a question of technical knowledge of the craft.

Ideally, writing feedback from peers should focus on two areas. The obvious but more time-consuming one is the technical aspect of the writing. It's more than grammar, spelling, and appropriate punctuation, though the first time a semicolon appears in a bit of game dialog should be the last. Technical feedback from another writer should include proper word usage, making sure unique characters have unique speech patterns, and other topics related to the act of placing words in a row to mean a specific thing.

It is very easy when writing to look at the screen and see what you want to be there instead of what actually is. That's how a ton of mistakes slip through, and that's exactly why technical peer feedback is important. Someone who is reading your work without attachment or anticipation of what they know is coming next is someone who is better equipped to see it for what it is.

Yes, game writing can be slangy and abrupt and ungrammatical when it gets to the dialog that gets shouted out during endless rounds of deathmatch and battle royale, but even there, the basics need to be used. Good technical feedback understands the idiom you are working in and takes that into account. It helps you say what you want to say more clearly and more effectively, and it makes you look better when your writing goes in front of other eyes.

It's basic, and it can be a little boring, but the alternative is dire. Having writing go out with basic errors in spelling, grammar, usage, and so forth is inviting tidal waves of derision. Plus, a basic level of professional competence at wordslinging should be expected.

This, incidentally, is where I take a moment to digress and make a plea for editors in the writing process. An editor can be a hard sell to a studio, as their function is something that can be viewed as redundant to the writers' function. After all, having someone whose job is to make sure the writers wrote right feels to an outsider like an indictment of the writing. Any professional writer who has worked with an editor will tell you, however, that the level of attention, skill, and detail from a dedicated editor can elevate work above the merely acceptable. And that's before you turn the editor loose on, say, Marketing copy or the content of social media posts.

Then there's commentary on the quality, which is like trying to wrestle a golem made out of yogurt. There are no absolutes in writing feedback. Yes, stuff feels bad or good, but quantifying why, what works or doesn't, is much harder. It's often best to pick out details and see if they create a pattern that reveals an underlying issue than trying to diagnose it all from 10K feet. And this sort of feedback should always be couched in specifics whenever possible. "I don't feel this particular element pays off" is more useful than "this doesn't work for me."

13.4 Approval Feedback

Approval feedback descends from Olympus above like a thunderbolt, and it determines whether a piece of writing proceeds into development and gets released into the wild. Regardless of who's giving it, however, there are certain guidelines that can ensure that the feedback can be as useful and efficient as possible.

It is a common misconception that this form of feedback is simply a binary choice: Yes (Approved) or No (Not Approved). A simple No, while decisive, is useless for fixing whatever problems the approver has with the document. It leaves the writer playing a guessing game as to what they might have done wrong, what needs to be emphasized or de-emphasized or thrown out altogether, without providing any positive direction for making things better.

Therefore, the choice should be redefined as Yes (Approved), No (Because of X), where X is a list of the issues the approver has with the doc, or No And Start Over Because What I'm Actually Looking For Is This Other Thing. Ideally the third one almost never happens. One would hope that before the writer got to work on the doc, they were involved in a clear discussion as to what purpose the doc would serve and what points needed to be hit in it. If that's not communicated before the writer starts – or if the writer ignores the direction they're given for reasons of their own – then the odds of having to do a complete rewrite go up precipitously.

What is most likely to happen, at least on a first pass, is a No Because of X. The latter three words are key. It is not enough to tell the writer they did something unsatisfactory. They need to know what and why so they can fix it. The feedback needs to be clear and actionable. "This is what is needed that is lacking" is actionable feedback. "I just don't like it" generally is not.

To be fair, the approver may not know why they don't like something. Many people are good at instinctively realizing something is wrong, but few are good at pinpointing exactly what that is right off the bat. The responsibility then is to dig down and try to get at the reasoning for the reaction, because there is always a reason, and sharing that reason is what will make the next iteration better.

Digression time: I used to work with a Creative Director whose response to writing he didn't like was to suck air in through his teeth and say, "I'm just not feeling it." This, in and of itself, was not particularly helpful. Eventually I learned that in order to get actionable feedback from him, I had to pin him down in discussion and start asking questions. What didn't he feel? Why not? What elements did work, allowing us to remove them from the discussion? And often it wasn't the first thing that he called out that was the real reason he was unhappy, or the second, or even the third. Eventually we got to the kernel of actionable information, but it was through the process of questioning that we found the answers, and that's a process you may have to embrace to achieve useful feedback.

13.5 Actionable Feedback

By useful, I of course mean actionable. Actionable feedback is something the writer can pick up and use to make a revision that will hopefully show improvement. It gives them direction and narrows down the need, and it is thus result-oriented.

The best feedback for a writer points them toward a fix without leading them by the nose to it. It allows them to generate their own solution instead of parroting back what they hear. It inspires creative approaches and new solutions that combine the approver's needs and the writer's abilities. It encourages progress and action, not paralyzed waiting. And it lets them pick up and use the feedback to a positive end instead of passively receiving it.

Giving it can be hard. The natural urge to provide a specific solution is strong and natural. After all, it checks a box on "problem solve." However, that's not likely to be the best result. It makes more sense in the long run for someone to rein in that initial reaction and instead try to give the writer something they can use to solve the problem in their own way.

Asking questions about what might be missing is a strong move in this direction. Asking for clarity if writing isn't getting its point across is another. Questioning intent (without accusing) can go a long way – "Why did you make this choice?" yields better results than "What is this crap?" "Have you considered?" is another good prompt if it comes with an idea and not a specific phrasing.

It takes practice, but the benefits to all concerned are immense. It yields better writing and better results. It builds a good working relationship where the writer feels trusted and empowered. And it provides a concrete bit of evidence as to what the approver is looking for that the writer can take into account when composing the next deliverable.

13.6 Feedback Tips – A Digression

Needless to say, all of this can take a while, and some of the feedback produced can be highly subjective. With that in mind, there are guidelines that can make the process of giving feedback easier and more likely to yield good results.

If you are in a position to be giving feedback to a peer, always make it about the writing, never about the writer. Focus on the words and whether they do the intended job in the best fashion possible, rather than on the skill or motives of the person who arranged them in the first place.

Never say, "I would have written it like this." That is not feedback. That is rewriting. It offers nothing to the original writer and instead shoves them out of the process. Only offer specific rewrite proposals if asked for and under time pressure, and even then frame them with "Have you thought about something like this?" This allows the original writer to both learn and save face and to build on the suggestion and come up with something even better.

Don't dictate; collaborate. You're not coming from a position of authority; you are critiquing a peer. Phrase your feedback in a way that lets the original writer accept it and interpret it according to their needs.

Because, if you're working with other writers, they're there for a reason. They have something unique and special they are bringing to the table, and that needs to be allowed to express itself. Trying to pour their deliverables into your particular verbal Jell O mold defeats the purpose of having them on the team. Sure, it can sometimes fall to someone in a leadership role to enforce tonal and other consistency, but that's making sure everything fits in the same sandbox, not forcing everyone to work on your particular sandcastle.

That's still peers talking to peers. Sometimes the feedback comes from somewhere else. This is Approval feedback, and it can be devastating if done wrong.

13.7 Taking Feedback – A Hidden Skill

So much for giving feedback. What about taking it? If you're experienced, it's one thing. The more feedback you've gotten, the better you probably are at extracting actual information from it. No feedback is 100% accurate, but it can still be 100% useful. Like I suggested, a significant percentage of the time, the literal phrasing of the feedback does not pinpoint the real problem. Sometimes you have to dig and find the actual concern underneath. Sometimes you dig and there's nothing there at all. And sometimes the concerns are spot on, and your path is clear.

Never accept every bit of feedback unquestioningly, and never reject every bit of feedback automatically. Each response needs to be examined on its own merits. Is it directly actionable or prescriptive? Does it make sense as is, or is it pointing to a symptom as opposed to the deeper issue? If a change is requested, what is the impact of that change? Yes, Dansky's First Law of Game Writing is always in play, but depending on where you are in production, the fix isn't necessarily comprised entirely of words.

If the feedback is good, your work is easy. Implement what makes sense, patch up the rough edges, and you're done. And if a note inspired you to build on it, that's even better. Draw attention to it in the next round of feedback (if there is one). And always thank people who put in the genuine effort to give good feedback, even if not all of it is useful. They may not have provided something you can pick up this time, but the appreciation builds bridges, and then maybe they'll be in a position the next time to hit a home run.

When the feedback is unclear, the most important thing to do is to ask good questions with no agenda to obtain clarity. Ask openly and sincerely, "Can you explain what you meant by this?" and follow up with more specific questions. If you have counterpoints, feel free to make them here, but do it respectfully. "I see what you're saying, but that doesn't take into account X, which we've already built," is a good response. "We just can't do that" isn't. "That would be dumb" is right out, even if you think it in your heart of hearts. You may have to go back and forth a couple of times to get at the real source of the commenter's disquiet, but that's OK. Just keep asking in a way that encourages the other person to open up, rather than dig in and get defensive. That encourages them to unload with the heavy artillery instead.

Remember, you should also always know when to surrender. A debate on feedback that goes on too long, becomes too contentious, and costs too much time (and money) as a result is a lose-lose proposition. It doesn't matter if the facts are on your side in cases like this. You can quote studies, emails, dictionary definitions, whatever, and still not move the needle. Recognize when that is happening and don't waste more energy or capital. You'll need both for later.

Even if you "win" in a discussion like this, the way you won is going to color future engagements. Beyond that, the chances of you "winning" are low because you simply don't have the authority to make the decision. I have seen a freshly minted writer, after an extended series of exchanges, tell their Director that said Director had failed to convince them of a point. The Director's response was simple: I don't have to convince you of anything. You have to convince me.

The new writer made the requested change.

13.8 How to Handle Bad Feedback

Unfortunately, sometimes you get feedback that is, to be blunt, bad. Whether it's someone pushing their own agenda in an unhealthy way or just a counterproductive idea. You have to learn to identify these and defuse them. Ignoring them doesn't work because people get upset if they're ignored in silence. Implementing them without pushback or question doesn't work either, for obvious reasons. You need to develop your radar for bad feedback, often by asking yourself, "What does this ask me to do?" Furthermore, you need to learn how to counter with gently explaining why it is bad and what you are doing instead. Bring receipts, back up your position (especially if following the bad feedback is going to cost extra time and money), and take into account how important the actual issue is.

A graceful retreat should always be an option, particularly if it's a relatively unimportant point and the other party is dead set. Conversely, leaving them room to retreat and save face is also a good idea, as making people in positions of authority look bad is seldom a wise career move. Entrenching on every single bit of feedback and refusing to accept anything sent your way gets you a reputation as hard to work with, and that's difficult to live down. By all means make stands that matter, but make damn sure they do indeed matter, that giving in is going to break things elsewhere and cost time and money and God knows what else. When you do make that stand, be sure you have plenty of ammo to back up your position, and bring facts rather than personal taste to the table.

All of that, though, comes with experience, and if you don't learn how to take feedback and use it early on, you may not make it to ripe professional old age.

13.9 For the Beginner

It's not easy, though. In fact, one of the hardest things for an inexperienced game writer to do is to learn how to take and use feedback.

There are a lot of reasons for this, the most common of which is a failure to separate the writing from the writer. Like I said, if you are getting professional-grade feedback – and if you're not, that's a whole other problem – it should focus on the words, not the person making them. It is about the writing, period. It is not about you, and it should never be about you, your worth as a writer, or your value as a member of the team.

You should learn to make and maintain that separation. If someone says that you need more differentiation between your character voices, they are saying exactly that. Make the active effort to have your characters sound different from one another. Don't dig in your heels. Just take the feedback with good grace and implement it in your own way. That will make the game better, which is the point of the exercise.

At moments like that, no one is saying, "You're a bad writer and you suck because your first draft wasn't made out of rainbows and ice cream." If you find yourself taking it that way reflexively, you need to stop, take a deep breath, and ask yourself why. Then, you need to figure out, with help as necessary, how to stop doing that. If you take it personally when it is not intended as such, you are going to poison your own well. People are not going to want to work with you if you don't listen or you get defensive or, worse, aggressive. They are not going to want your work if every edit becomes trench warfare on the Western Front and getting it requires more time and energy than it is worth. Where that leads is, unfortunately, inevitable.

Actively avoid that. Even if your first reaction is to counterpunch, hold back. Listen. Ask questions about what is being said. Maybe explain your intent and ask how that failed to come across. Bear in mind, though, that the voices of those who have already made the mistakes you might be making for the first time have value that you can take and use.

Every senior worth their salt knows that personal attacks are the worst way possible to improve someone's writing and the least effective way to punch up a deliverable. Using that approach is actively counterproductive. Firing on your own troops is no way to win a battle.

13.10 Building Trust

What has to evolve in this space is trust. You need to trust that the feedback you are getting is intended to help your writing improve. When you reach that headspace, then you can look at the feedback objectively and apply it where it belongs, which is to say, to the words. At the same time, your lead needs to be able to trust you to take feedback in the spirit that it has been given, that you are not going to view it as an attack on you or your creative vision to be resisted at all cost. If you do feel that way, entrench and vow to die on the hill of an inconsequential detail; you are not doing yourself or the game any favors. Sooner or later that situation is going to get resolved with the hammer coming down.

Nobody wants that. Juniors don't want to get it because, well, it's not pleasant and can have repercussions down the line. Seniors don't want to do that because the good ones prefer to let team members bring their own voices to things. Allowing juniors to learn and grow and improve through doing makes the writing team better, and what lead doesn't want that? On the other hand, being forced to do a prescriptive mandate means that the process isn't working. And if you're on the receiving end of that hammer, you're probably not going to like it much, either.

Again, this doesn't mean you have to take every bit of feedback literally. It's better if you don't. You need to be able to take the feedback, run it through the filters of what you're trying to do, and come up with a solution that's organic, not imposed. That's what everyone wants. If I, as a senior, have to tell you exactly what to write, I'm not saving any time by having you write it. Learn to pick up the ball and run with it, to look at the feedback and ask further questions as necessary, and to answer the questions it raises on your own terms.

13.11 Training Your Critiquers

Because good feedback is the start, not the end. It is there to make the writing better, to drive the next step in the writing process instead of shutting it all down. And it's not a one-time thing, either. You can extrapolate basics from one bit of critique, but odds are there's going to be a lot of writing in your game, and it's all going to need close attention from someone who isn't you.

You want, ultimately, to teach people how to give you consistently actionable feedback. Better feedback received more consistently will enable you to turn around better revised drafts faster. Cleaner feedback delivered more clearly will save you – and the person who gave the feedback – the time that otherwise would have been spent on back and forth on what the feedback was getting at. It's a win-win.

This means teaching people how to give useful feedback. This is *not* a case of telling them what you want to hear. It *is* a case of telling them *how* you want to hear things, and there is a very real and sizable difference between the two.

To do this, there's a do and a don't. Do give positive reinforcement for stuff that you can use right out of the box. Let people know that feedback you can use is appreciated. Bring them the revisions that feedback inspired and let them know what fueled it. Don't, if feedback isn't useful, let it sit there. Ask the questions that will lead to it becoming actionable. Show patience and appreciation for what's there, and build the path to better instead of dropping down a wall. With repetition and reinforcement, they can give you more of what you need, and you can get to a better place. That, in turn, will produce better writing. But it can't happen without good, actionable feedback on every level.

13.12 Weaponized Feedback

The worst-case scenario is when the feedback you get is not feedback at all. In some cases, what you receive has little or nothing to do with the work and everything to do with promoting the agenda of the person giving the feedback. You will get nothing you can use, only negativity that sometimes crosses the line into abusive language and *ad hominem* attacks.

I wish this weren't the case. The thing is, I've heard too many stories and seen too many things.

What's going on here is simple. Your work is not the point. There is something else at play that you are in the way of. Maybe you were hired by someone whom the person giving feedback doesn't like, and hitting you with nastiness is a way of striking at them. It could be the person giving the feedback wants to give your job to someone else and, as such, is greasing the skids for your departure by claiming your work is bad. There could be personal bad blood or differing political viewpoints. Or maybe the person giving the feedback is a bona fide asshole, more interested in asserting their own authority than in getting good work.

Protecting yourself from this is always difficult and, to be honest, sometimes impossible. If someone high enough on the food chain wants you gone, then sooner or later they will probably get their way.

What you can do is limited but important. Always keep receipts, whether they be chat transcripts, recorded meeting videos, or emails. Create an archive of this stuff where either A) they said stuff they later slammed you for doing or B) they were unprofessional, and keep that archive someplace safe. When it starts, let any allies you have in the building know. A friendly Director or producer can stand up for you and challenge the bullshit from a place of greater safety. At the very least, this can buy you time to find something else.

And always, document everything. You never know. If they're malicious and vengeful, they might reach out to their contacts in the industry to try to poison the well for you. It is best to have ammunition to return fire if that happens. Taking the "high road" and sitting quietly by while your professional reputation gets trashed is not an option. No one else is going to stand up for you if you don't stand up for yourself.

13.13 Positive Feedback

That's a negative. With that in mind, let's end this chapter on a high note and talk about positive feedback.

One big misconception is that negative feedback is the only form of feedback. This is absolutely not the case. When giving feedback, you should always make a point of calling out the good stuff, the stuff that stands out and that you want more of. Even if the deliverable as a whole isn't great, you should be able to find *something* in it to praise and encourage. It could be a single turn of phrase, or it could be a specific character or bit of narrative logic. Whatever it is, even if it's a lone jewel in the mud, rescue it and treasure it and call it out for what it is.

This has multiple benefits. It confirms what you want, giving the writer you are giving feedback to a guideline for future deliverables. Say what you like, and they'll know to give you more of it in the future. That's a win.

Doing this also makes you seem more approachable. If the messages you send are consistently and exclusively negative, other writers are not going to feel comfortable talking to you. They will go into any conversations expecting the worst, and they will probably end up dreading or even avoiding talking to you about this stuff because they know it's just going to be a steady rain of unmitigated unpleasantness.

There is a third reason, however, and it's the best reason. Giving positive feedback encourages the writer you're working with. It makes them feel good about their work. It helps them feel valued and a part of the team. It energizes them to do more good work and to not be fearful or tentative. By calling out the good bits on a regular and consistent basis, you are helping to develop that writer into a better professional.

The best part is the writing. It's the easiest thing in the world to pluck the good quotes and run with them.

14

Loops and Boundaries

14.1 Introduction

One of the most important things you need to do as a game writer is to build your feedback and approval loops and then make them airtight. Finding the right people who are in the right positions to tell you what will make your work better is invaluable. Figuring out who can and should approve your work so you can set down the pen and let it move forward to other aspects of the team is vital. Do that, and you have established the boundaries and processes of your workflow in a way that is going to make everyone happier.

Conversely, if you don't lay down hard, tight boundaries, then you will inevitably spend as much time fighting for the right to do your work as you do doing it. Not creating a tight loop for feedback means that everyone and their uncle will feel free to comment and then raise hell if you don't act on their comments. This gets worse the more people are involved. The math is simple. The broader the range of commenters you get, the greater the probability of your getting contradictory feedback, which makes it impossible to make everyone 100% happy. It is important to note when that happens that, if you are spending your time pushing back against people trying to tell you exactly how to do your job, then you are not actually doing your job.

14.2 Approvals

Similarly, if you don't get a formal, airtight approval system in place – the finished work goes to these two people, and that is it, and then it gets handed off if they approve – then you will get sucked into an endless cha-cha of one step forward, two steps back. If a whole committee of folks needs to approve every bit of writing, the odds of getting them all to agree in a timely fashion are roughly zero. If people outside the established workflow have the authority to step in and reverse approval decisions, they almost certainly will, and this has all sorts of negative consequences.

For one thing, it screws up the deliverables of the people downstream from you, who thought they had usable material to work with. It undercuts established processes, rendering them less authoritative and encouraging more people to feel comfortable interfering in them. It messes with your workflow, because instead of moving on to the next task, you have to return to an old one. That steals time from your next task in a way that makes it less likely to be polished and more likely to get reversed as well. Beyond that, it has a negative impact on your work and standing in the team, having what was deemed good and shippable suddenly and publicly be described as neither.

DOI: 10.1201/9781003592983-14

This is not to say that every bit of writing needs to be rubber-stamped and sent on its merry way without a second thought. Good approvers can and will send writing that is inadequate back for rework instead of sending subpar stuff on to serve as other teams' raw material. If they're good, they'll also provide their reasons for doing this, giving you the tools you need to make revisions quickly and efficiently and causing as little drag on the process as possible. See the previous chapter's discussion of actionable feedback for more on that.

And if things are super awesome, then time for this sort of iteration has already been baked into the schedule. That means there's no actual hit on productivity because your reworking of material even at this late stage in the writing process was anticipated and planned for.

14.3 Identifying Sources of Feedback – Good and Bad

Every game writer should actively be looking to build, reinforce, and protect good and appropriate sources of feedback. Let's take a moment to think about what that means and about the whole concept of feedback.

It is an absolute baseline of professional writing in any field, including video games, that you need other eyes on your stuff to get it ready for a wider audience. No matter how good and smart and perceptive you are, there are things you absolutely will not see in a piece of writing because it came from inside your head. Because of that, you have the benefit of knowing exactly how it's supposed to read, what it's supposed to be conveying, and all that other good stuff. You have, in a very real sense, jumped to the ending because you know how the story goes.

The thing is, though, that the rest of the world does not share that particular cheat code. Things that are crystal clear to you may be obscure to others. Points you think you made may not land cleanly. And things you try to say subtly or indirectly may slip past audiences entirely.

This is where finding people to give you *good* feedback comes in. You absolutely need people who can read your work in the context of what it's supposed to be accomplishing and tell you where it has succeeded or failed. You need to know where the leaks in the dam are so you can plug them. You need to know where the possible misinterpretations might be so you can head them off. You need, bluntly, to be told where you can do better.

And this is absolutely fine. Nobody gets it right on their own. You can't. You do not contain the multitudes that your audience does. Thus, getting the responses from people who are not you, who are not reading it with all your accumulated knowledge and experience and, yes, baggage, is doing you an invaluable service. The absolute best thing you can do is humbly and appreciatively take the feedback and use it to make your stuff better.

That is not to say that you have to take every bit of feedback as a direct mandate from Heaven, to be acted on unquestioningly. As a writing mentor of mine once told me, lots of people are very good at telling you that there is a problem, but most people are terrible at telling you exactly what the problem is, and when they tell you what they think it is, they're most likely going to be wrong. The proper approach to getting feedback is to look at it critically and see what it's trying to address. If it's a word choice, hey, that's a simple thing and not too deep, and you can change it or not or bring in a different word that you think is better if you like. If it's something deeper, though, it behooves you to sit down and try to figure out what the real issue is.

If you get feedback from multiple sources and they all pinpoint the same area, that gives you something definite to go on. If it's one reader who calls something out, then you need to figure out whether it's a real issue or just a personal preference that you can safely sidestep.

14.4 Prescriptive Feedback

Feedback that tells you exactly what to do, depending on when it arrives, can be useful, or it can be a straitjacket. If you're absolutely up against a deadline and multiple rounds of feedback haven't gotten you over the finish line, that's when you can expect prescriptive feedback in a positive way. The thing needs to be done, the thing needs to be done in this way, and the thing needs to be done now. Take that knowledge and use it next time.

Getting "Do this specific thing" right off the bat, on the other hand, is prescriptive and generally is an expression of what the reader would have written if it had been their deliverable instead. This is often less than helpful. Most likely, they are not as familiar or engaged with the material as the original writer.

As such, that direction (because it is not a suggestion) has a high chance of being made without context. It comes down to not taking into account all of the details it might contradict and ways in which this deliverable may be attached to other pieces of writing elsewhere in the game. Other problems – or at least lengthy explanations and knock-on tasks – will almost certainly result.

This, incidentally, leads to one of the biggest issues with other departments' approach to game writing. By and large, critique of a writing deliverable is done outside of context, in isolation. And game writing doesn't work like that. You need to be aware of the game's entire narrative and where any given piece fits into the larger whole. You need to understand its specific function – foreshadowing, exposition, setting up a later development, paying off a previous hook – and write it accordingly. As such, in order to work harmoniously to support the game's larger experience, not every piece of writing needs to blow the doors off. Not every character dialog needs to be fraught with tension and conflict. All any given deliverable needs to do is fulfill its specific function as part of the greater whole and help produce a better player experience in the process.

But when a deliverable is viewed and reviewed in isolation by folks who do not have a mandate to hold the entire story in their head, things get funky. Because there may not be an immediate payoff from a specific bit of writing, there may be demands to punch it up, to add conflict, to make it self-contained. This gets repeated over and over again, and the end result can be a narrative that has a flat, maxed-out volume, where every moment is the most important and loudest moment, and none of the pieces fit together. It is absolutely understandable to want each piece to be the best it can be, but what it can be has to be dictated by the larger needs of not just the scene, but of the game as a whole.

As a writer, you have to preemptively push back against this approach in order to preserve the quality of your work. You have to establish context before submitting a piece for feedback. You cannot let the conversation be established on faulty assumptions that will create cascades of problems down the line. The folks giving feedback need to be briefed on what exactly the deliverable is for, how it fits into the larger whole, and why it is necessary in its current form. Maybe there will be pushback on one or all of these points, but what matters is that you have laid out the basic framework of the discussion instead of letting someone else do it. That in turn means you have done what will help you address your needs instead of letting the conversation go sprinting off into the weeds.

14.5 Saying No (or Not Like That)

You can, in fact, say no to feedback, more or less. Like I said, not every bit of feedback is accurate, useful, or helpful. Some are most definitely harmful. You need to break yourself of the habit of confusing feedback with mandate. Sure, sometimes word will come down the pike from a lead or a Director that a certain thing must be changed, and when it's phrased like that, then you do what you're told or you start polishing up the old resume. Even in those cases, there's often wiggle room that allows you to do the best job of addressing the issue you can, instead of transcribing the words provided to you from above.

I have been on the giving and receiving end of notes like this. There have absolutely been times when one of my reports delivered stuff that simply did not get the job done. On a first pass with time to revise, that's one thing. When we're up against a deadline and the deliverable needs to be done immediately, that's another. In the former case, I'm happy to give actionable feedback in the form of suggestions and prompts for inspiration, hoping the writer can come up with something good – and not necessarily what was in my head because their voice is and should be different from mine. However, if time is tight and I know exactly what I need, I have no trouble framing it and demanding its delivery.

You should always try to do this in a way that doesn't alienate or demoralize the writer you are speaking to in the process. That often means cushioning mandates in reinforcement of why you're asking the writer to do something instead of doing the rewrite yourself. In my case, it's because if I'm working with a writer, it's for a reason, and that reason is their unique voice. I don't insert myself actively into rewrites unless I have no other choice and the clock is ticking. It's just that sometimes, the clock does indeed tick, and I'm the fastest solution.

On the receiving end, I understand that if it has come to this, then the time for debate is past. My job – and yours – is then to address the mandate as best as possible in a way that ends the discussion and allows the deliverable to move forward. Sometimes that means doing exactly what is asked for.

Sometimes there's a little wiggle room to get creative while still addressing the point. Regardless, there has to be a focus on the specific issue, on resolving it, and on doing it in a way that doesn't open up other discussions and issues that will stop things dead in their tracks. Is this always the best possible writing? No. Writing is one whirring cog in the big machine of game development, and sometimes the best writing and the best solution aren't the same thing.

That being said, feedback that comes with less of a mandate and less time pressure can sometimes be refused or transformed. You can never ignore it, because people who give feedback like to know they have been heard, but you can refuse it in a way that will help defuse further conflict.

The process is simple. Read the note, assess what it is asking for, and then decide whether doing it makes sense. If it doesn't, do what you have to do – or not do – instead. If someone asks why a change wasn't made, let the person who made the note know that while you appreciate the feedback, it doesn't work because of a specific reason. Then *give* the specific reason – maybe it's word count, maybe it's because of the cost of doing it, whatever – and then move on to achieving a fix that works for everyone.

Feedback that can be passed on usually tells you to do something that breaks something else. Maybe it's character motivation, maybe it's world logic, or maybe it's flow. In any case, a fix that causes new problems is no fix at all. It's a way of shifting problems around and creating more work. If implementing a note means that you're going to generate new ones, you're better off not making the change in the first place. Other bits of feedback that you should not address – and that you should resist addressing – are ones that run counter to the intent of the deliverable or that fight against what has been established elsewhere. With a little practice, these sorts of notes become obvious, and you can spend less and less time debating over whether to pay them heed. Just hold them up to what you are supposed to be doing with the deliverable, and see if they match.

All of this is utterly vital. You need to know what good feedback looks like and what bad feedback looks like and how to deal with both. But equally as important is setting up the mechanisms for getting that feedback.

14.6 Feedback Mechanisms

The first step is establishing who needs to be involved. A lot of times, a lot of people will ask to be included on communications loops because they are afraid of being left out or of losing status by not being involved. This is not conducive to fast, efficient workflow. Figure out who needs to see your stuff first.

If you're working with other writers, building an initial feedback loop with them can be incredibly valuable. These are people who speak your professional language and who can provide feedback in language you can understand and use. Their words may not carry the weight of a mandate, but there is a good chance they have expertise behind them that makes them of instant utility.

If you have team members like that around you, take advantage of them. Use them to iterate and polish before kicking stuff up the ladder, and make sure you are doing the same for them. This builds awareness on the team of each other's styles and what each of you are doing and helps create more harmonious deliverables instead of ones that are contentious. You may even want to loop your lead into this first, informal round of feedback, or you may want to save them for later when things get more formal. It depends on the team structure for your project. Bear in mind that getting that help from peers before exposing your work to the harsher critics who sit in high places can save you pain in the long run.

Inevitably, though, you need to turn over your deliverables to those higher powers. What is vital here is identifying who those folks are who need to be in on the conversation. Is it the Art Director who is going to be in charge of building the pertinent assets, the Creative Director who is overseeing the entire creative vision, the Design Director who needs to make sure what you've got matches the gameplay, and, of course, the Narrative Director and/or the Lead Writer? Not all of these people may be perfectly equipped to provide feedback on writing, but they are experts in their own areas, and you can meet them in the middle to explain how your stuff touches theirs.

What you don't want, however, is everyone jumping in demanding the right to see everything. There is no reason for the entire design team, or for junior Marketing folks, or for other people who don't have any expertise in writing but who want to make sure they're "involved," whatever that means, to start clogging up the pipeline.

The simple fact is, the more people who have to read it and provide feedback before you can make next steps, the longer it's going to take to get all that feedback. People have other tasks, many of them associated with their primary functions, and as a result, giving you feedback gets back-burnered. Time stretches. You have to chase people for the very feedback they insisted on giving, and your well-scheduled deliverable becomes a time-crunch nightmare.

14.7 Defenses Up

If you are in a position to do so, gatekeep your feedback loop aggressively. If you are too junior to do this, relay your concerns up the ladder to your lead and your producer. Get them to fight the battle for you. That's part of their job.

If someone wants in whose presence doesn't make obvious sense, challenge them and don't back down. Keep the extraneous, non-expert voices out of the conversation because they will only make your job slower and harder. Hold close the people whose opinions do matter, and educate them in how you want to receive feedback. If you get a good note, call it out and thank the person who gave it. If you get a bad or unusable one, have a follow-up discussion as to how it might be better next time around. In a word, train them (but don't let them know you're doing it). Having a consistent, tight loop of people who know how to give you what you need is manna from heaven.

And above all, do everything you can to exile the people who feel they need to "contribute" to make it look like they are integral to what is going on. They are not interested in improving the work. They are interested in making themselves look good, and the best way is to find something negative to harp on, regardless of whether doing this is within the scope of the feedback loop. What is important to them is not making your work better; it is them being seen doing something to justify their position. If you get saddled with one of these, be relentless in dealing with them. Keep them out if you can; make sure their ridiculous contributions are seen as ridiculous by everyone else if you can't. Don't actively mock them, but an earnest "Did you really mean" can go a long way.

14.8 Timeliness Is Next to Getting It Done

The other half of the equation is getting the feedback in a timely fashion. Some folks turn stuff around fast, some, in geologic time. Unfortunately, sometimes people don't get to it. Maybe the reasons are good. There might be a crisis elsewhere that needs to be dealt with, for example. Maybe the reasons are not that good after all. It doesn't matter. You need that feedback to do your job, and if you don't get it, you're the one who's going to look bad.

Nagging and reminders only go so far. Ultimately, you have to pull out all the stops. Get help if you can from producers and other people in the feedback loop. If you are in a position to do this, do not be afraid to call them out publicly with a message saying, "I am still missing feedback on this deliverable from these three people, and the deadline is Thursday." If you are not, get your producer, who is functionally married to the schedule and has a vested interest in keeping to it, to do it. If necessary and with their help, you can use the nuclear option: Stating that after a reasonable time allotment for feedback, you will take silence as approval and move forward.

Nobody is going to believe you when you say that until you put your foot down and do it, incidentally. Then the feedback will almost certainly come flooding in once they realize you're serious. Just be careful to have backup before you try it.

The same holds for the actual approval process. Writing deliverables that are not approved are not being worked on. They're not getting sent to Voice Directors and actors. They're not going to artist if they're going to adorn in-game artifacts and models. They're not being handed to Marketing for their needs to get the word out to players. They are just sitting there, and again, if they don't eventually become useful, the blame is going to land with you.

The best tactics here are slightly different. Pare the number of approvers down to a bare minimum, with the active support of your producer. Make it painfully clear to all involved that the approval process needs to be a swift up-down yes-no so things can progress. Enlist allies to keep more people from inserting themselves into the loop, again to keep things from slowing down. Particularly in spaces like this, your resistance may be read as being precious or artsy, insulting language that is a cover for not respecting your work or opinion on it. Now is not the time to fight that battle. Instead, let others do it for you. Have them make the case for why this needs to happen fast for the rest of the team's sake. There are times to be front and center, but this isn't necessarily one of them.

14.9 Why Delays Are Bad

Make no mistake, slow feedback is a disaster waiting to happen. Sitting there waiting for someone with approval authority to turn a document around and not getting it in a timely fashion can be a nightmare. Yes, those folks generally have other stuff on their plates demanding attention. When "low priority" becomes "no priority," though, or when your entire two-week sprint of rewrite time gets spent waiting, you've got a problem. You've also got a situation where, because of it, the writing's not getting the polish it needs to match that achieved by the rest of the game, and rest assured, when that happens you're the one who's going to hear it.

In the end, what matters is building a successful method to get your deliverables polished up and moved to the next phase. Once you build that machine and get it humming, it tends to be self-reinforcing. Success breeds success, which breeds increased familiarity and efficiency. If you tend it and trust it, it will help you do your job better. There are tasks for a writer beyond the act of writing that will allow you to thrive professionally, and this is one of the most important ones.

15

Leveraging Production

15.1 Introduction

Without a formal production process, games don't get made.

I mean, sure, there are exceptions, with solo devs that labor on their own schedule to occasional miraculous effect, and I have nothing but admiration for the people who can pull this off. The rule of thumb is, however, the bigger the project gets, the more you need a stable, clear process to succeed.

This is where game producers come in. It is their job to wrangle the schedule and the resources, and by the resources I mean the people, to best effect to get the game made. There are a Noah's Ark's worth of elements that go into a game – design, engineering, UI, features, audio, writing, art, and animation – and all of them are done by various people who may or may not be talking to one another at any given moment, and somehow someone has to keep track of it all to make sure everyone has what they need to do their jobs and everyone delivers what they are supposed to.

This includes writers. As a writer, you need to know what to write, when to write it, who to write it for, and what the parameters of the writing are. All of these tasks need to be assigned so there's a person responsible for getting them done, and all of them need to be tracked so progress can be gauged and steps, if necessary, can be taken to provide needed support.

As such, you need to be friends with your producer. If there is writing in your game, the odds are good there is a producer assigned to manage it. Producers' entire job is Making Sure Things Get Done, and they often have an unholy love of project management software and spreadsheets. That being said, a good producer who understands how you work can do wonders for your productivity, the quality of your work, and your satisfaction with your job.

That means, of course, talking to them. Your producer may not just be in charge of writing or narrative. Depending on how much there is, they may have other departments in their portfolio as well, and you want to establish a relationship to make sure you don't slip through the cracks.

That means reaching out and talking on a regular basis. It means educating your producer on what you do and how you do it and what it's good for. This shouldn't happen in anything but a spirit of sharing. Most producers don't know how game writing works. By giving them the straight scoop on timelines, processes, and the like, you are giving them information they need to do their jobs better. You are not imposing; you are not demanding. You are sharing and educating, and everyone benefits from it.

DOI: 10.1201/9781003592983-15

You also need to communicate what you need to function to a producer. Sometimes it's time. Sometimes it's more resources – a producer can make the case for another writer on the team in a way that a writer generally cannot. Sometimes it's building the budget and getting the permission to hire a needed sensitivity reader or subject matter expert to make sure your writing is accurate and respectful. Sometimes, frankly, it's protection from above. A good producer should be able to bring evidence to bear as to how things went down in cases when they went down poorly, and if the fault lies elsewhere, they can stand up for you more effectively than you can for yourself.

And most important of all is finding out what you actually have to do. This doesn't always get generated by a producer. A lot of task lists fall out of meetings with other departments who will work with you to establish the things they need, but the formal assigning of tasks should always go through a producer because that's what producers do. They are the point of contact for folks outside the writing group, and they are the arbiter of what gets assigned to whom.

15.2 The Magic What and Institutional Knowledge

With that in mind, you want your "what" to be as helpful as possible. Getting clear direction on deliverables is very important. This goes beyond the creative side of things. You also need to know things like what is the expected word count (very important when you are writing things that are constrained by available on-screen real estate with character limits) or what characters Marketing wants to appear in a given teaser trailer. Knowing precisely what tools you have to use and what goals you have to meet keeps you from swinging blindly at a target that is never defined. More than once, I have had to go back to producers or Directors who assigned out writing tasks without thinking of the actual functional information needed to do the task requested to get this precise sort of clarification. They knew what it was, but they didn't realize they had to communicate it. But checking with them was far better than having them be upset when they didn't get what they had never asked for.

This, by the way, is why, on a certain level, having keepers of institutional knowledge is a double-edged sword. Yes, it is helpful in the extreme having a writer on staff who has been making a particular sort of deliverable forever and knows the parameters in their sleep. Still, if that information gets siloed in that writer's head, and the rest of the team is used to going to that writer and that writer alone, then things are liable to get hairy if they are out sick or on vacation or employed elsewhere when a need arises. This is why you make sure that knowledge is shared and why you make sure the people defining tasks define them in a way that is useful.

15.3 A Part of the Machine

Understanding the vast humming machine that the game writer is a single part of is hard for a lot of writers, particularly those who got their start in other media. In game writing, you cannot simply sit and wait for the muse to arrive bearing a dry martini and a fully formed deliverable's worth of inspiration. The things you create are needed by other people on a schedule and with dollar signs attached. Lines of dialog that are going to be recorded need to be written, polished, and approved to allow them to be handed off to actors and Voice Directors and the like. Bits of scrawled graffiti need to be delivered to the artists who are going to paint them on map walls. UI text needs to go to the UI team to implement. And everything needs to go to Localization sooner or later, and as far as they're concerned, sooner.

What this means is that you are not writing for yourself. You are writing for your teammates, the folks downstream in the flow of making the game. In some ways, even if your job as a game writer is to harness and exercise creativity, you are simultaneously a worker on a psychic production line. You take what is passed to you, add what is needed, and send it on down the line. There is no room for being an artist, not when there are deadlines.

As a result, brinkmanship and waiting until the last minute are bad business, because other people are depending on you to do their jobs so they can in turn do theirs. Gum up the works, and the entire delicate structure totters. The numbers of people and the sums of money involved in large games these days are vast enough that even small delays can be catastrophic. And if you're causing a delay because inspiration hasn't struck on the 25 variants of "Reloading!" you were supposed to deliver last week, there will be precious little sympathy extended your way.

15.4 The Perfect Really Hates the Good

Hand in hand with this is the notion that your writing must be perfect before other eyes can see it. This is not true. The perfect is very much the enemy of the good. It beats the good up at recess and takes its milk money.

I'm not saying you should not strive to do your very best in your writing. Obviously, you want to create the very best work that you can. You want to bring all your powers to bear on it, you want to polish it until it gleams blindingly bright, and you want to finish knowing you have done your utmost to make it right.

Unfortunately, these goals don't always line up with the demands of production. As such, you have to learn when "good enough" stops being a lame excuse and starts being a statement of useful fact. Otherwise, you end up learning it the hard way.

You should absolutely do the very best you can. You owe it to yourself, your coworkers, and the game to put in the full effort your job requires to produce superior work. The drive to improve, to add that last perfect detail, is strong because, as writers, we hold in our heads what the writing could (and maybe even should) be. The temptation to tinker endlessly, to not give up the deliverable until there is absolutely nothing left to do but put whipped cream and a cherry on top, is incredibly seductive.

It is also, unfortunately, potentially destructive.

There are times, lots and lots of times, when the internal customers you have on the team do not need perfection. They do need *something* to work with that *approximates* the shape of what the final text will be so they can start working. In that case, holding back the deliverable in order to keep tweaking adverbs is massively counterproductive because you are keeping other people from getting to work. I know it's hard to know when something is "ready," but even the best chef will occasionally taste the dish in progress to get a sense of how it's progressing and how close it is.

Again, this is not saying to throw your first rushed effort to the lions. You absolutely should not share a draft that is incomplete or unformed. Here is where that definition of "good enough" comes into play. You have to ask yourself: Is it good enough for other people to understand what I am saying? Is it good enough for people to give useful feedback? Is it good enough to represent the final intention? Is it good enough to start – not end – the conversation? Is it good enough for the next person in line to use? That's what a workable, positive "good enough" means.

You must resist, then, the voice in your head that says you cannot let anyone see anything until it is as good as it can possibly be and every word cuts like razors and shines like diamonds. If you want to achieve perfection in a first draft and will be satisfied with nothing less, then you are going to fail, and people will fail with you. I understand that this approach often goes hand in hand with fear, but this is where you have to be brave. This is where you have to trust your talent and your work to stand on its own in its first encounter with other people. This is where you have to learn to start to let go.

As I frequently tell writers working for me, "We write in Legos, not gems." Ideally there will be time for iteration to find the perfect word choice, the absolute best that a thesaurus has to offer. In the meantime, though, any word that gets the point across and conveys your intent can be plugged in effectively enough. You've got to build before you rebuild. You need the basics in place before you can work on the fine details.

Let me be clear. You need to give yourself permission to be something less than perfect in order to be effective. This can be scary. It is perfectly understandable to be afraid of putting your work out there for people to see, especially people who seem to demand perfection right off the bat. It can be nerve-wracking to give over a script, wondering if there are things you missed. It can be flat-out painful to let go because once it's out of your hands, you can't control it anymore.

But you have to, because if you don't, the game can't move forward. The longer you hang onto a first draft trying to get it sparkly, the less time there is for others to look at it and use it. There is also less time to give you feedback for revision so you can make it better in a way that works for other people, instead of guessing in a vacuum. Breathe deep, let go, and tell yourself it's not all or nothing, because it can't be.

15.5 Follow-up Detachment

Incidentally, one of the side effects of investing too much in a first draft is the likelihood of being unable to produce a second draft in a timely fashion and without gnawing your own wrists open. If you get too close to a particular solution for a writing task, you run the risk of seeing it as the only solution to that particular problem. You view your deliverable as the optimum choice, and tinkering with it runs the risk of making the whole thing collapse. And when you are asked for rewrites, you sit there and you ponder, and you find yourself paralyzed as you slam up against the unyielding walls of your emotional involvement in your own work.

You know what? Sometimes it's OK if it all does crash down and you need to build it again. The truth is, though, that most of the time, you don't need to do anything that drastic. What you do need to do, however, is to take a step back and look at your writing from a less fraught place. Frequently, the best way to do this is to walk through the material with someone else, calmly and with detachment. Let them ask questions and offer alternatives. Don't put too much pressure on yourself. Feel free to explain why you did what you did, but be open to other ways to achieve the same effect. Relax your grip on the material before you crush it to powder and draw your own blood. You'd be amazed at how much better it feels.

15.6 Goals and Timeframes

Moving on from that, one of the most important things you can do as a game writer is set reasonable goals for yourself and communicate them to the people making schedules. Very few people know how long a writing deliverable is going to take. This includes a great many writers and definitely includes most of the people outside of the narrative group in any given game. It's not necessarily a question of malice or willful ignorance. It's that producers, unless they have worked closely with writers before, have no experience of it and therefore simply do not know.

This is derived in part from the notion that writing is a mysterious task best performed in silence and solitude, and possibly in conjunction with eldritch chanting. While this is a romantic and oddly appealing myth to perpetuate, doing it is ultimately counterproductive.

Why? Because this approach silos off useful knowledge of the writing process from the folks who most need to learn about it: Directors, producers, and other folks at the top of the food chain. If they don't know your needs and abilities, they can't set reasonable expectations for how long it's going to take to do a task, how many people are required, and all the other pertinent details that go into a reasonable workload.

In a perfect world, you could rely on these folks to identify the gap in their knowledge and seek to rectify it by asking pertinent questions, scoping the task before setting due dates, and making decisions based on that information. Unfortunately, we do not live in a perfect world. Folks in positions of authority tend to have a lot of plates spinning. They may not know what they do not know and should seek out, they may think they know but they don't, or maybe there's someone feeding them bad intel on how long a writing task takes.

In the end, it's immaterial. As a matter of self-preservation, it behooves any game writer to provide an education about what their task entails, whom it is going to impact, and how long it should reasonably be expected to take. This needs to be communicated to the producer who is setting the schedule and then pushed up the ladder. This, then, will ensure that the understanding is clear as to how long something is going to take in order to do it right.

Why is this important? For one thing, no one ever gives the writer too much time to do a task. There is an ingrained perception, often fueled by the "evidence" of last-minute, desperate writing binges to get something done, that writing tasks don't take all that long, even the big ones. If the people making the schedules know, and you absolutely must be honest with them about how the sausage gets made, then they can hopefully create a work schedule for you that is conducive to doing good stuff. This means schedules with enough time built in to get feedback, iterate and polish, and maybe even do a table read so you can hear your work in real time. If you don't, if you try to make yourself look good by shaving off needed time or thinking you can somehow find a way to switch into Beast Mode endlessly and at will, you need to check yourself before you wreck your entire writing team.

Be smart. Be honest. Be proactive. Do this, and then you can do your real job right.

15.7 When Not to Write

Writers are trained to fight for the chance to write all the things. There is a reason for this. If you cannot point to a task or a series of tasks you are assigned, they may start wondering why they are keeping you around. Thus, writers fight for the chance to write everything, even if it produces a workload overload that leads to some very bad places. Even writers with secure positions will leap at the chance to get more of their work into a game.

What you have to understand is this is not necessary and is often wrong.

Very few games need all of the writing. Fundamentally, each game has an appropriate amount of writing. For some games, this is a lot. For some games, it is none. Most, unsurprisingly, land in the middle. What this means is that as dangerous as it is to have a game where key aspects of writing don't make it into the finished product, it is sometimes just as bad to have too much writing.

It's simple. Not everything needs to be explained in minute detail. Not every minor character needs a four-page bio. Not every conversation between two patrolling guards, or even two major characters, needs to be ten minutes long. Your space combat game does not need an endless, detailed, scientifically plausible treatise on how the ship shields work in-game, because everyone knows the cliché of "Shields up!" and understands instantly what it means.

Yes, there are games that specifically cater to lore-hounds, and if you're working on one of those, go to town and pack a lunch. Chances are low, however, that you're working on one of those games, which means you don't have carte blanche to scribble away. Figure out what the appropriate amount of writing for your game is and target that in order to budget time properly and do it well.

In many ways, the whole point of game writing is brevity mixed with efficiency to serve utility. Every line of dialog should serve one of two purposes: It should give the player a piece of gameplay-pertinent information, or it should deepen their understanding of a character, a situation, or the world. Furthermore, it should be delivered in a way that supplements and reinforces the act of play instead of derailing it and locking players into reading, listening to, or watching stuff that is actively preventing them from doing what they want to be doing. Dialog should not be excessively long or florid unless the scenario and characters expressly call for it, and even then, you want to more give the sense of that sort of thing than indulge in baroque linguistic linguine.

As a result, if you are thinking about writing something for the game, ask yourself: What purpose does this line serve? If you have a good answer, great, go ahead. Even then, resist the urge to overwrite, over-explain, and overdo. Some things are better left as hooks and enticing mysteries.

15.8 Where Do You Fit?

What does a functional production cycle look like? That depends on a lot of things: The size and type of the game, the budget, the allocated resources, demands made by outside partners like Steam or Sony or Nintendo, and more can all impact things. There is no single model that I can map out for you here, but I can draw some broad outlines.

Writing's role in production can generally be broken down into two categories: Proactive and Reactive. Proactive is infinitely preferable. It's what happens when calm, rational decisions are made up front about what sort of writing deliverables are going to be needed when, how many people are needed to do them, and how big they're going to be. These estimates are usually off, but that's OK. They're a starting point, and it is possible to make adjustments with goodwill as you go along and see where everyone's best guesses fell short.

With this approach, the types of deliverables you get asked for change over time. In the early stages, you're not going to be doing a lot of dialog or even bark writing. You'll be working on the plot, the character and enemy descriptions, the game world, and more things like that. You will be building foundations, using documents that players ideally will see very little of.

That's OK. That's what is needed to get other team members rolling. Then the cycle progresses, and it's time to start thinking about smaller chunks of the game, levels, missions, or questlines. Here's where you might start writing some placeholder dialog. Next, as things get more granular, you start being asked to write more and more specific things. Maybe it's the core dialog for the Golden Path through the quest. Once that's in place and people can playtest with placeholder recordings, it'll be time for tweaks and improvements based on player feedback. And once that's locked down, it'll be time to start crafting things like background chatter and barks if the game calls for them.

It's not hard and fast, but that's the way it can work a bunch of the time.

Then there's Reactive. Reactive writing happens when, at some point along the way, someone uncovers a screwup or a gap or a line that's aggressively not working, and you need to react to the sudden need. This sort of thing tends to be fast turnaround and high pressure, and more often than not you only get one bite at the apple. It can be as small as "We need a line to tell the player to do this specific thing!" It can be as big as "We know you are already in the recording studio, but in between lines can you please write our entire tutorial, which we forgot about until yesterday." Either way, you need to do it, you need to do it immediately, and you need to do it without complaining to your game writer friends until much later, when no one else can hear you and you're all swapping stories of the unbelievable things you were asked to do over a round of tasty beverages.

Obviously, this is not ideal. The more Proactive things are, the more time you have to pace yourself, iterate and polish, and make sure that you're doing your best work. Last-minute panic can sometimes drive inspiration, but more often it produces substandard work because it's got to get done and there's no time to make sure it's getting done right. And heaven help you if the powers that be get used to you turning stuff around on Reactive deadlines without a hiccup, because they'll start assuming it's normal and reproducible, and that's asking for trouble.

15.9 Script Lock Is Your Friend

One writing-related aspect of production that is absolutely vital is script lock. Look, things can and will change up to the last minute, and sometimes you have to roll with that. There still has to be a cutoff, a point where no more changes are allowed except in emergencies, and everyone else has to stop fiddling around and asking for one more line. At a certain point, you have to have the script finalized, and not just for your sake.

You *will* need accurate line counts for the recording studio if you are going that route so they can schedule actors and block out session time accordingly. Wait until the last minute for that, and you're likely to find the studio you want to use short on time because other people have booked it, and your desired talent unavailable because they took other gigs while you left them flapping in the breeze. You *will* need to hand over completed scripts to Localization to give them enough time to do their jobs right and to interact with you to make sure they're getting everything across in translation that needs to be there.

Failure to do this leads to wasted time and money. It leads to rushed work. It leads to frustration at the perceived lack of respect. And because there is no fixed target, it can lead to a certain lack of rigor around the edges, where people always assume there's time to catch stuff until there suddenly isn't. I've literally been laughed at in meetings when I asked to set a date for script lock. When the bill came due, in the form of last-minute scrambles and expensive pickup recording sessions, it wasn't quite as funny.

15.10 No Quick Favors

While we're in the neighborhood, there's one thing that other devs will often try to do is circumvent the work tracking process. They will ask for "quick favors" and "small tasks" that "don't need to go through Jira" because they're, well, small and quick.

Except there is a very good chance that a given task as imagined by someone outside of the writing space might take a lot more time than they think. That's time you're supposed to be spending on your other, tracked tasks.

These things also tend to pile up. If you do one once, that invites an ask for another and another, and when someone *else* comes along and asks, you feel bad about saying no to *them*, and it snowballs. A task that takes half an hour may not seem like much, but when you get hit with a series of them, they add up to a significant portion of your work week.

Also, since these tasks aren't being tracked, they are free to balloon wildly. After all, no one is watching them or reining them in. This can mean what starts as a one-paragraph write-up turns into a massive exposition dump, or a quick trailer script draft gets sent back for endless rewrites as the goal-posts on the initial task rumble hither and yon. If the task isn't described in a ticket, after all, then the people asking for it are free to have it morph wildly on you without constraint. You have no recourse when it does, and they're still asking for more.

This hurts you in a lot of ways. As noted previously, it chews into the time that is formally allotted to other tasks. It also potentially exposes you to multiple types of bad news. There is the possibility that the task you get asked to do is not one that should be done, and by putting time and effort into it, you are getting yourself into trouble for aiding and abetting. There is also the fact that a completed task that is not in the tracking software is functionally invisible to Production. You might as well be working on ether. And at the end of the month or the sprint or the milestone, when it comes time for them to look at the metrics, your efforts are not going to show up. This sort of work is not going to count in your favor, even if it helped someone else on the team. You are putting yourself in the crosshairs as "unproductive" because the velocity of your completed tickets will be impacted by the off-book work you have done. That, in turn, will turn up in performance reviews and promotion discussions and questions of whether or not you're worth raises or promotions or even keeping on the team.

Don't do it. Protect yourself. If the task you are being presented with is described as being of such importance that it has to happen for the sake of the game, make them back up that assertion. State your terms.

Tell the person asking for the task that you will be happy to do it *if* they talk to your producer and get it turned into a work ticket. If it's that important, they will be willing to put it into the system to make sure it gets done. If they're not willing to do that, if their first response is "But it's just a small thing," then you know where you stand on this one. If they're not willing to make the effort to support your work because it's mildly inconvenient to do so, then maybe they shouldn't be getting that work as a freebie.

This is one I learned the hard way, and because I was a trusting soul in my younger days, I had to learn it twice. It cost me time, and it cost me money. Because my hours on these projects were not formally accounted for since I wasn't formally tasked, I was not eligible for bonuses given to the team. It cost me credits that I should have had for my work. And it cost me time that should have been spent elsewhere, doing things that would be formally appreciated.

Don't do this, no matter how much you like the fellow dev who is asking. Use process as a shield. It gets used as a bludgeon often enough.

15.11 Metrics and Writing

People rely on metrics to make informed decisions, which is generally not a bad thing. Having good evidence as to what works and what doesn't can help planning and resource allocation to produce what players want most effectively.

The problem is, what those metrics are measuring can be wonky, based on what questions are asked, who's asking them, and what gets left unasked. When the subject of those metrics is writing, then things run the risk of going off the rails.

Writing questionnaires is serious business. There are two-semester courses devoted to this topic in statistics programs at fine universities. There is a skill to composing questions that produce useful, actionable data.

Sadly, a lot of studios do not use trained professionals to put together their feedback prompts. The work is instead done by some combination of Marketing, business, and team leadership, and the results are not always great. There are instances when the questions are worded so vaguely that no useful data can be gleaned from the responses. There are times when questions lack nuance or context. There are even times when the people putting together the questions have their collective thumb on the scale and phrase things to produce the result they wanted all along.

Data like this is often not useful. It can, however, be dangerous if used unquestioningly. If there is anything about writing at all in these things, it's usually a simple up-down "Did you like the story?" That leaves a lot of territory uncovered and leads to responses that lack context or nuance. These in turn can get boiled down to simple sentiments like "Nobody likes the writing," which don't paint a complete picture but which can drive design, resource, and business decisions.

If possible, try to get in on the writing of the survey questions. Be a voice in the room if you can for writing when the questions get composed. If you can't get directly involved, then at least push your concerns up the ladder to someone who is. It's not great, but it's better than nothing. If you can talk them into asking three questions instead of one, that's a huge win.

16

Dealing with the Negatives

16.1 Overview

One of the absolute constants of a game writer's professional existence is disrespect. Sometimes it is intentional. Sometimes it is unconscious. Regardless of the source, there is, wired into the DNA of the industry, a suspicion of and disdain for writing as an element of game development. This can manifest in any number of ways, but it's never-ending, and it's something you have to watch out for. You have to in order to take care of yourself professionally.

It's kind of ironic that video games don't respect writing, seeing as so many early classics were text-only adventures. *Zork* and *Planetfall*, and their ilk, were in a real way primarily writing, with no graphics or action or gameplay other than typing. Writing has been an essential part of the history of games all along, and yet that fact largely gets disregarded.

16.2 Why Do They Say Such Things?

There are several reasons for this. One is that, once games moved into a graphical space with fast-twitch action gameplay, the very task of writing was often back-burnered. It got deemed secondary in importance because at that point the tools did not exist to get writing into actual games. Sure, there was often glorious supporting material – any gamer of a certain age has fond memories of the cloth maps and thick manuals that used to come with boxed PC games – but the actual games had few mechanisms, if any, for displaying writing to players. As such, the task of writing generally got fobbed off to the lead designer because, well, they wrote documents, and documents were made of words, and thus they could handle this word thing, too. While many designers worked hard and did their best with this scenario, the simple fact remained that they were designers, not writers, and not everyone had both skill sets.

Not helping matters was the fact that writing was seen – and still is seen, in many cases – as something external to the game, as opposed to an integral part of the player experience. Writing got bolted on at the last moment, a coat of paint on an existing game designed to give it a vague context and produce Marketing copy. This ultimately became known as "the narrative wrapper," a phrase that by definition suggests that writing is external to the game itself. It may be around the game and contain it, but it's not "of" it, and as such it is automatically lesser.

DOI: 10.1201/9781003592983-16

This is something I have experienced multiple times. On more than one occasion, I would be approached with an urgent task to create a story and maybe some dialog and cut scenes for a game that was already locked down in terms of its feature set, mission design, and gameplay. There would be no time to do anything but hammer a quick solution out, and certainly no way to suggest ways in which the narrative elements could maybe be integrated into the game itself. The work I did in these scenarios was always external to the actual play experience, but when you get asked, "We go into the studio Thursday. Here's the game. Can you write it for us?" There isn't always a lot you can do. (Afterwards, of course, the writing inevitably gets nitpicked, but this is a "water remains wet" scenario.)

As a result, coming into the more modern eras of game development, writing was squarely behind. Things have not improved across the board, either.

16.3 The Dilemma of Writing

At its core, writing is not a technical task, nor is it a quantifiable one. Most other disciplines in game development have a pretty simple gauge for how good their work is – does it work? Does the feature function? Does the art asset represent what it is supposed to? Does the lighting solution allow for gameplay in a space?

Writing, on the other hand, is purely subjective. One person's good writing is another person's nightmare trash scenario, and while there are certain professional standards that must be met – grammar is your friend, spelling is important, and so on – there is no way to look at a piece of writing and say, "yes, this is good" or not in absolute terms. The best you can do is ask, "Does this writing meet the needs of the task it is supposed to fulfill?" and go from there.

The good news is that leaves a lot of room for interpretation. And in that interpretation, there are a lot of ways that encourage disrespect for writing that get expressed. Someone in a senior position who is not a writer, who may not read, and who probably has no professional training in the techniques of writing is nevertheless in a position of authority over writers and writing, and their opinions can be devastating.

What must inescapably be dealt with, however, is the fact that writing is, by and large, not a technical task. While the rise of the narrative designer role and the evolution of writing in games have led to writers often being assigned technical tasks related to the implementation of their writing in-game, that is a secondary and derivative task set that follows on to the primary one: Writing. People have been writing for a very, very long time without the aid of compilers or renderers or other complex technical solutions. Developers from other aspects of the team can and should take pride in their technical knowledge and expertise. But because writing does not require anything of that sort, and because game development is an exercise in technology, writers are seen as lesser, not a part of the team. Their task is viewed as less complicated, and thus, easy. Which, as we all know, is nonsense. Still, the perception persists.

This, unfortunately, ties into the demon twin sibling of "writing is easy," "anyone can do it."

16.4 Anyone Can Write – Or Can They?

Let's start with the basics. Not everyone can in fact do it. Writing is a craft as much as an art. It requires skill and practice and talent and time. Occasionally there are geniuses at it, the same as there are geniuses in any form, but those are few and far between. The rest of us have to work, and work hard, to get good at what we do – to become, in a word, professional.

A lot of folks outside of writing don't see that or don't want to see that. Their position is that because they use words for certain things – emails or texts or whatever – every use of words is fast and easy and doable by anyone. They refuse to respect the professional nature of the role and its specifics, and people (and projects) get burned as a result.

People who are not professional video game writers assume that anyone can be brought in to do the task, making writers interchangeable. They believe that since the tasks are easy, they don't need to be supported with time or resources, and that since the tasks are easy, they should be perfect in the first draft.

That is a lot to unpack. That is also a lot to confront. So let's take it apart, one item at a time.

The notion that anyone can do a writer's job is a patently false one. No one looks at other members of a dev team and thinks they can slide in and make character models or build levels or code features or produce animations from the word go. All of these other professions are regarded as exactly that: Professions. As such, they are treated with respect for what went into acquiring that professional status.

Writers tend not to get that. Instead, folks outside the field feel free to jump in and do rewrites, often making things actively worse in the process. Protesting this again gets the writer labeled as defensive, sensitive, or precious, or worst of all, "not a good team player," when if the situation involved literally anyone else on the team, there would be hell to pay.

Part of the problem is that these folks genuinely do think they can write, and write well, and that the first thing that comes to their mind is the perfect, golden solution. This is bunk. A good professional game writer creates a deliverable in the context of the rest of the writing and narrative direction of the game, taking into account character and plot needs in the process. They understand that no piece of writing exists on an island and that it's a connected body of work. One deliverable builds on top of the last, even if there is no immediate, direct connection.

Furthermore, the work required to make the writing professional-level and good takes time and iteration. Dashing something off on the first pass may be a decent conversation starter, but nobody in the writing field genuinely thinks that their adverbs don't stink. With professional status comes an understanding that the work takes time and effort and that the myth of lightning inspiration producing flawless texts is Hollywood nonsense.

I recall a conversation with an Art Director who was looking over a first-pass writing deliverable. It wasn't perfect, but their response was to state their intent to rewrite it to their specifications. When I suggested that a better route would be to provide feedback to let the writer iterate and improve, the same way artists take feedback and iterate on concept art, they were practically speechless. The concept had never occurred to them.

16.5 Hold My Beer

This is hard to confront and hard to admit for a lot of people, and in avoiding it, they create more problems. The most common is that when they are asked for feedback on writing, they dodge and bob and eventually say, "It's easier if I just rewrite it myself." This is because providing useful feedback is hard, and coming to grips with the content in a way that permits the feedback to be good is also hard. With that comes the recognition that crafting this stuff is hard, too, and that blows the paradigm out of the water. Rather than accept that the deliverable may in fact have some depth and heft to it that cannot be addressed with the simple wave of a magic wand, they pivot to doing a fast rewrite that makes them feel good about their contribution. They get to present their vision without communicating it in concept form or having it exposed to feedback, and by doing it this way, they express their disdain for people doing the hard work of writing.

Yes, there are times when a writer is not meeting an expressed request for a vision, even on multiple drafts. There are massive differences, however, between a writer who gets a formal directive and explicit feedback and still misses the target for whatever reason and someone who, when confronted with a deliverable they need to understand to critique, simply decides that the writer can't read their mind and produce what's in their head and doesn't take the effort to communicate it.

Dealing with this is hard, and sometimes impossible. When someone above you on the food chain injects themselves like this, there is no one to tell them no, and as a writer, you can't complain too much or you get slapped with all the bad labels. This is, of course, unfair. Labeling writers who stand up for their work and for the integrity of narrative and writing as "troublesome" or "precious" instead of taking their concerns seriously is bad business. It demotivates the writers. It encourages other team members to disdain input from writers and to think poorly of them as well. It produces bad writing, as writers become gun-shy about taking risks for fear of being slapped down publicly.

Meanwhile, the writing that does go out, often without going through an iterative feedback and rewrite process because it came from on high, is often not very good. It's one thing if the person doing the fast rewrites has experience doing the job and can provide a valuable, professional take. It's entirely another to get the back end of "I'm thinking of a deliverable, no, that's not it, why can't you deliver what is in my head that I haven't communicated to you?"

16.6 How Do You Fight It?

To combat this, your options are limited. If there is time, do a feedback pass on the rewrite. Ask if there's time for you to do another pass now that you have an example of what's wanted to serve as reference. Enlist other team members, like producers, to slow the roll on slamming first-draft rewrites into the game.

And whatever you do, do not react in anger. Doing that will get your feedback disregarded. It is perfectly OK to feel anger at this kind of treatment, but expressing that anger in a professional space generally doesn't work too well. Instead, phrase your feedback in the form of questions. Does this new line adequately communicate this needed bit of information? Would this character use that language? Is this new version too long, and can we say it more efficiently? Keeping the temperature down and forcing the discussion into a space where it's about technique, not feelings, can sometimes triumph where pure anger cannot.

16.7 Writer versus Game Writer

Along with this is the notion that writers are largely generic and thus can be swapped out without consequence. The simple fact is that not every writer is good at every type of writing. I've been brought in to clean up after acclaimed writers whose work in other media was highly regarded and excellent but who could never grasp the basics of leaving room for the player to be the star of the show. They were great writers, but they were not great game writers.

The job of game writer, as noted earlier, has its own unique demands and requirements and language and skills, and you can't grab someone because they ran a good *Dungeons & Dragons* campaign on one hand or wrote a good episode of a *Law & Order* spinoff on the other and expect them to hit the ground running or even to ever learn to run at all.

One of the interesting spinoffs of this perspective, incidentally, is the politics that often swirls around filling the game writer role. Often, particularly in large companies, there is a brutal political struggle around whose favorite writer gets the job. This can lead to some awkward fits of writer and role. It can also lead to some real and appropriate hard feelings when someone who is eminently qualified for a position gets passed over for reasons that aren't quite load-bearing. This in turn leads to strained working relationships, and all sorts of bad things derive from that. Meanwhile, the powers whose ambitions to choose the writer were thwarted don't always take things lying down. There can be plenty of after-the-fact campaigning, sandbagging of the writer who got the role, and slow-rolling content to make the current writer look bad. Make them look bad enough, and maybe it might be time for a replacement, and thus the whole dance starts again.

In moments like this, the "writers are replaceable" canard gets revealed to be more "writers someone doesn't like are replaceable." It is, in a word, nasty.

16.8 How Do They Do That?

Like anyone else in game development, game writers work at their craft. I know this for a fact, because I've been running round table discussions at the Game Developers Conference for nearly 20 years, wherein discussing craft and becoming better at it is the focus of what we do. Everyone doing this job who is worth their salt wants to get better at it. They want to learn and grow and improve, and by and large they do.

The simple experience of having shipped a game and come under the equivalent of live fire helps you level up. Working with other writers who know stuff you don't helps you level up. Getting professional feedback, which tells you where to improve, helps you level up. And the end result of all of that is someone who is demonstrably better than someone randomly pulled in because they are more pliable or, God forbid, cheaper.

This is emphatically not to say that the industry does not need to constantly cultivate and add new talent. Understanding that, it should be a supplemental model, done to constantly refresh and expand a talent pipeline as seniors age out or move on to other industries. What I'm trying to say here is that there is definite value in specific writers who have demonstrated that they are good at writing games and who can probably do the job faster and more efficiently than someone who is going to have to be trained up from the starting blocks.

And I will repeat myself here: Not all good game writers are good writers for all games. I freely confess I would be terrible at writing a dating simulator. Dating simulators are good and popular and fun games, and millions upon millions of people enjoy them, and there are writers out there who do an excellent job of making them compelling and fun (even the one where you're dating pigeons. In fact, maybe especially that one.). I know I can't do it right, because my writing brain isn't wired that way, and trying to plug me in to do one would be a tragic mistake for all concerned. I am comfortable with this; I would refuse any offer of a gig like that, and I wish only for the writers who are good at it to succeed beyond their wildest dreams.

16.9 You Are Number Six

Ultimately, writers are absolutely not interchangeable. Each professional writer draws from a specific base of knowledge and experience, combining that with their vision and their skill to approach the job in a unique and productive way.

Thus, it falls on individual writers to demonstrate their worth as individuals and to do it in concert with coworkers who understand and value them. Don't drop off deliverables and hope people see the unique elements you put in. Instead, when you deliver, provide a summary that calls out the stuff you're proud of to put it in people's faces. Make them aware so they know to look for it.

In addition, leverage your peers appropriately and respectfully. Make sure that coworkers who use your deliverables and who collaborate with you audibly support you. Ask them to send notes of appreciation to your lead and producer. Build a paper trail of people saying your stuff is good. Establish yourself as a good, productive coworker with strong relationships that will take time and energy away from production to replace. And if there is a specific area or character that you can own (with permission), do it and make sure everyone knows that's your area of expertise. It's a lot easier for folks to defend you – or for you to defend yourself – if you can point to specific stuff you do that nobody else does. Generalists may do a lot of the heavy lifting, but if you can call out something where you're a star, it's easier for others to create a narrative around and assign value to your presence.

16.10 Here Comes Another One

Then there's the question of resources. Because writing is not valued, it is often not supported. As a result, writing teams aren't big enough to do all the tasks needed (as opposed to the ones projected). Editors, who provide tremendous value, are often a fever dream. Writing windows are short and frequently get eaten by other departments' issues. Money is not there to hire actors to do table reads of scripts. Other departments' time and effort are not available to support narrative-themed initiatives. Writing-adjacent tasks are deemed low priority and thus get done slowly or not at all. You get the picture.

It ends up turning game writing into the equivalent of a cooking competition show, where contestants are given 15 minutes and a random grab bag of ingredients to make a meal to serve to gourmet chefs. Writing without these resources – without adequate time or support or attention – means that the writing isn't as good as it could be. Because the writing isn't as good as it could be, it often gets singled out as a weak spot, and the writers take the blame for not being able to consistently conjure up miracles. Rarely do post-mortems focus on the writing process, as there are usually issues deemed more important to tackle, and unfettered by observation, the cycle repeats and repeats and repeats.

Some of this comes from a failure to understand what writers do and how long it takes, as opposed to the myths. This results in tasks being created without being accurately scoped, and if they're not scoped, then it's impossible to assign the right amount of time to get them done. Of course, this requires asking writers how long it will take them to do something and what a task involves. I've seen situations where people outside of the narrative group have come up with narrative tasks and passed them off to producers to assign without ever contacting the writers and narrative designers to see what the tasks, inevitably referred to as "a little thing," require in reality. When the situation inevitably blows up, there is shock and surprise and then embarrassment when what had been asked for (in terms of time and effort and steps) gets laid out in detail, as opposed to what had originally been imagined. Regardless, this sort of thing clutters up production schedules and deliverable pipelines. It causes cascading problems down the line, and it all comes from people not reaching out and learning in order to optimize writing.

16.11 Getting Needed Help

The best way to counter this is with time and money. Work with production to lay out your tasks – all of them – and how long they take to do right. Hand in hand with that, figure out what wasting your time costs. Be able to demonstrate how much extra it will cost to not do things the right way. Do this rationally and calmly so that it's clear you're advocating for the project, not yourself. And bring visuals to support your points. Words don't always stick, and people don't always read.

Getting additional resources to support writing is a long, slow, hard road. The victories don't come often or easily. Because writing is seen as a lower priority, other hands reaching out get filled first. If, however, you consistently make the case as to why these resources are needed, even a few more days here and there, then sooner or later, there might be movement in your favor.

16.12 If at First . . .

The last quill on this particular hedgehog is the idea that writing should come out perfect the first time. This is an impossible fantasy, born of the notion that writers are suddenly struck by inspiration such that they can then channel their muse into spotless prose at supersonic rates of speed. Television, movie, and novel writers perpetuate this thing, and they really should know better, though to be fair, horror writers are a bit over-fond of "writer who has writer's block and thus gets eaten by a monster as a result" plotlines.

The simple fact is that first-pass writing needs iteration and feedback to achieve its optimal form. To quote a hoary writing axiom, the purpose of a first draft is to exist. It is to get words down to allow you to start messing with them and improving them based off something concrete. It may be that most of your first draft survives. It may be that none of it does. It doesn't matter. What matters is that it exists as that first rough hewing of the block of marble. From you will eventually produce the equivalent of Michelangelo's David, if Michelangelo's David was a list of a dozen variations on "Reloading!"

As a writer, you literally cannot know everything that is going on with the game when you first sit down to write a script for a mission. Stuff changes. Features evolve, arrive, or go away. Levels get reworked based on technical considerations or artistic ones. Missions get redesigned or chopped. Budgets change. Stuff gets cut. There are questions of timing. The list goes on and on and mutates every 30 seconds to boot.

As a result, the first draft of a writing deliverable is inevitably going to have to be tweaked to match the new reality of the game. At the same time, a first pass is a first pass, and it can be made better once the basics are laid down and you can focus on the details. With that understood, there has to be time and will to do those multiple iterative passes, the same way every other department on the development team gets time and resources to iterate and polish.

Or, to put it another way, nobody in their right mind would put a first-pass character model in a game. Nobody would put a first-pass mission space, or a first-pass lighting solution, or a first pass at weapons balancing for a combat system, or literally anything else. There is an understanding there that anything needs to be polished and tested and improved before it meets the paying audience. That understanding often does not get extended to writing. Because writing is devalued from the get-go, there is the expectation that writing deliverables will arrive fully formed and flawless. When that doesn't happen, the fertilizer hits the fan.

This is not to say that some writers don't buy into the myth and think that their first-pass deliverables are made of angel tears and starlight. These folks give the rest of us a bad name when they reflexively push back against any change, when they demand other departments make changes to suit their previously undisclosed narrative ideas, and generally act like entitled, petulant children.

As discussed elsewhere, writing is not here to drive the train, and making ultimatums based on a clever turn of phrase is a great way to get yourself shunned by your team. There has to be a basic understanding that it's all part of a bigger project and that some compromise is inevitable and utterly necessary. If you find yourself working with a writer who thinks the project revolves around them, it's time to raise the red flag. If you are a writer who thinks the project revolves around them, it might be time for some self-reflection about your place in the cosmos.

16.13 Conclusion

In the end, it comes down to understanding how writing is regarded in game development, and the answer is often "not well." Sure, there are games that are writing-driven, many of them spectacular successes, but there are a million excuses made for that success to credit everything but the words. That has to stop. There has to be respect and understanding and collaboration between equals if we're going to provide the best content possible and do the best work that we can.

As a writer, I don't get into it with a character artist about their choice of a particular shade of red on a model. If asked to provide feedback, I will, but I will couch it in terms of where it's coming from, not dictate terms. At the same time, I expect character modelers to read the character descriptions I provide that have been approved and implement the pertinent bits I have written for their use.

I've had experiences where a character description was based around one very specific physical feature – it was the whole selling point of the character, the thing his entire backstory was hung off of – but when it came time to approve the character model, lo and behold, that feature was nowhere to be found. When pressed on it, the Art Director sort of shrugged and said, "Oh well, too late to change it now." The character, predictably, came across as entirely generic and failed to find any traction with the audience. The end result was wasted time, wasted money, and wasted opportunity.

By the same token, as a writer, I do not need to be endlessly arguing specific word choice with folks who do not possess a level of writing expertise. Feedback is always welcomed but when it gets down to the level of granularity where you're doing multiple email exchanges with Director-level team members over which adverb to use on a line no one will ever hear, then things have gone off the rails. There needs to be trust in place to allow you to do your job by means of your expertise and experience. There needs to be an understanding that wasting Director-level time on whether to use "stealthily" or "quietly" in a character description for half a day is expensive and ultimately unnecessary. Alas, when they think they know best, sometimes the best thing you can do is concede and hoard your ammunition for another, more meaningful fight. If it doesn't matter that much, retreat gracefully instead of wasting your moral capital on a fight that was never worth winning.

In the end, it is imperative that the game industry get educated about writing because we are a part of the process. Anything that makes it harder for us to do our jobs makes it harder for the game to get produced. But there are decades of myth, some of it willful, that need to be dismantled before there is real and lasting progress.

It is often assumed when someone makes a statement like this in public that they are demanding that writing be given authority and autonomy over the whole game. Nothing could be further from the truth. What professional game writers want most of all is to be regarded as an equal part of the team, ready to produce what is needed and given the same time, respect, and resource as their professional peers. That is something that needs to be repeated, loudly and often. The places where there is professional inequality in terms of what's allowed and what's supported need to be identified and rectified. The more of this stuff gets realized, the better game writing output will be, and the better the game experience will be for players.

And yes, there is hope. When I started doing my roundtables in the mid-2000s, the professional issues people raised were stark. Writers were not being involved at the start of projects. Nobody was hiring more than one writer. Writers were not being sent to recording sessions, where they could do on-the-spot fixes to improve quality. The list of problems was long.

The good news is that today, for all of the ongoing problems, those original issues have largely been addressed. Progress has been made. We're in the room and in the recording studio more often than not. It's a series of wins.

Now, the people attending the roundtables have all new issues to discuss and address, because those first few vital goals have largely been achieved. With time, hopefully more will be as well.

In the meantime, though, you still need to fight like hell. All of us do.

17

How They Will Try to Screw You

17.1 Overview

There are a lot of times when being a game writer is not fun. There are frustrations that are largely unique to the role, and they come at you from all directions. Knowing that they are out there helps to a certain extent, but it only goes so far.

There is, after all, a reason I titled this book what I did, and that is because on a lot of levels the game development industry really does hate game writers. Note that I did not say "game developers" are the ones doing the hating. The vast majority of the literally thousands of developers I have worked with over the years around the world have been cool, fun, nice people who bore me no ill will and who were generally pretty great to hang out with after the figurative whistle blew. They showed interest in my work and were supportive of the efforts my fellow writers and I made to make the game better.

No, it's the industry that hates game writers, and it is set up in a way to perpetuate that hatred. The production model that we have, particularly on bigger-budget games, is particularly constructed in a way that makes writers' lives harder, devalues their contribution, and prevents them from doing their best work. It grinds down egos, frequently asks the impossible, and shows little or no respect for the work that they do.

That, in my book, is pretty much the definition of professional hate.

And I don't blame most of the people who perpetuate this. In a lot of cases, asking them to realize this is what they are doing is like trying to get a fish to understand the concept of being wet. They've been doing things this way for long enough that it's invisible to them, and knocking them out of that orbit can be difficult and professionally risky. There are very few game writers – I can think of maybe a half dozen – who can go into a studio head's office and say, "You're doing it wrong," and then come out still employed.

So we put up with it. We learn to cope, we find workarounds, and we win small victories where we can. That absolutely doesn't mean we have to like it or accept it. The whole problem is not going to get itself solved in one fell swoop. There are too many aspects and too many angles and too many years of ingrained habits to change. Maybe, though, by taking it apart, we can look at smaller battles to fight and possibly win and thus drive things forward one step at a time.

DOI: 10.1201/9781003592983-17

17.2 What's Going On?

Let's start at the beginning. As noted in the last chapter, one of the most common obstacles game writers face is the superior who is not a writer but who thinks they are. This person may be nice. They may be well-meaning. They may accurately spot deficiencies in the writing team or in the deliverables that need to be addressed. But their method of addressing it is to pick up the pen themselves, which is destructive on numerous levels.

There is, of course, the obvious: People who are not good at a job should not be doing the job. The odds are very good that someone on a gaming development team who is doing another job, especially at a very high level, is not good at writing because their professional development has been focused elsewhere. It is not impossible, but it is exceedingly rare for someone to ascend Olympus with professional-grade writing chops as a side hustle. The smart money bets the other way.

And even if by some miracle the Creative Director or whoever has writing skills, their focus should genuinely be on the game as a whole, not your specific area. There are plenty of other departments that are inevitably having their own issues that will require their attention, but writing disproportionately draws hawk-like scrutiny that demands personal involvement on a granular level.

What results is almost always a problem. If the higher-up does indeed insist on writing, the writing team is now forced to deal with what is most likely verbiage that is not up to snuff. Because it is imposed from the outside of the writing process, it will most likely not be well integrated into the rest of the writing. Because it is dropped from a great height, editing or revising it becomes a political question as much as a craft one – do YOU want to be the one to tell the Creative Director that their stuff is crap and risk your career as a result? On the other hand, letting it go unchallenged reinforces the bad logic behind its creation and leads to more of the same down the road.

And that's if you even do get a chance to look at it. Sometimes it gets bolted straight into the recording script without passing Go, collecting $200, or being checked for basic competence and accuracy. The end result is generally not good.

The levels of interference vary. Sometimes they will make script notes where they want to tussle to the death over a specific word choice. Sometimes they will offer material, unsolicited, that you are expected to make work. Sometimes they will fail in their actual task, which is to provide actionable feedback, and instead say it is easier to rewrite to get what they want. All of these make your job harder as a writer and make the writing worse.

Unfortunately, there is often very little you can do about something like this. Obviously, people in positions of creative authority on a team can and should express their opinions on the writing as it comes along, and no sensible professional writer would ever object to that. But thinking they can do your job on top of their own and do it better than you? That's fantasy, one that makes the writing worse while robbing the rest of the team of that person's time that they spent doing your task instead of focusing on their assigned tasks elsewhere.

Underlying this is the fact that many decision makers do not understand how writing works or the benefits it provides, and they do not understand that they do not understand, and on top of that, they do not see this as a problem. It comes down to a word-based version of the Dunning-Kruger effect. They think, because they use words every day, they know how to use them professionally.

This is the same sort of logic that leads 6% of American men to think they could beat a 1,700-pound grizzly bear in hand-to-paw combat because they won a schoolyard fight in fifth grade. Most people know their way around a kitchen enough to make a grilled cheese sandwich; very few of them would equate themselves to professional chefs as a result. There is a failure to understand that while the basics of using words are one thing, doing so on a professional level to achieve specific effects with delicacy and precision is something else entirely. It requires training and practice and all the sorts of things that go into any skilled profession.

The difference is, people look at art, for example, and don't think they can do that. This is in part because of the barrier to entry put up by specialized software and techniques, and in part because it's pretty damn easy to tell if a piece of art, be it a texture or a character model or a level, looks like the thing it is supposed to. Most of what is jokingly referred to as "engineer art" or "designer art" is, honestly, crap. And there's nothing wrong with that – it's intended to be a placeholder, with the explicit understanding that the grownups are going to come along any minute now and replace it with something better.

The same goes for code, or audio, or animation. There is a clear understanding that what the professionals in those arenas do is, in fact, the work of highly trained professionals, and that, as such, the work in question is best left to said professionals. In all my years in the industry, I have never seen senior project management look at, say, a character model they didn't like and immediately go to work on the asset instead of communicating their feedback.

Yet that respect often does not get extended to writers or writing. Instead, there is the relentless drumbeat of "it's just words," as if words were purely weightless and easy. Nobody says "It's just art" or "It's just code." On the other hand, with writers, there's an implicit "there is nothing special about what you do," even when the evidence points heavily the other way.

The flip side of this, of course, is that people are very quick to jump on writing they don't like. They often don't pull punches when they do it, either. But that's all they've got. They're rarely good at saying why something is bad or what target isn't getting hit. They bring out the knives instead.

Understand this, too: There is a world of difference between "Bad" and either "Not what I wanted" or "Not what I expected," but the chances are you're not going to hear it.

Actual bad, a good chunk of the time, is bad. Maybe the writing's not in character voice and is jarring as a result. Maybe it's overwritten, or too wordy, or too long for the time or screen real estate allotted. Maybe it's ungrammatical or uses words incorrectly. Whatever the case, if it's bad or even "not as good as it could be," "why it is bad" deserves to be called out cleanly and clearly to allow the issues to be addressed. There is absolutely nothing wrong with bad writing being identified as such. No one's stuff is pure, unvarnished gold 100% of the time. Every writer should be humbly ready to have their inevitable mistakes identified so they can fix things before the words meet the player.

"Bad," though, can be awfully subjective. Without a "*why* it is bad," it feels like personal preference, if not a personal attack, instead.

Because "Bad" is the catchall word for all sorts of disapproval, and a lot of times it is the wrong one.

There is nothing wrong with a lead or a Director saying, "This is not what I wanted," to a deliverable. That should be a starting point, though, a place from which what was wanted instead gets described. It becomes slightly more problematic if there was never any indication of what was wanted given before writing started. It gets painful if there was an unverbalized expectation that was not met despite never having been given voice. And it gets downright ugly if a certain direction – or freedom of action – was given only to be rescinded, overwritten, or erased from the conversation.

That takes us into the territory of "Not what I expected," which is often code for "Why did you not read my mind?" If expectations are set, they have to be communicated. Otherwise, the only way they can be reached is blind luck. Expecting writers to be psychic, to win the age-old game of "I'm thinking of a deliverable, no, that's not it," is wasteful in the extreme. All it does is serve to reinforce the power dynamic and put another negative mark in the ledger.

As always, it comes down to simple communication. People in positions to expect deliverables need to communicate the requirements and expectations they have to allow them to be created in timely and professional fashion. Punishing writers for not being able to go full Charles Xavier produces nothing good. Not good team dynamics, not trust in leadership, not good writing.

Nothing.

Then there's the question of self-fulfilling prophecy. Team and studio leadership that goes into a project thinking writing is always bad is not going to support the writing because, after all, why spend precious money on something that's going to be bad, right? This leads to writing (and narrative as a whole) not getting the resource, support, and time it needs to achieve a level of polish equivalent to the rest of the game. Then, when the game releases, the undercooked writing stands out in contrast to the rest of the assets. The gaming media jumps on it and calls out the writing as bad. And the people who helped create the problem in the first place feel justified for having done it in the first place.

It's an incredibly difficult cycle to break, particularly if it has gone on for several iterations. You are not going to change the minds of people who can point to the desolation of their own creation and say, "See?" The best hope there is for someone new to come in, if not at the decision-making level, then at least at a high enough level that they can successfully champion writing in the face of the headwinds of opposition.

On a less elevated level, there are coworkers who will not be on your side. They may not like writing, thinking it takes away from gameplay. Maybe they resent having to collaborate with writers and thus rein in their creativity that little bit, claiming that the writers are trying to tell them what to do. (Note: Don't tell them what to do. Have a respectful conversation instead.) They may even simply ignore your approved work, and, unless there are consequences for doing so, they will then feel empowered to keep on doing it.

Fighting this means checking in early and often to make sure they're not trying to sneak something through. This cuts off the "it's too late to change it" excuse at the knees. Also, if you call something out on a dev level and changes don't happen, you should elevate it to a lead and producer level and let them lead the charge.

This speaks to a larger truth, incidentally: You should not feel like you are alone on the team. A lot of projects do shove writers off into a corner, intentionally or otherwise, but you cannot survive, much less thrive, under those circumstances. In order to endure, you need to reach out and build bridges on multiple levels. You need a good relationship with your producer, making sure they know what you do so they can champion you to the rest of the team. You need good relationships with fellow team members on your level, letting you inform and support each other's work. And once you demonstrate the value of what you are doing and how it benefits them, too, you'll have allies on the team, making it that much harder to isolate and dismiss you. If you can build a relationship with someone on the Director level, even better, though beware of the politics of what is called "skip-level." You don't want to be seen as bypassing the chain of command or leapfrogging team members. Doing this will breed resentment among those who think they got sidestepped.

Building allies, though, does not mean setting yourself on fire so someone else can make s'mores. Remember that you are under absolutely no obligation to make excuses for, enable, or assist people who are screwing you. This includes both people who are actively working to make your job harder and those who are disinterested in doing the things they should that will save you pain. Both types, unfortunately, can be found in the game development world.

Writers are in a precarious position on a team. We are often viewed as the most expendable team members and the ones most easily replaced. We are also bullied with labels like "precious," "artiste," and "not a team player," all of which result in a very head-down approach to a lot of stuff that goes on that shouldn't. Very few writers want to risk rocking the boat and getting retaliated against as a result by team members with longer tenures, more secure roles, and friends in high places. People simply don't feel safe calling out bad behavior.

As a result, most writers seek to avoid making waves. The approach gets internalized, and pretty soon, you're making excuses for the people who make your professional life worse. I've heard "Oh, they were busy" far too many times to explain why another department skipped a step in the process that would have involved writing or why a deliverable that kept writers bottlenecked was late. Rest assured, on those same teams the same leniency was not necessarily extended to the writing staff.

There is a constant stream of reasons either coming from writers or coming from the folks who screwed writers and then picked up and parroted by the writers themselves as to why it's fine that writing got hosed. That doesn't benefit anyone, even the ones starting the cycle of bull. The assets that come out of this are generally subpar because it's short-term cover for incompetence or laziness. Alas, it's surprisingly effective too much of the time.

Even worse than making excuses is actively helping them. Picking up tasks they half-assed and then dumped is a too-common occurrence. Written assets going out the door as Marketing text or social media posts or blog content without getting a writer's eye on it – and a fact check for content – is a regular thing, too. Then there's the ever-popular "This is an emergency and we need it now!" maneuver, which too often is the result of someone else waiting until the last minute because, of course, you'll bail them out.

All of these inevitably turn into you having to scramble to turn their grit into a pearl. Whether it's doing an emergency rewrite with a deadline bearing down in a matter of minutes or finding errors in something that went out and engineering a fix that others didn't even know they needed, it frequently falls on the writer to step in, step up, and deliver.

This is not a healthy professional relationship. It should not be encouraged. People who fail to meet their deliverables and professional obligations need to be called out on it, or they will keep doing it. Without consequences, they have no reason to stop, and they may indeed be encouraged to press the advantage.

The more they do it, the worse your professional life will get, and that will be bad in all sorts of ways. It will shift blame onto you. It will shift extra work onto you. It will make their lack of planning your emergency time and again. It will, ultimately, wear you down and make it harder and harder to get out of the bad situation as this diminishes you professionally.

If you see yourself in this sort of cycle, break it as quickly as you can. If the ask comes your way, answer but loop your lead and your producer in on the response. This stuff thrives in silence. If they're violating an agreed-on process, call that out by quoting old emails or Teams chats or whatever. Do not give them wiggle room. Do not let them justify. And most of all, don't fight this fight alone. Get your producer involved from the get-go, because it's their job to make sure your deliverables are solid, and this is hurting that. Document every interaction, and keep receipts.

Above all, though, stop participating. Yes, it may be tempting to play nice if someone fails you to avoid looking like the villain. You don't want to go over the top right off the bat. Remember, as easy as it is to make excuses and roll over, it will get that much harder with each succeeding incidence. Don't. If you catch yourself making excuses, stop. The people relying on you to clean up their messes need to take responsibility. If you find yourself anticipating the next emergency because it's *always* an emergency, get ahead of that. Poke the people in question about their progress early and often and publicly. Don't let them guilt you with "It's for the good of the game!" because if it was that important, they would have taken care of their responsibilities, too.

17.3 Value Your Work

This leads to another trap that you may get led into: Not valuing your work.

Your work is worth something. It comes from the unique place of your talent and your expertise and your skill and your experience. It has intrinsic value because of that, and it has value because of the need it fills for the game.

There will be those who try to tell you, though, that it is worthless, and as a result they should get it for free. That your time and effort are worthless, too. That, after all, is the whole faulty logic behind generative AI, that writing is a problem to be solved and not a process to create something more than a checked box. Don't listen to them. Put a price on your time. If they want you to add a little something to your workload, turn around and demand it be put into the production schedule to make sure you get credit for the work. If they ask for writing but don't want you to bill the hours, tell them it's pay to play. They wouldn't dare ask an engineer to code for free. They shouldn't dare ask you.

Put a price on your time and your work, then. If someone wants you to do a contract gig, value your time when you give them a price. It's too easy to undersell and undervalue yourself because the industry trains writers to think our time isn't worth that much. Shake that off and give yourself credit, and with credit, give yourself a decent hourly rate. You can always reduce it if you have to in negotiation to lock down the gig, but trust me, you are not going to be able to negotiate up.

The same goes, incidentally, for time spent giving lectures or doing chats or whatever else. If you want to do one out of the goodness of your heart, that's generous and kind of you. Just keep track of how many hours you're giving away doing that. Understand that doing this comes with a cost, because you could be doing something else with your time besides giving your knowledge away for free.

I know, I'm a fine one to talk. I do a ton of freebie work and chats with students and judge student contests and whatever else. But I do so with my eyes open, knowing the trade I'm making in exchange for the thing that benefits me: Developing the craft of what we all do. I am very lucky in that I am in a position to do more of that than some, largely because I don't sleep much, but even so, it's a conscious choice that has been carefully weighed. You owe it to yourself to do the same. Only give away what you can afford to. Don't promise the time you need for yourself. There is no absolute goal to be met, only what puts you into a good place. Too much can be as harmful as too little, as you burn yourself out, overload yourself, and maybe even start to resent the people who are taking up your time.

Which can be a little unfair. After all, each of them maybe thinks they are only asking for an hour. What they don't realize is that a half dozen other people asked for an hour, too, and wham, that's another workday added to your docket. It's up to you to value and protect your time in a way that works best for you.

Finally, you have to be proud of your work and your skills. There are people with vested interests in belittling your contribution. From the credit thieves to the jealous wannabes who would kill to have your job, from the people who don't think your work deserves the time and resources to be done well to the people who think they can do it better than you, from the coworkers who resist collaboration to the folks who don't give you what you need to do your job, they all work to make your life harder and your work worse. Understand that they are out there and that you will have to deal with them. Even if the vast majority of developers are good people who want to make good games, there is a chance of snakes in the garden and worms in the apple.

As long as you know that, you can look out for them and take steps to protect yourself. Just remember that nobody has your best interests in mind more than you do, and relying on others to take care of you without acting to take care of yourself is to invite disaster.

17.4 The Lying Game

A lot of the stuff in this chapter is about stuff that maybe happens through ignorance or misunderstanding or ego. It's certainly bad and certainly wrong, but not all of it comes from a place of greed or malice.

But sometimes, they lie to you, and you have to be ready for that.

They will tell you to do things, and then when you do them, they will swear they never asked for you to do it in the first place. Then, you will be the one to get in trouble for wasting time and money.

They will offer you projects that will be urgent and exciting and cool, and then when it's time for support, silence will suddenly descend. When it lifts, either the project in question will have been canceled ages ago without telling you, or it will have been handed to someone else without telling you, or they might even claim that it never existed in the first place and that you're hallucinating the whole thing.

That is, if you even get an answer. I have seen projects vanish into the carnivorous mists multiple times, never to be seen or even referenced again. Some of them were transmedia projects. Some were game pitches. All of them I had been specifically directed to write up pitches or even full scripts for. All of them, I had been told, were vitally important.

Then, poof.

At times like that, it's best not to chase after phantoms. If they disappeared your work, nothing you can do will resurrect it. Continued pursuit of something the higher-ups clearly do not wish to discuss any further is not going to do you or the work any good. Chalk the lost time up to skills development or suchlike and move on. In the meantime, I would absolutely never suggest keeping a copy to prove you did it in the first place and, if appropriate, filing the serial numbers off and slapping on a fresh coat of paint in order to present it to a different audience.

I'm not going to go into stuff like gaslighting because that can happen to anyone and isn't writer-specific. The painful truth is that at some point in your career someone is going to lie to you. It might not be out of malice, as they might be making up an excuse as to why a deliverable is late or why they've failed to turn around feedback on something you wrote. Or, maybe you've presented them with an issue they don't want to face for whatever reason, and therefore they will come up with all sorts of spurious logic to avoid having to make a decision they don't want to. Maybe they're busy and forgot that they never said the thing to you they wanted to say to you, which is OK as long as they don't insist they said it to you.

Folks who do these sorts of things can sometimes be talked around to a better place. Leading with "You lied!" may be cathartic, but it puts the other person on the defensive in a way that makes ultimate benefit unlikely. As tempting as it is to seek vengeance, you can do yourself more harm than good. It's far better to start with "I'm sorry, I don't remember that conversation. Could you refresh my memory?" and allow a graceful recovery that doesn't make you the object of embarrassed wrath.

Then again, there are the people who either don't care or are actively trying to harm you. They will lie about what you said or didn't say. They will ascribe motives to your work that you never dreamed of. They will steal your work if they think it's worth their while, erase your contribution completely, and lie about their having cooked it up in the first place. Often, the people who do this do it a lot and thus are very good at it. They have friends who will back them up and possibly patrons higher up who will cover for them. They will have planned for this and put resources in place, and they will have anticipated your responses because they've seen it all before. Trying to fight them with something as primitive as the truth is not bringing a knife to a gunfight; it's bringing a spork to an artillery duel.

Normally, there are things you can do to protect yourself from this. Keep receipts, emails, and chat logs. Make sure you know your company's retention policies, as they might routinely delete older emails or threads. If a conversation is face-to-face or doesn't get recorded online, write up notes and send them around to confirm what was agreed upon and discussed. Less malicious types may be open to correction when presented with evidence, and while more malicious ones may not care, there's a reasonable chance HR might if it comes to that. And of course, there's always the old-school option of printing everything out and making sure you have secure hardcopies of everything.

Honestly, though, if you find yourself dealing with someone like that, make your plans and pull the ripcord as soon as possible. There is no long-term benefit to working with people who do that. They will take the best you make in order to profit from it themselves and leave you out in the cold, or worse. Respect yourself and your work, and go find someplace that will do the same.

18

Raising Up the Next Generation and Keeping the Old One from Fossilizing

18.1 Overview

It is trendy to say things like "No one entering the game industry now needs to hear anything from anyone over [insert arbitrary age here]." On the surface, it's a bold statement of intent because clearly the old have nothing to offer except outdated views and lessons on how to yell at clouds.

And yet . . .

The industry I joined in 1999 is dead. So, too, are the one I worked in during the 2000s and the one in the 2010s. I have seen emergent gameplay decried as boring because it lacked spectacle, and I have seen it trumpeted as the ultimate goal of video games. I have seen the rise and fall and semi-rise of the silent protagonist. I have seen PC gaming declared dead about six separate times, and I have seen single-player games declared dead equally as often.

There has been change and growth and, yes, death. Things have moved in cycles, and things have disappeared forever. That's how it goes. The thing is, though, that each succeeding iteration of the industry is built on the mistakes, successes, and painstakingly acquired learnings of the one before.

18.2 What Has Gone Before

Does everything old apply in perfect congruence to what has come after? Of course not. My first video game project had a team of roughly 15 people, and there was worry at the studio that it was maybe too large. These days we're making games that can take the better part of a decade to make, using upwards of a thousand devs and requiring budgets creeping ever closer to a billion dollars. Trying to cram a giant of a game into best practices designed for a team the size of a small regional high school's baseball team is insanity.

More to the point, no one is trying to do that, regardless of how many straw man arguments to that effect are made. Where there is worth, however, is in taking those old lessons and seeing what can be extracted from them that could be applicable today. And again, these aren't intended to be constraints. These are intended to be pieces of information that can be picked up and adapted to new circumstances.

They are not bibles or holy writ; they are folk wisdom and tools. The wheel does not need to constantly be reinvented. Older lessons, hard-earned, can still hold true. And they can be used as the building blocks for the new lessons that grow out of new forms of game writing from new voices using new technology.

DOI: 10.1201/9781003592983-18

In that spirit, it is right and proper for those of us who have experience to share it with those coming up behind us. This is not to say that we should be imposing strict regulation and demanding faithful imitation. We made mistakes. We worked on different sorts of games, with different demands and different needs. It simply doesn't map perfectly, nor should we expect it to.

What we can and must do, however, is refine what we have learned in order to pass it on. We need to examine our experiences and extract the stuff that remains cogent, that can help make writing better even if it originated in a game from – God forbid – 2016. We should not expect or want disciples who will carry on our approaches unthinkingly. We need to use what we know to empower our artistic heirs, who can then take up the craft we have embraced and helped evolve in a way that they can then make it theirs.

They're going to do things we can't imagine, just like we've crafted things that would have been deemed impossible by those before us. We are links in a chain that leads into the future, and we need to ensure that every link is strong.

18.3 Why Help Others Up?

The cynic will ask, "What's in it for me?" They might see this as training up their eventual replacement. The selfish temptation to climb the ladder, then kick it over so no one can climb up after you, is real and all too prevalent.

It's also a bad, short-sighted idea.

If you are a senior writer on a team with younger or less experienced writers, there is a very good chance that, at least at the beginning, they are not as good at the job as you are. This means they can do less work, and that their work is going to need more attention from you, which means less time you spend writing. Investing time in less experienced writers to help them improve makes your life easier, because it's generally going to make them better. If they write better, they can be trusted to do more and more complicated tasks. If they write better, that also means you have to spend less time giving feedback because there's going to be less feedback to give, and that gives you more time to write your stuff. And finally, if they write better, the writing as a whole is going to be better, which means more praise for the writing from fans, media, and influencers, and that makes you look good.

There are secondary benefits as well. Professional trees are very much a thing. The folks you help today are the leads of tomorrow, and they might be the ones asking you to do a consulting gig or noting your influence on social media. That in turn makes you a little bit of a hotter property, and someone more junior may seek you out in a way that elevates your name.

And then there's the last one. We are here, one and all, because we love games. We want good games to play. The more we do our job in terms of training up those coming up behind us, the better the games they will make, and that, too, is part of our professional legacy.

Also, it means we'll have more fun, and that's always nice.

18.4 How to Help

How do you do it?

Start by being honest with yourself. Look back at your CV and think about what you learned, good or bad, in each game. Maybe there was a great takeaway, like I got with Sand Guy on *Far Cry*. Maybe there was a negative lesson, something you tried but now know to avoid. Extract that and then expose the next generation to those gems.

Giving conference talks and posting videos or LinkedIn screeds is one way to do this, sure. Another is talking. If you've got juniors on your team, make your knowledge available. Tell stories. When giving feedback, drop in wider advice than how to fix a specific line, and give context for it if that helps. Make yourself available as an approachable resource. You don't want to turn into Grampa Simpson, but the occasional "Oh yeah, we ran into something like this on another project I did, and this is how we solved it" can go a long way toward avoiding wasted time.

Don't lock everyone into your nostalgia trip, but do make your past experience accessible. Offer up what you can in bite-sized chunks so they can pick and choose what might work for them, and don't try to force anything. Yes, if you're a lead or a Director, sometimes you want to mandate approaches that you know will provide optimum results. But there's a gap between that and "Do it this way because that's how we used to do it in the Aughts, young whippersnapper."

You might also want to generate, if you have the authority and bandwidth, exercises to train up certain skills that you've shared. Practice can be useful, especially if it's shared with other team members. This allows everyone to bounce off everyone else. These are also ways people can learn without necessitating you sitting there with them, investing your time directly.

If you get the chance, you should take the opportunity to introduce people to the wider professional community. There is tremendous value to be gained in making people feel like they belong and that the people whose work they have perhaps admired are now their peers. That opens a plethora of doors, from asking questions of people who were previously seen as unapproachable, to helping with job hunts or finding new hires, to having someone to talk to about the job who gets it. Professional support is invaluable. Community is, too, when it comes to slaying the dragon of impostor syndrome that lies in wait for us all.

Dig into your mental (and electronic, and oh my goodness, actual paper) files. Find the good stuff. Dust it off and share it in a way that people will listen, picking it up and running with it themselves. And bring them into the wider professional world to help them keep growing beyond what you can offer.

18.5 Mentoring

When it comes to the transmission of knowledge, there's nothing that beats direct mentoring. This goes for passing the knowledge both ways. Establishing a clear, direct relationship with a formal, agreed-on goal is a great way to build a comfortable way to share what you know and what you want to learn.

Not every mentorship has to be a result of a workplace interaction. If you are in a place where there's a team with writers younger than you, you should actively seek out the time and resources to mentor them. If you are on a team with writers senior to you, you should actively seek out the time for them to mentor you. Making this a formal part of the work relationship allows you to explore more broadly applicable topics as well as stuff directly related to current deliverables. It allows for playing the long game, looking at stuff needed in six months, and laying the groundwork for tackling them effectively now.

Also, it's of benefit to the company if they'll allow it. Supporting formal mentorship is the sort of career development a writer rarely gets, and having something like that in place is attractive to talent on both ends of the relationship.

However, if you're a senior who wants to share knowledge, you don't have to stop at the office door, virtual or otherwise. If you maintain a social media presence as a game writer, there is a non-zero chance that students and young game writers will approach you for advice. I always try to respond as long as the approaches are reasonable and respectful of my time and expertise. You don't need to spend your time on someone who wants to have all the secrets poured in their ear so they can claim expertise without effort. Reasonable requests and well-thought-out questions can always be fruitful prompts for discussion.

That's informal. There are more formal ways to seek out someone to mentor. The IGDA can be a method of making connections, whether on the national/international level or at a local chapter. Similarly, local game jams or college game dev programs or clubs can also be things to reach out to if you want to share your knowledge. You may have to make the first approach, strolling around the floor at a game jam or reaching out to the school and offering your time. Smart students and schools will jump at the chance. It's sometimes a difficult fit with universities, as very few game development degree programs offer much in the way of writing classes, but hopefully you're a good enough writer to craft a persuasive email.

You can also even step outside the formal game development world. I have given workshops at conferences, conventions, and educational settings, teaching the basics of game writing to writers and interested individuals from other fields. Some of the attendees have even gone on to embrace game writing professionally. Find people who want to learn, and teach them.

Don't think you have to be a wizened elder to do this. Even if you've only been in the business a year or two, you know more than folks who haven't cracked the code yet. Share what you feel confident sharing in a mentorship context, and never be afraid to say, "I don't know" or "That's something I haven't dealt with." The knowledge you *can* transmit is still invaluable, particularly if you don't leaven it with guesses or hearsay.

There is a secondary benefit to mentoring someone. Those relationships tend to endure. The junior you teach today inevitably goes on to another company and maybe starts doing some mentoring of their own there. Through your work, you've built up a professional peer group and watched your knowledge get passed down through professional generations. That's doing some real good that goes beyond you and into the wider community.

18.6 But Wait, There's More!

That's all fine, but there's a sneaky second upside here. Just as juniors can learn from you, you can and should learn from them.

Because if you don't, you're going to fossilize. What you know will get steadily less and less applicable, and you will become steadily less relevant in turn. Your hard-earned knowledge is great, but if you intend to remain professionally active, you need to keep adding fresh stuff to it.

The best source of current knowledge is those very people you're trying to elevate. They have a very different perspective on things than us olds, or even not-so-olds, do. They play differently than old-timers like me did or do. They're looking for different experiences. They want different types of characters and challenges. Different things in games (and out of them) are important to them, from customization options to the way they share their experiences.

And you need to know all this stuff if you want to keep making content that they are going to want.

A good approach is to try talking to them. Listen. Let them show you. Ask what they're playing and why, and then try it yourself. You may suck at it, but at least you have the experience to share and understand. Talk to them about games, and their perspectives, which will vary wildly from yours. Find out their professional ambitions and how they plan to achieve them.

All of this is going to help you. It's going to keep your game dev brain far more limber than it might be otherwise. It's going to keep your conversation and your approaches fresh because you're feeding them something new. You're going to see innovation you'd miss if you stuck to your same old, same old. And you might even pick up a little excitement at the idea that, yes, we are all getting paid to make games from those to whom it is still new.

One of my annual projects is running the Student Game Narrative Analysis Competition for the Game Narrative Summit at GDC. Participants are asked to submit a narrative analysis of any video game of their choice, and the winners get to do poster sessions at the Summit.

A lot of students enter. I am the lone judge. I have to score a whole lot of entries. And I wouldn't change a thing, because every year I get a jolt of energy from doing this. Reading their papers, I learn about games I've never heard of, let alone played. I get to read their takes on classics of the form and cutting edge, coming from a place that I've never been and can never go. I get a crash course in what's important to them in game writing, year over year. In short, I learn, and I am better at doing my job after doing the judging than I was before it.

For this, I am grateful.

It can be hard admitting that you don't have all the answers or that the answers you do have no longer apply. At the same time, it can also be liberating, opening you up to new knowledge and approaches that will reinvigorate your work. That's a trade-off worth making, and always will be.

19

Building Your Name, Keeping Your Credits

19.1 Overview

In the end, all you really have as a game writer are two things: Your credits list and the actual texts you created. They are the proof of what you have worked on, the documentation of your professional path. They are also what will help get you jobs, speaking engagements, consulting gigs, and the like. They are the bulk of your professional bio and the easiest way to garner respect from people reading those bios. They define your body of work, and ideally, they should be able to speak for themselves.

19.2 Acquiring Your Work

Documents can be problematic to obtain. Most companies are very protective of their development documents, even for games that are over a decade old. As a result, having legal access to your work is sometimes iffy, though the fact that there's so much game content available on YouTube softens that blow a bit. I may not be able to show someone the script document for the hoary beast that is *Splinter Cell: Conviction*, but I can sure as hell feed them a dozen links of highlighted scenes full of witty banter.

If you are on good terms with an employer, you should ask if you can keep script documents and the like as portfolio samples. This is especially important for a game that doesn't ship, as odds are that work will not be available as a video elsewhere. If the project (or the studio) is going down the drain, it is worth a shot to ask if you can take home stuff that isn't otherwise going to get used. They'll probably say no, but they don't always, and it's not like you have anything to lose at that point.

If you're engaged in ongoing employment, on the other hand, you need to be careful about the ask. Studio leadership may well see it as a precursor to jumping ship, even if you're just building your personal archive. If you go this route, make sure you are very sure the person you are asking understands why you are asking, and set the parameters of what you are asking for very clearly. If it's text assets like a cinematics script, you stand a better chance than you might asking for full cinematics renders.

If they say no, you don't have many options. One popular move is to grab the documents anyway, then rewrite them in a way that changes the names, places, etc. Enough that they can't be traced. Other folks will find YouTube videos of their work and painstakingly transcribe them, rebuilding their assets on their own. Then there are the folks who gamble that what they do will never get back to their employers and copy scripts wholesale. I do not recommend doing the last in particular for obvious legal reasons, but I can't stop you, and I'm not going to try.

DOI: 10.1201/9781003592983-19

Once you have scripts and other documents for your portfolio, you want to pick the best bits to show off your skills. Again, there are no absolutes. Tailor the pieces you include in a given iteration of your portfolio to the role you are applying for. Not every game wants to see the biggest and loudest thing in your arsenal. Some want to see character moments. Some want to see stuff that's in their genre.

Pick and choose. Just be sure to be surgical when picking and choosing. You want to pick things that make their point quickly and immediately. Including a script for a seven-minute cut scene is asking HR reps to do more reading than they are probably willing to do. And, if you have a choice between a script sample from something that was a hit and something that wasn't, the hit is often the better choice. The more people who see your sample and get a positive hit of recognition, the better.

But that leaves credits, and credits are tricky.

19.3 Securing Your Credits

In many cases, you will have to fight for your credits. People will take any excuse, particularly if there is a bonus involved, to downplay your work or claim it for their own. People steal credits. People say they did work they did not do. People say you did not do work that you did, and the lie gets posted on industry credits sites before the truth gets out of bed in the morning.

The most important thing is, of course, to make sure you are credited appropriately for your work. In a fair and just world, this would happen automatically. In that same fair and just world, we would all have pet unicorns that poop rainbows. Hence, it falls on each of us to be vigilant in protecting our own good names professionally.

What that means on the ground is this: If you are a contractor, negotiate your credit before signing a contract. If your role changes during production, renegotiate to accurately reflect your new level of contribution. Do not think that folks will take care of it for you because it is the right thing to do. They may forget. They may dislike you and want to make you look worse than you are. They may not understand the full scope of your contribution and need to have it spelled out for them (with receipts). Do not sleep comfortably until your proper credit is assured ***in writing***.

If you are in-house, it gets trickier. There are formal processes in place at a lot of studios – your job title is X, you get X credit – but these often don't reflect the realities of development. Again, building bridges with your producer types and keeping them updated on what you are doing minute to minute can go a long way. Because when the game comes out and you are listed as "Dialog Assistance" for a game you wrote the entirety of, it's too late.

Particularly damning is the habit many studios have of stripping the credits of team members who left the project before ship. It doesn't matter how much they might have contributed to the game; the second they depart, they get bumped over to "Special Thanks," or worse. Tons of good work gets functionally erased from the record this way, leaving the people who did it without recourse.

Credits, therefore, are slippery things. Many studios will double-check a writer's claimed credits against the game they are claiming credit on, but as has been seen, even the shipped credits of a game can lie. There are plenty of people out there eager to claim credit for work they did not do to slide into opportunities they may not quite deserve. And there are people who are quite happy to take credits away from you that you worked hard for.

19.4 Defending Your Credits

Warning you against credit thieves may sound like paranoia, but I assure you, it is not. In my role as an advisor to the Game Narrative Summit, I was once asked to review a talk pitch from a guy claiming to have written a certain game. Which was fine, except that I had actually written that game, was the only writer on it, and had never heard of this person. Another game I made massive contributions to, I was credited as "additional writing" because since my hours had been billed a certain way, I was not officially "on the project." They were, however, quite willing to use my work. I have even been given credit in conversation and online resources for games I had absolutely nothing to do with and which I had no intention of claiming credit for. I shot that down quickly, because there's very little percentage in being called out for stuff other people did.

Don't let any of that happen to you. Guard your credits and your contributions like a dragon on its hoard. Because, and this is the sad truth, no one else will.

In practical terms, that means a few things. Beyond checking and double-checking your credits in the game you are working on, make a habit of making regular stops to view your credits lists on various professional sites. Make sure they are up-to-date and accurate. If something's not right, dispute it if you can. Keep evidence of everything you've done and worked on in a way that won't get you in legal trouble.

Don't stop there, though. Collect testimonials from coworkers who were there and saw what you did and plaster them across your social media and job site profiles as appropriate. Don't be afraid to claim credits you deserve but never got on your resume. Just a parenthetical "Uncredited" can suffice to stake your claim, or at least open a conversation.

You owe it to yourself and your work to claim every credit you deserve. Now, you may have credits in your personal history that you don't want to show off because the games in question were terrible. That's fine. It is not mandatory to give a complete accounting of missteps on a document specifically designed to make you look good. I always made a habit of never mentioning [redacted] and [redacted's redacted: redacted redacted] when putting myself out there. If someone asked, I wasn't going to lie, but you want to lead with your best, not your worst.

And honestly, even the worst game you worked on that shipped is still a shipped title. Working on a clunker is a rite of passage for a lot of devs, and the fact that you survived the entire production cycle even on a game that was a flaming bag of poo is to your credit.

As for games that don't ship, those count, too. How you list it on a resume can vary depending on whether it was announced or not. If the title was announced but never shipped, claim the announced title. If it wasn't, you shouldn't use the internal name for it because no one is going to know what the heck you are talking about. You are, however, perfectly within your rights to note "Unannounced Title" as what you were doing for a two-year stretch that is otherwise barren of employment.

The point is to get recognized for the work you did.

19.5 Building Your Rep

Hand in hand with building a credits list is building your professional reputation. You do this with credits, of course, but that's far from the only way.

The truth of the matter is that these days, as a game writer, you also have to be your own marketing department. It is conclusive actual-proof-of-Nessie rare. It is unusual for a company to promote one of their writers in these dark times, unless that writer was a pre-existing celebrity whose fanbase they hope to tap. The chances of them propping you up in front of cameras for interviews, sending you on press junkets (on the rare occasions when those happen), or otherwise promoting you as a key figure are small. After all, doing that builds your value. That means they might have to pay you more or lose you to a competitor.

To paraphrase a notable movie bad guy, you have to do it yourself. Some of it you can accomplish on your own; some you will need permission and possibly support for. But it helps to shotgun blast all possibilities out there, because the more eyeballs and ears you hit, the more people will know you and your work. The more people know you, the more you will be talked about and referenced, too. That pays off down the road.

Social media is the place to start. Figure out what you are most comfortable doing, whether it be streaming, writing blog posts, posting on social media sites, doing a podcast, or some combination thereof. The important thing is to have a clear identity in the way you present yourself and then to provide regular content. This establishes your personal brand and builds an audience that comes to expect, anticipate, and share your content. Focusing on writing is a good base, but finding your own unique spin on it or area of expertise can help you stand out.

Speaking engagements are also very helpful for building your brand. These tend to build on one another. Find a conference you want to speak at, apply, and then use that acceptance to make yourself more attractive to the next one. The audiences you talk to may range from a few dozen to a few hundred in person, but pretty much every conference these days records and posts their content, so your message can extend its reach massively.

Some companies insist you get approval for a conference talk, which makes sense because they don't want you saying anything embarrassing or that might become a leak. Marketing departments can be fanatical about "controlling the message," even if they had you write the message. Get those permissions as quickly as you can. You will want to have your talk ready to go even before it gets accepted at the conference, because the PR department and possibly Legal are going to want to look at it in order to know if you should be allowed to submit in the first place. Get ahead of the curve if you can. Prep talks that interest you and then target conferences that might want them. Yes, conferences like GDC are the highest profile ones, but there's much to be said for picking smaller conferences that offer a more self-selected audience for your material. Furthermore, smaller conferences will also let you polish your presentation skills to prepare you for the bigger stages.

There's also a side benefit of speaking at conferences, especially ones with a writing or narrative focus. That is networking. Introducing yourself to your fellow writers and making connections is a valuable professional asset. If you're speaking, getting yourself out there as an authority in the community is incredibly valuable. If you're not, most sessions have follow-up informal time with the speaker. Make the most of those by asking sharp questions and engaging in respectful discussion.

19.6 Best Behavior

It goes without saying that you need to behave professionally in this context. Do not stalk people you want to meet through the halls, even in jest. Present yourself as a professional by being polite, recognizing others' experience and thoughts, and bringing value to the conversation. Don't try to tell everyone you run into your absolute, sure-fire, original solutions for every problem, because there's a good chance anything you've thought of they may well have thought of, tried, and discarded already. Don't be dismissive or rude, and do not trash anyone's work, even if you don't like it. You may not be talking to the writer of a particular game you hate, but there's a reasonable chance the person you are talking to may be friends with one of the writers on that game and isn't going to take kindly to you trash-talking.

And above all, bring the best version of yourself out to play. You are at a conference as a professional, representing your work and your employer (if you have one). Don't get sloppy drunk. Don't behave inappropriately regardless of what your standing in the industry is. Do present yourself as someone that your peers are proud to recognize and whom they will cheerfully signal boost or recommend for jobs. I've said this before, but it bears repeating. For all that games are a massive global industry, it's also very small in some very real ways, and the writing community is tight-knit. Be a bad actor, and word will get around quickly. You'll want to avoid acquiring that kind of stink if you want to keep working.

One of the downsides of conferences is the potential expense. If you're lucky, your employer or the conference will pay for your travel, lodging, and food. This is not the norm at a lot of companies. Even if you're a speaker, there are a lot of people at any given studio vying to go to the big conferences. That includes studio management, producers, engineers, artists, designers, and Marketing folks, among others. Writers tend to be way down on the list of who gets personal development money for things like conference attendance, so it's wise to start lobbying in advance. It's also wise, unfortunately, to start saving.

The good news is, though, that if you do enough shows and build enough of a reputation, then conferences and schools will start asking you to come speak. Sometimes they'll want to do this remotely. Sometimes they will want you on-site in order to lovingly feed you to the wolves. Sometimes they even pay you a speaker fee or honorarium to do so.

And all of these have a vested interest in promoting you. The conferences want people to attend, which means they have a reason to champion your talk. The colleges want to show value to their students and get them excited, so they'll pump you up as well. Get enough of that, and it starts taking on a life of its own. You might even, if you're looking for trouble, find yourself in a place where people think you should write a book.

19.7 Conclusion

This is an ongoing process. There is no resting on laurels allowed, not if you want to remain pertinent and visible. As your star rises, you will need to pick and choose wisely as to which shows, social media outlets, or interviews make sense for you in terms of cost and benefit and time. Cultivate your public persona to be appealing and professional, and make sure you are always on or near the public's radar. You don't have to do the big thing constantly and every time, but you do need to not let yourself be forgotten. There are a lot of people out there looking for the same limelight you've been working to acquire, and it's easy to get lost in the shuffle. But the hard work pays off on lots of levels: In the people you meet, in the professional benefit to yourself, in the good that you can do by sharing your knowledge, and in the doors that will open to you, one after another, of new experiences.

20

It Ain't Easy, But It Just Might Be Worth It

20.1 Introduction

And here we are, at the end of all things, and the giant eagles are not coming to save us.

If you've gotten this far, you've seen a whole lot of information about how hard the job can be. About how much more than just the writing it entails. You've seen the big and the small, the high level and the low. You've seen stories to inspire and stories that produce despair, and probably even a couple that make you want to pick up torches and pitchforks in order to storm the castle.

Which leads to here and the big question: After all this, why do it?

It's hard, after all. Hard to break in, hard to stay in, hard to do the job, and hard to get recognized for it. There are a million people out there telling you they can do your job better than you can, many of whom would cheerfully give up an internal organ without the benefit of anesthetic to have your job. It can be exhausting, frustrating, and thankless.

And yet.

You know what? There are a lot of reasons.

The first one is the simplest one: Because there is very little on this planet cooler than getting paid to tell stories to thousands or even millions of people. Our job is literally to write, something that untold armies of people wish they could do. Yes, there are obstacles and hardships and utter nonsense we have to deal with, but in the end our life's work is to use our unique skill to help people have fun.

That, I think, is worth doing. Even though not every game we write is pure sunshine and gumdrops, by and large our work produces joy. It makes people happy. It, in collaboration with the work of our teammates and peers, gives people something worth jumping into instead of staying in reality, at least for a little while.

My friend, that is priceless. We put a price on our part of it anyway, as well we should, but in the end, our writing can help create some genuine good.

Tied into that is the notion that we do a lot of heavy lifting on creating worlds and characters that people identify with. Our work helps give them safe virtual spaces where they can explore being someone else for a while, someone who can do things they can't and win victories they never will. It gives them a place to experiment and fail and try something else and learn. Our writing is a big part of that, and that's incredibly important. I have had people tell me how important my writing on a game was to them, how it maybe gave them comfort in a bad time or let them come to grips with themselves in a way they couldn't in the real world. That is genuinely good, and writing for games can help achieve that. We, as writers of games, can help achieve that.

DOI: 10.1201/9781003592983-20

Then there is the fact that as a game writer, you are in the early stages of helping forge a tradition. Your work is laying down some of the foundations of the craft going forward. You are part of a rising form that will grow and endure, and its continued development from your contribution will, in a very real sense, be your legacy.

This means a lot of things. It means your work, and the information you pass along to your peers and the juniors who come after you, becomes part of their professional bedrock. They then will adapt it and use it and pass it down themselves. It's a tiny, but real, form of immortality. It's part of the collective body of knowledge that will evolve and grow as more games get made and more writers take on the challenge of what we do.

Now, the notion that games are a young medium is demonstrably false. Video games date back three quarters of a century in one form or another. Games with lots of writing were around in the 1980s, when text adventures were all the rage. We are not freshly hatched, though we like to pretend we are to excuse some of our failings. In my opinion, as an industry, we were forced to grow up too fast because there was too much money to be made, and the attempts to cram what we do into the Hollywood model because it was understood and profitable were always faulty.

That being said, writing as a respected aspect of video games is relatively new and fragile. I've been doing this for 25 years, and I have seen game writing grow and change and blossom in ways we never dreamed of when I was writing "wall of text" briefings for tactical shooters in 2002. We have seen the arrival of massive open-world games with titanic stories. We have seen small projects with old-school graphics that nevertheless broke people's hearts. We have seen innumerable games with good and interesting writing all standing under the big tent that is game writing, and we have always made room for more.

I have had the privilege and the honor of contributing to that growth and change in my own small way, alongside so many other smart and talented people. I treasure beyond words the fact that my contributions have been a part of helping create this form, and I feel that as game writers, we are just getting started. That's another reason to do this, because even if you're writing barks on the shovelware tie-in game for a bad TV movie, you're still adding to the body of work. You're still a part of something bigger.

Many years ago, a student came up to me at GDC and introduced themself as an aspiring writer. I shut them down, respectfully and immediately, and said, "Do you write? Then you are a writer. There is no aspiring. You're already doing it." To be fair, doing it doesn't mean you're experienced at it or an expert at it or even good at it, but it means you're doing it, and that matters. The big tent should be welcoming to all. There is no conditional second tent for those waiting to accrue enough credit to get in, no line for people to stand in before they get their ticket punched. If you do it, you belong. And if you don't do it and you want to, then start doing it. Join us.

And one of the reasons I say to join us is that, by and large, video game writers are some of the smartest, most thoughtful, and most talented people it has been my pleasure to know. I take pleasure in their company and their conversation, and I take pleasure in their work. The professional community of game writers may not be stainless, because honestly, no group of human beings is, but the overwhelming majority of game writers I have worked with, learned from, mentored, fanboyed on, given the prompts to for an improvisational writing competition, chatted with, or said hi to in the hallway at a conference have been people worth knowing. There is a real benefit to being part of a strong, supportive professional community, drawing strength from it when you need it and offering support in turn when you can.

Another reason to do this is the challenge. As game writers, we are exploring new territory with every new game we help develop. We are pushing the boundaries of interactive entertainment in a way that no other form can. (Be quiet, tabletop RPGs. You're fundamentally different, and I can prove it.) We are facing challenges in our work that are new and exciting and, in many cases, unprecedented.

Guess what? We're meeting them. We are rising to the occasion and creating those new things, overcoming those heretofore impossible obstacles by inventing new ways to write and new ways to interact with gameplay and design and art and all the rest. We have blue water ahead of us, and every new project is an invitation to dive in. Don't be discouraged by signing on to a game that doesn't seem to offer this opportunity. One of the most difficult challenges of my professional career came on a racing game, one of the last places you'd expect to find it. Innovations from stuff that otherwise gets lost get noticed by sharp-eyed folks and rescued as inspiration for other games. Your best work always matters, because you never know how far it will go.

You know what else? There is an amazing feeling that comes with seeing your words, in conjunction with voice acting and audio and character modeling and animation and level building and everyone else on the team, come to life. To see and hear them realized in a way you might not have been able to accomplish on your own. To watch them get presented to fans and players, and to see them pick your stuff up and run with it, quoting it and otherwise letting you know through their actions that they dig it. To have seen your act of creation realized and made manifest, and to have the world declare it awesome.

There are very few feelings in this world better than that. Even the most grizzled veteran – and I was once identified at GDC by a pair of junior devs who told me that they had flat-out been ordered to seek out "the grizzled guy" – still gets a rush when their writing goes live. As for the first time your writing goes out into the world, it's mind-blowing. It's an experience worth seeking out and a memory worth cherishing.

But the best and final reason to do this is because we can. As game writers, we have a unique opportunity. We have somehow emerged to be the ones gifted with the opportunity to do something that has never been done before. Through all the nonsense and heartache, the long hours and the sleepless nights, the endless rewrites and the edits that make you tear your hair out, we still get a chance to do something great that so few other people ever get a chance to do.

That's why I'm thankful. That's why I get angry when we're prevented from doing the best we can do. And it's why, ultimately, I keep doing this crazy thing, and why I want you to join me on the journey and in the trenches and deep down in the word mines, too.

Now, let's write some games together.

FSC
www.fsc.org
MIX
Papier | Fördert gute Waldnutzung
FSC® C083411

Kolibri 360 GmbH
Ferdinand-Jühlke-Straße 7
99095 Erfurt, Deutschland
produktsicherheit@kolibri360.de